Our Own Minds

Our Own Minds

Sociocultural Grounds for Self-Consciousness

Radu J. Bogdan

A Bradford Book
The MIT Press
Cambridge, Massachusetts
London, England

For information about special quantity discounts, please email special_sales@ mitpress.mit.edu.

This book was set in Stone Sans and Stone Serif by Toppan Best-set Premedia Limited. Printed and bound in the United States of America.

Library of Congress Cataloging-in-Publication Data

Bogdan, Radu J.
Our own minds : sociocultural grounds for self-consciousness / Radu J. Bogdan.
 p. cm.
"A Bradford book."
Includes bibliographical references and index.
ISBN 978-0-262-02637-6 (hardcover : alk. paper)
1. Self (Philosophy) 2. Self-consciousness (Awareness) I. Title.
BD450.B564 2010
126—dc22

2010005415

10 9 8 7 6 5 4 3 2 1

Control of a [mental] function is the counterpart of one's consciousness of it . . . Consciousness and control appear only at a late stage in the development of a function, after it has been used and practiced unconsciously and spontaneously.

Lev Vygotsky, *Thought and Language*, 90

Conscious updating is vital to social life. People interact too fast, they change their evaluations of one another too rapidly, and they perceive the incredible subtleties of social life too quickly for anything but a fully attuned conscious mind to track. . . . It is the immersion in culture, rather than any feature of the brain, that defines our truly human modes of consciousness.

Merlin Donald, *A Mind So Rare*, 86, 254

Contents

Preface

For a good number of years my thinking about the human mind, and specifically about how it came to be designed the way it is, and why, has been dominated by several intertwined themes. One is that the human mind is unique because it is designed during a unique ontogeny that responds to unique challenges. A second theme, implied by the first, is that the uniqueness of human ontogeny is best analyzed by looking at it in evolutionary terms. This evolutionary angle, in turn, leads to a third theme, which is that the unique pressures that shape the human mind during ontogeny are primarily social and cultural. Children's minds handle social and cultural challenges through a suite of ontogenetic adaptations that gradually assemble unique mental capacities such as communicative meaning, word reference, propositional thinking, autobiographical memory, imagination, reflexive thinking and more. This is the fourth theme. Given its indispensable role in handling social and cultural tasks, the great assembler or mind designer, or at least enabler—according to a fifth theme—is children's intuitive psychology (also called, professionally, 'theory of mind' or 'mindreading').

Against the background of the other four themes, this fifth and last theme has animated my research in recent years. First, I looked at the evolution of intuitive psychology and the role it plays in the mastery of social relations and cultural practices (Bogdan 1997). I later looked at how intuitive psychology drives the development of novel mental faculties, such as reflexive thinking or thinking about thoughts (Bogdan 2000), and predicative thinking (Bogdan 2009).

Taking again a developmental perspective, the present book turns to consciousness, and specifically its functional design, in an attempt to understand how and when it comes to be, and why. The answer to the why and when questions is that children's functional capacity for consciousness is assembled during development out of a variety of ontogenetic adaptations that respond mostly to sociocultural challenges. The answer to the how-it-comes-to-be question is that the functional design of consciousness has its executive roots in self-regulation, with intuitive psychology serving as the chief self-regulator.

This last answer also anticipates the functional sense in which I construe consciousness throughout this book. It is the consciousness of one being related to various targets in the world (things, events, situations) and of the affordances or opportunities that this relatedness opens up for thought and action. I will call it *self-consciousness*. This is not the ordinary meaning of being conscious of oneself or conscious of one's mental and behavioral states. It is the more basic and broader meaning of being conscious of the self's mental and behavioral relatedness to—and involvement in—the world. The basic idea behind this unusual concept of self-consciousness is that it is vital for any organism to regulate—that is, guide, monitor, evaluate and correct—its relations to the world and their affordances. Such self-regulation provides an organism with a *sense*, experienced or registered in some fashion, of how it relates to the world and to the effects of this relatedness. This sense *becomes conscious*—as self-consciousness—when self-regulation operates under certain parameters. In my analysis, these parameters reflect primarily *executive* abilities initially recruited and assembled by an *intuitive psychology* that handles the *sociocultural tasks and practices* that growing children must assimilate, reproduce and master.

Thus the answers to the questions that animate this inquiry converge on the following central idea: that the functional design of human consciousness develops out of a self-regulatory machinery that adapts to and handles the major sociocultural challenges of human ontogeny. And I will argue that this development goes through two major phases. Before the age of 4, children develop a world-oriented or extrovert form of self-consciousness, but lack a mind-oriented or introvert self-consciousness. It is only after 4 that children begin to turn toward their own minds, and in particular their own attitudes, mostly under the sociocultural pressures handled through a self-directed intuitive psychology. Children's understanding of their own attitudes, which I call *self-understanding*, thus becomes the platform for—and the driving force behind—the development of their introvert self-consciousness.

A major implication of this analysis is that self-consciousness may be uniquely human, possibly with some roots in nonhuman primates and other intensely social mammalians. The uniqueness of human self-consciousness is generated by a definitely unique ontogeny immersed in distinctive social interactions and cultural practices—very demanding, constant and escalating in complexity—which force the children's unique intuitive psychology to take a self-regulatory job that recruits and assembles a suite of executive abilities. The joint exercise of these abilities installs self-consciousness as a mental disposition.

Phenomenal consciousness is not on the agenda of this book. Yet it is an implication of my analysis that its manifestation is ultimately grounded in the executive design of self-consciousness, although the proximal cause of phenomenality most likely resides in the biochemistry and wiring of the brain. Nor are powerful phenomenal kinds of experiences, such as emotions and feelings, on the agenda here. Important as they undoubtedly are in our conscious lives, and in those of many animals, I take these kinds of experiences to modulate and enhance the more basic mental and behavioral relations to the world and to ourselves. Self-consciousness emerges primarily from those relations.

The overall message of this book, then, is that minds cannot be conscious, *simpliciter*, without being functionally self-conscious. The reasons why young human minds—and apparently they alone—develop self-consciousness is that they face extraordinary and escalating sociocultural pressures that cannot be handled without setting in motion a complex executive machinery of self-regulation under the guidance of an increasingly sophisticated intuitive psychology. Sometime in childhood, but not very early, novel sociocultural challenges force this executive machinery to turn toward the children's own minds. From then on, self-consciousness becomes introvert and children's minds become what we intuitively take to be *our own minds*.

At different stages in the gestation of this book I was fortunate to have the critical reactions, suggestions and encouragement of friends, colleagues and audiences who heard or read and discussed various fragments of what went into the final version. My warm thanks to Dan Dennett, Marc Jeannerod, Keith Lehrer, David Olson, and Wolfgang Prinz, and to lively and inquisitive audiences at the University of Arizona, Bilkent University, the University of Bucharest, and the Max Planck Institute for Human Cognition in Leipzig. I was also fortunate to be able to inflict some of my ideas on three good students in an advanced undergraduate seminar at Bilkent University—Emre Erdenk, Ozge Ordal and Saniye Vatansever— who responded with good questions and spirited conversation. I *tesekkur* them very much. And I thank, with gratitude, the reviewers of the MIT Press for their detailed critical comments and constructive suggestions.

Finally, I am grateful to the good people at MIT Press who brought this book to print—first senior editor Tom Stone and later his successor, senior editor Philip Laughlin, assistant editor Marc Lowenthal, copy editor David Dusenbury, and production editor Deborah Cantor-Adams. This is my fourth book with the MIT Press, and I want to take this opportunity to thank this remarkable institution—and its legendary Bradford Books imprint in particular—for a longstanding, consistent and rigorous dedication to cognitive science and philosophy of mind, for the craftsmanship of its books, its commitment to keep them in print and, last but not least, its thoughtful pricing policy.

I Issues, Data, and Theories

1 Setting the Stage

1.1 The Project

This chapter provides a guide to the main argument of the book and the concepts it employs, stipulates the terminology, and previews central questions and the answers to them.

Clues from Blindsight

A much-discussed clinical case, blindsight has become a rich source of empirical data and theoretical insights about consciousness. Blindsight will make other appearances later in the book, but here its job is to introduce our main theme.

Blindsight is a case of unconscious vision in the blind field. The blindsighter is not conscious of the scene in the blind field, and not conscious of seeing or being visually related to that scene. Only when prompted by the experimenter does a blindsighter recognize, often much above chance, various items in the blind field, including their size, shape, use and even color, and move and act successfully in the same blind field. On his own, a blindsighter has no *intent to act*, no *means-ends initiative* that structures and animates the intent, no *monitoring* and *control* over what he registers unconsciously in the blind field, nor is he able to *share the information* from the blind field with other faculties, such as thinking, remembering, planning, speaking or acting.

The italicized words in here refer to *executive abilities* that handle information as well as mental and behavioral activities. What blindsight suggests is a correlation between these executive abilities and visual consciousness. I think that the correlation is deep, systematic and goes beyond the visual domain. Consciousness, I will argue, results from the work of the mind's executive machinery.

Blindsight also raises an intriguing question about the evolution of consciousness. A blindsighter can engage in a good deal of successful visuomotor cognition and action without consciousness. Most animal species operate in some perceptuomotor modality or several, without the assistance of the various executive abilities that are absent in blindsight. Are these species conscious in those modalities? Do they *have* to be conscious? Even though there are no definite answers to these questions, I take blindsight to suggest the strong possibility that consciousness may be absent in many if not most animal minds. Consciousness may be a very rare commodity on the phylogenetic market. If so, the question is why.

The successful yet unconscious perceptuomotor cognition and action of both blindsighters (in the blind field) and (possibly) most animal species suggest that the real reasons—meaning the most potent selection pressures—for consciousness should be sought in domains *other* than perceptuomotor and more generally mental interactions with and actions on the physical environment. Two questions follow from this suggestion. What is the nature of these distinct pressures? And is consciousness a direct adaptive response to these pressures or an indirect outcome of other adaptive responses that make it possible?

In a nutshell, my answer to the first question is developmental and identifies sociocultural tasks and practices as the most distinct and potent pressures that children face in their first years of life. To manage such tasks and practices, children develop an intuitive psychology, whose regulatory operation recruits and assembles a suite of executive abilities, such as those absent in blindsight. These abilities in turn bring consciousness to the young minds. So motivated, the answer to the second question goes for the indirect option: consciousness is likely to be a byproduct of more direct adaptive responses to sociocultural pressures. This is the general idea. Its elaboration can be anticipated as follows.

In Very General Terms

From almost the first days of life, everything surrounding human infants is social and cultural—*social*, in the sense of intense interactions with adults, first in coregulation, face to face exchanges of facial expressions, gestures and vocalizations, nonverbal and later verbal communication, and sundry joint activities; and *cultural*, in the sense that these interactions are structured in patterns of behavior, as activities and practices, standardized and conventionalized in, and thus shared by, a community. Very young children are intense socializers, and puzzled but curious witnesses of the strange and challenging culture around them, much before they are competent locomotors and manual handlers of physical items in the world. They are Vygostkians before becoming Piagetians. And even when they become—and progress as—Piagetians, most of their time and most of their mental energy and activities are still spent as Vygotskians. This asymmetry is bound to impact on the design of their minds, and self-consciousness is a result of this impact.

Consciousness is a key feature of our mental design—for many thinkers, the key feature—and its development is therefore bound to reflect the sociocultural impact. And yet, relatively little has been researched and written on the ontogeny of consciousness and on how it is shaped by the sociocultural environment. Consciousness is a multifaceted phenomenon that notoriously defies easy and neat explanations. A narrowly focused approach may be more successful. This inquiry will focus on the ontogeny of consciousness, as it responds to the major sociocultural challenges to children's minds.

Children's minds begin by being conscious *of* things, events and particularly people around them, and later of their own thoughts and attitudes. Being conscious of these various items, their minds cannot fail to be conscious of how they *relate* to the world and how this world-relatedness affords further opportunities for thought and action. This, I will argue, is the primary phenomenon. It is the consciousness of the self as it relates to items in the world or in the mind—a conscious sense of self-to-target relatedness, as I will call it. With some trepidation, I abbreviate this sort of consciousness as *self-consciousness*.

I will suggest that self-consciousness, so understood, develops gradually during childhood, from being oriented toward the outside world in early years to being oriented also toward one's own mind—or, more accurately, toward what one's own mind relates to and does—in later childhood and beyond. This development is driven mostly by the sociocultural tasks and practices that children must assimilate and engage in competently. In order to do so, children must figure out how adults do it, and why. And that figuring out calls for understanding how adults relate mentally and behaviorally to sociocultural activities and to the world in general. That understanding takes the form of an intuitive psychology (also known, professionally, as 'theory of mind' or 'mindreading'), which is more rudimentary and oriented toward other minds in early years, and more complex and also oriented toward one's own mind in later years. The latter orientation amounts to representing one's own thoughts and attitudes or *self-understanding*, as I will label it.

This book is about why and how understanding minds, first others' and later one's own, drives the development of self-consciousness, first world-bound or extrovert and later also mind-bound or introvert. The central argument aims to show that sociocultural tasks and practices call for the development of intuitive psychology. The latter has a *self-regulatory* role in children's assimilation and handling of sociocultural tasks and activities. This intuitive psychology handles its self-regulatory job by recruiting and assembling a suite of *executive abilities*, such as intending, controlling, attending to, monitoring and so on, that end up installing self-conscious-ness and driving its development. It is the asymmetric development of the intuitive psychology—other minds first, one's own later—that, through its self-regulatory exercise, drives a commensurate asymmetric development of self-consciousness.

The central argument of this book can be diagrammed schematically (and simplistically, for now) as follows:

sociocultural tasks and activities → intuitive psychology (other minds first, one's own later) → self-regulation of children's mental states directed at other people and later at their own minds → recruitment and assembly of executive abilities → that install self-consciousness (first extrovert, later introvert)

The arrows mean different things—selection for the first arrow, probable causation for the second and third, and strong correlation for the last. The last arrow is the most critical for the argument. To get it as close as possible to a nonaccidental link and perhaps to causation, the rest of the book aims to tighten and constrain from various angles the correlation between executive abilities and self-consciousness. Blindsight will be a major prop in this effort, as will a suite of developmental data. In order to clarify further the direction of this inquiry, the next sections will preview its key concepts and main themes.

1.2 Central Concepts

What follows are preliminary profiles of the central concepts employed in this inquiry. These profiles will be amplified and sharpened in later chapters.

Self
Life means self-determination. It is biologically imperative for any organ-ism to distinguish itself from the world through mechanisms that ascertain

what happens inside or is caused by the organism, as opposed to what happens or is caused from the outside. Failure to make this distinction amounts to extinction. *Selfhood* will be construed here quite minimally in the basic biological terms that reflect the work of such mechanisms. So construed, the self is not an entity or set of internal states but rather results from the executive ways in which an organism distinguishes itself from the world and registers its interactions with the world as self-initiated. When self-identifying mechanisms—or *self-mechanisms*, as I will call them —function properly, the organism can be said to have a very basic and minimal *sense of self*—a sense, that is, that its internal states, operations and actions are its own and generated by itself. When the internal states and operations are mental, we can talk of a *mental self*. An organism may lack this sense of a mental self, at least partly, when some self-mechanisms are impaired, as they are in some forms of schizophrenia.

It is important to note that this minimal and most basic sense of self-hood, as ownership and agency, is implicit in the work of an organism's self-regulatory machinery and is subpersonal, so to speak, and therefore quite distinct from the much higher-level ordinary or personal sense of self. The latter is normally reflective and built around memories, values, feelings and much more. This latter sense of self is not on the radar of the present inquiry. But self-consciousness is, and it originates in the basic sense of ownership and agency. I use the word 'sense' liberally in order to leave open the nature of the mechanisms involved, their mode of operation and how this operation is internally registered, whether consciously or not. But I am not assuming—indeed, I am skeptical about—the possibility that a sense of self results from an explicit representation of some internal entity, state or relation.

Target-Relatedness

While distinct from the world, as self, an organism is actively and purposely related to the world. Its *relatedness* to worldly targets expresses the fundamental biological fact of having goals or being goal-directed. Once the organism's self-mechanisms are operative, its goal-directedness requires relating to various targets of its representations and actions, so that we can talk of a *self-to-target relatedness*. A target can be a physical object, event or situation, a mental state, an imagined fiction or an abstraction.

Philosophers often label the mind's target-relatedness *intentionality* (or sometimes aboutness), so that self-to-target relatedness would become *self-intentionality*. To avoid confusion with the ordinary sense of intentionality, as having an intention, I will stick to self-to-target relatedness or just target-relatedness. The notion of target-relatedness refers to a general dis-position of organisms to engage the world in various types of relations—sensorimotor, behavioral, mental. In the mental domain there are different *modalities* in which the organism's target-relatedness is exercised, such as perceptuomotor, communicational, affectuomotor, thinking and so on. I will use the adjective *modal* to indicate the property or operation of a modality.

Just as selfhood reflects the biological autonomy and distinctness of an organism, and a sense of selfhood registers and measures their normal parameters, so the self-to-target relatedness reflects the world-directed posture and modus operandi of an organism. The normality and success of this relatedness are registered and measured by specialized mechanisms, in order to secure the organism's survival and prosperity. A *sense of self-to-target relatedness*, not necessarily and not often conscious, thus results from how the organism's target-relatedness is internally registered, monitored and managed.

Self-Regulation

Self-regulation is the main explanatory concept on the executive side of my analysis. It is the most basic biological phenomenon, the manager of life, and is exercised at every level, from immunological and circulatory to mental. In particular, it is exercised to distinguish selfhood from the world, to register and check upon the self's representations and actions in relation to their targets, and to broadcast the findings to other mechanisms for appropriate measures and reactions. Self-regulation is thus at the heart of selfhood and its relatedness to the world.

If the theme of self-regulation is played in a major key throughout this book, how self-regulation actually works and delivers the goods (so to speak) is much less known, at least at higher mental levels. This is why the actual operation of self-regulation will be described in a minor key. On my reading of the neuropsychological literature, this operation is essentially one of anticipatory simulation. As noted in chapter 4, such simulation is likely to explain eventually the functional design of consciousness, but at the present stage of scientific knowledge this is just a promissory note.

Self-Consciousness

I note from the outset that I do not propose a theory of self-consciousness, nor do I have a tight definition of self-consciousness. A working notion will do for the main purpose at hand, which is to identify and explain the developmental grounds for self-consciousness, as both origins and reasons.

The basic idea is that, exercised in some dominant modality such as vision or thinking, the regulation of self-to-target relatedness renders the self's sense of that relatedness and of its affordances conscious, when certain conditions obtain in the mind, the world and their interaction. The mental conditions are mostly executive and respond to external conditions, mostly sociocultural.

Self-consciousness thus means a conscious sense of self-to-target relatedness and of its affordances. By *affordances* I mean the opportunities for further thoughts and/or actions opened up by one's sense of target-relatedness. If I am conscious of driving a car, which means conscious of handling the car on the road, I am thereby conscious, depending on the context, of various things I can do with the car in its relation to the road.

The internal conditions in which one's sense of target-relatedness and its affordances becomes conscious are analyzed below as *parameters of self-consciousness*. They identify the mental abilities, mostly executive, whose joint operation, subject to self-regulation, installs self-consciousness as a mental competence. Metaphorically speaking, self-consciousness is like a platform raised and secured above many interconnected pillars, most of which are executive in nature.

This inquiry, far from being exhaustive, aims to identify the key executive abilities and self-regulatory practices that are internally sufficient to generate self-consciousness, and also identify the external conditions that cause those abilities to join forces and produce that outcome. The list of such abilities includes intending, control, top-down attention, multitasking, global availability of information, intermodal interfaces and others. These are abilities whose joint exercise is taken by a spectrum of functionalist theories to define and possibly explain consciousness.

I subscribe to this functionalist consensus as a plausible account of the mental conditions in which self-consciousness is manifested. In what follows, I assume this functionalist analysis and focus on what explains the development of self-consciousness. My hypothesis finds the best explanation in the regulatory job of children's intuitive psychology, as it recruits and assembles executive abilities whose joint exercise generates self-consciousness. Taken separately, the exercise of executive abilities need not— and most often is not—conscious. When the exercise of one or another such ability is conscious, it is because self-consciousness is *already* installed and active. The focus will be on the factors and conditions that lead to the installation of self-consciousness in the first place.

As anticipated, the notion of self-consciousness adopted here is not the familiar notion of a self-image or of being conscious of oneself, reflectively—as when one is ashamed or proud of oneself or made suddenly aware of oneself when, for instance, talking too much. Also, the notion bears little resemblance to those employed in social psychology or psycho-analysis. Nevertheless, as I construe it, the notion of self-consciousness has a distinguished philosophical pedigree, going back at least to Kant, and is at the center of recent accounts of consciousness which will be reviewed in the last chapter.

Self-Understanding

Intuitive psychology, as the competence to figure out minds, is a pivotal notion in the argument of this book because its self-regulatory job creates the conditions that install self-consciousness. When its self-regulatory duties require representing other minds and their sociocultural activities, intuitive psychology is responsible for the development of early extrovert self-consciousness. When the same duties require it to represent the thoughts and attitudes of one's own mind, intuitive psychology is respon-sible for the later development of introvert self-consciousness. It is not my aim here to explain our intuitive psychology (but see Bogdan 1997, 1993, 2003, 2005a, 2005b) or the self-understanding that results from its exercise. The aim is to explore their formative role in the development of self-consciousness.

Despite the ambitious title of this book, its focus will be on one's own thoughts and attitudes, such as desires, intentions and beliefs, and not on other kinds of mental states, such as emotions, affects, feelings and moods. Besides economy of argument, the main reason for this choice is that the former are the primary links to the world and therefore the primary sources of self-consciousness, as understood here. On some accounts, emotions and possibly feelings may also be representational, but in more complex mind–body–world packages, and their inclusion would have greatly com-plicated the analysis. Yet again, I need to stress that there would be no emotions and affects to speak of unless organisms *first* self-regulated their conative and cognitive relations to and actions on the world. When I talk here of consciousness of minds and of understanding minds, I mean nar-rowly minds populated by thoughts and attitudes.

Self-This and Self-That

Besides the self-hyphenated concepts introduced so far, I have a few others in store, which are meant to simplify the discourse and save some trees. I will use the prefixes 'self-' and 'other-' to indicate the ownership of thoughts and attitudes, ascribed to self or others, respectively. Thus a 'self-attitude' (such as 'self-belief') means one's own attitude (e.g., belief), while an 'other-attitude' (such as 'other-belief') means the attitude (belief) of someone else. The same with ascriptions of thoughts and attitudes: 'self-ascription' means ascribing a thought or attitude to oneself, while 'other-ascription' means the ascription of a thought or attitude to someone else.

Installation

A leitmotif of my analysis is that self-consciousness is *installed* by executive abilities, such as intending, metacognition and multitasking, which are recruited, assembled and managed in a self-regulatory mode by children's intuitive psychology. Informally, I will introduce the notion of installation by analogy with language.

Language does not self-install, once the children's minds are turned on and activated by appropriate inputs. Although primed by evolution to discriminate and register the sounds of possible languages, the children's phonetic software for their specific native language is installed gradually by persistent exposure to the actual sounds of that language. The same is true of the grammar of a native language and the acquisition of its words. In each case, the innate predispositions for phonetics, grammar and word acquisition take the form of a spectrum of patterns of neural connections that the inputs would wire into specific configurations. This, very roughly, is how the various components of language are installed in children's minds. The spectrum of candidate neural patterns, the sorts of relevant inputs and the activation paths through which the latter configure the former, are all evolved dispositions. Yet the actual animation of these dispositions in children's minds is effected by contextual immersion in and flexible adjustment to particular domains of language, with variable yet specific patterns of sounds, words and phrases. All of this takes place during a definite period during early childhood—the 'window of installation opportunity,' as we may call it.

The installation of a complex mental competence, such as language, takes place in two complementary phases—one evolutionary, the other developmental. Reaching into the remote past, this evolutionary phase installed innate predispositions; the developmental phase finishes the installation by having (usually) domain-specific inputs activate the innate predispositions along specific paths and set up specific patterns of neural connections. The latter configure the competence in question.

I take the installation of self-consciousness in children's minds to be in some (but not all) respects analogous to that of language. Instead of phonetics, grammar and word acquisition, we have a set of executive abilities, an intuitive psychology and the underlying machinery of self-regulation, which all constitute the predispositions selected long ago by evolution, in a first phase, for various reasons unrelated to consciousness. Also selected a long time ago, in response to sociocultural pressures, were the job and ability of intuitive psychology to recruit and assemble executive abilities in a self-regulatory pattern capable of generating self-consciousness. This capability is activated and configured by actual inputs originating primarily in the sociocultural activities that children assimilate and master at different stages in their ontogeny. My account of the installation of self-consciousness will assume the evolutionary phase and focus on the developmental phase.

I propose two windows of installation opportunity—before the age of 4, for extrovert self-consciousness; and after 4, for its introvert version. In both phases, the child's intuitive psychology brings and wires together a set of executive abilities in the form of a dispositional network of neural patterns.

With this conceptual and terminological preview behind us, I will rephrase the project of the book in terms of the central questions that will be explored in developmental terms.

1.3   Central Questions

The major questions are the following:

1. *the sense of selfhood question*: what enables an organism to register its target-related mental states, attitudes and activities as its own (ownership) and as initiated by itself (agency)?

An organism may register not only its mental states, and what they represent as targets, but also the very relatedness of those states to their targets and its affordances. Thus the second question:

2. *the question of the sense of self-to-target relatedness and its affordances*: what enables an organism to register, monitor and do something about—in a word, to 'sense'—the relations of its mental states, attitudes and activities to their targets and affordances?

Since in most organisms this sense of self-to-target relatedness and its affordances need not be conscious, and in most species it is not, the next question is

3. *the self-consciousness question*: what makes an organism conscious of its own mind's relatedness to targets in some dominant modality; and, in the

human case, what makes one conscious of one's own attitudes as target-related mental representations that have affordances?

A human mind cannot be conscious of its own attitudes without recognizing them as attitudes. Thus the next question:

4. *the self-understanding question*: what enables one to conceptualize and understand one's own target-related attitudes and their affordances?

Once one's target-related mental states and attitudes are understood conceptually, and one is conscious of them, we may ask perhaps the most philosophical of questions, which is

5. *the self-knowledge question*: what enables one to know, in what manner and to what degree, that—and what—one perceives, remembers, thinks or desires?

It should be noted in passing that this self-knowledge question was understood in the ancient Greek philosophy of Plato, for instance, differently from what it became for Descartes and modern philosophy. In the former, at issue was the knowledge of formal, moral or aesthetic truths—of the Forms themselves, as Plato put it. It is knowledge as an ideal that guides one's life and mind. In the Cartesian tradition, still dominant today, the much narrower and inward-looking question (as formulated in question 5, above) is about accessing and being certain of one's own mental states and their contents. Also, in passing, I note that there is lively debate in the developmental literature as to whether children before the age of 7 know their own minds, in the sense of understanding their first-person access to and authority regarding their own mental states (P. Mitchell et al. 2009). The argument of this book predisposes me to side with those who deny such knowledge to young children, but this is just an educated guess, and will not be pursued further.

Having identified this fifth self-knowledge question, I will set it completely aside. This book is only about questions 1 to 4, in the above list—and is about them only to the extent that they illuminate the ontogeny of self-understanding as it interacts with that of self-consciousness.

Phenomenality Quarantined

The reader may have noticed by now that no question has been asked about *phenomenal* consciousness. Indeed, no attempt will be made here to discuss, let alone to explain the phenomenal—or qualitative, experiential or what-it-is-or-feels-like—character of consciousness. The aim, rather, is to explain the reasons for which and the conditions in which self-consciousness materializes and grows in children's minds. As noted, self-consciousness is construed in functional terms. Metaphorically: the aim is not to explain the bulb's light but rather what it takes to light the bulb.

I take self-consciousness to enable the manifestation of phenomenal consciousness. I am *not* saying that self-consciousness generates its phenomenal expression. I am saying, rather, that self-consciousness provides the functional matrix in which phenomenality is manifested. Metaphorically, again: it takes electricity, an outside grid, internal wiring, a bulb and filament, a switch and more to produce light. The light is the phenomenal consciousness, if you will. The bulb may even light up in brief, intermittent pulsations caused by sporadic electric bursts, in the way in which nearly vegetative patients—and possibly animals or human infants during their first hours and perhaps days of postnatal life—may have brief and intermittent phenomenal pulsations. It takes electrical impulses crossing a filament inside the bulb for the bulb to light up. That is the proximal cause of the light. Likewise, the biochemical impulses of the nervous system may be the proximal cause of phenomenal pulsations. Those pulsations become normal phenomenal consciousness when embedded in the robust functional matrix of self-consciousness. Phenomenal pulsations may be brief and intermittent not due to impairments in the biochemistry of the brain but more likely due to impairments or underdevelopment of the executive machinery of self-regulation that installs self-consciousness.

In short, I am not claiming that the phenomenal character of consciousness is reduced to the functional design of self-consciousness. The claim is rather that the latter makes the normal manifestation of phenomenal consciousness possible. Yet this claim—whether controversial or banal—is not (and I repeat, *not*) part of the argument of the book. Phenomenal consciousness is thereby quarantined for the remainder of the book except for some further thoughts in chapters 4 and 8. For those (a likely majority) who take phenomenality to be the essence of consciousness, this policy may look like an abdication from responsible explanation. I hope that the remainder of the present inquiry will make them think again.

Equally quarantined are some of the most potent and quintessential kinds of phenomenal experiences, such as emotions, feelings and pains. Besides focus and economy of argument, my decision is based on the belief—admittedly not demonstrated here, but defended in the literature (e.g., Dretske 1995; Tye 1995)—that these kinds of experiences are actually relational and have the job of modulating and enhancing an organism's mental and behavioral relations to the world and to itself. Self-consciousness emerges primarily from those more basic relations. Modulation and enhancement may be the role of and reason for phenomenal consciousness. But this may be a story for another time.

1.4 Developmental Answers

The answers proposed to the four central questions formulated in the previous section are all developmental. There are good reasons, both substantive and methodological, for choosing a developmental angle.

Why Development

One substantive reason is this. The roots of self-understanding and self-consciousness reach deep and early in development and even phylogeny, and can best be understood in these historical contexts. Going historical may enable science to identify the critical junctures at which human self-understanding and self-consciousness emerged, and to discern the reasons for this emergence. This approach can go a long way toward elucidating the nature and operation of self-understanding and self-consciousness.

Another substantive reason for taking development seriously is the following. The understanding and consciousness of one's own thoughts and attitudes are among the mental faculties that are uniquely human. This is primarily because of some unique features of human ontogeny. I speculate in the concluding chapter (and also elsewhere: Bogdan 2000, 2005a, 2009) that both self-understanding and self-consciousness are likely to be assembled during development out of many, often disparate capacities under pressures and conditions that are specific to distinct stages in human ontogeny. This is why only a close look at development could reveal the reasons for, as well as the roots and the resulting design of, these faculties.

The methodological reason for choosing a developmental perspective reflects my belief that intuition, introspection, even disciplined phenomenology and conceptual analysis, or a fine sense of the ordinary use of the relevant pieces of language—the chief instruments still in use by most philosophers of mind and consciousness—will not get us very far in exploring and answering the central questions of this book. Nor do I think that, on the empirical side, we can answer those same central questions by trying to find where the abilities involved in self-consciousness and self-understanding are localized in the brain. Even the most current models of their operation—whether computational, connectionist, dynamic or embodied—would not suffice to answer the questions I have put forward. One also needs some plausible and coherent hypotheses about why the faculties in question developed, out of which precursors or enablers, when they developed, in order to do what, and in response to what challenges. A developmental inquiry is best positioned to deliver such hypotheses. The one outlined at the outset of this chapter is my candidate. What follows is a preview of how I propose to argue for this hypothesis.

Outline of the Argument

The overarching theme of the next two chapters is the developmental asymmetry in how children relate, in different modalities, to the outside world and their own minds. According to current data, the great temporal divide seems to fall around the ages of 4 to 5, which I will simplify by referring throughout to 'age of 4' or simply '4.' So the first step in the argument, taken in chapter 2, concerns this asymmetry and consists in showing that prior to the age of 4—or during 'early childhood,' as I will call the period from birth to that age—children are mentally and behaviorally invested almost exclusively in the outside world, both social and physical. The evidence for this outward orientation comes from analyses of memory, thinking, intuitive psychology and lack of self-control.

Young children are of course conscious of their own bodies and actions, as they engage the social and physical worlds around them, and also conscious of the affective, communicational and perceptuomotor modes of such engagements. This is extrovert self-consciousness. It is consciousness not only of the world children face but also of their relatedness to that world in the dominant extrovert modalities; it is consciousness of the resulting experiences as well. What young children are not yet conscious of are their own thoughts and attitudes, as they relate to their targets and affordances. They lack introvert self-consciousness.

On my hypothesis, the main (though not only) reason for this asymmetry in the development of self-consciousness is the asymmetric development of intuitive psychology, which is first directed at other minds and only later at one's own. Chapter 3 brings further support for this asymmetry and criticizes some established theories of intuitive psychology that either posit symmetry or a reverse asymmetry—that is, understanding and being conscious of our own minds first, and of other minds later. Thus concludes the first part of the book.

The second part aims to explain the asymmetries in the development of intuitive psychology and, as a result, of self-understanding and self-consciousness. Chapter 4 takes its distance from the Cartesian view of consciousness and makes a case for the relational format of consciousness, which reflects its executive roots in the self-regulation of an organism's relatedness to targets and of its affordances. This self-regulation begets extrovert self-consciousness when the intuitive psychology of young children—which I label *naive psychology*—regulates their assimilation and handling of sociocultural tasks and practices by means of consciousness-generating executive abilities. Chapter 5 explains how young minds implement this scenario. It suggests that human infants already need and expect adult coregulation, and, as they turn into young children, the coregulation of their sociocultural activities is increasingly handled by naive psychology in a means-ends format. It is this coregulative means-ends format of children's naive psychology that recruits and assembles the executive abilities that underpin the emergence of their extrovert self-consciousness.

The next two chapters examine the older children's turn toward their own minds. Chapter 6 explores the premises for such a turn by re-analyzing some earlier philosophical accounts in developmental terms. It then distinguishes between the early naive psychology and a later common-sense psychology whose novel features enable a common understanding of minds, thus facilitating children's turn toward their own minds. The chapter concludes with the neuropsychological and cognitive developments after 4, which make such a turn possible. Chapter 7 explains the sociocultural reasons for which, and the new kinds of thoughts thanks to which, the self-regulatory work of commonsense psychology translates into self-understanding and leads to introvert self-consciousness.

The final chapter begins with some reflections on how the competence for self-consciousness may have emerged as a developmental byproduct of other competencies. It also acknowledges what the argument of this book has not covered sufficiently or at all, and why, and concludes with a comparative discussion of several other accounts of self-consciousness, marking similarities as well as differences.

2 Developmental Asymmetries

This chapter samples the evidence about the development of the main abilities that are either involved in or symptomatic of understanding minds and self-consciousness. I read the evidence as pointing to a robust asymmetry in the development and use of these abilities before and after the age of 4.

Section 2.1 draws a general profile of the young mind. It is a mind almost exclusively oriented toward the outside social and physical world, and beginning to turn toward itself only after 4. Section 2.2 notes that the resources of memory, both long- and short-term, required for accessing and dealing with one's own mind, are not yet up to the task. Although young children have a memory for facts and experiences, they do not yet have an autobiographical memory that can retrieve past attitudes. The latter is a form of memory that is required for self-understanding and introvert self-consciousness. Reflecting these memory limitations, young children's pretending reveals the limits of their imaginative thinking. So argues section 2.3. According to section 2.4, young children also have limited abilities for self-control in general and mental self-regulation in particular, both being required for marginalizing the outside world and attending to one's own mental states.

The last two sections turn to the major characters in our story—intuitive psychology and self-consciousness. Section 2.5 holds that it is the overtly expressed attitudes of other people, and not their own, that first engage young children's intuitive psychology in its early naive version. Section 2.6 introduces extrovert self-consciousness. I approach its development in two stages. In a first stage, consonant with the analysis of this chapter, I suggest that young children's consciousness is extrovert and blind to its own thoughts and attitudes. In a second stage, chapter 4 will explain why this is so.

2.1   Before and After 4

The Pull of the Outside World

A truism that captures well the orientation of young minds is 'out of sight, out of mind.' Perhaps the best known psychological observation vindicating this truism is Piaget's: the infant plays with an object; while he is still watching, the object is hidden under a rug or behind a pillow; but instead of searching for the object, the infant loses interest and starts another activity. Once out of the infant's sight, the object also vanishes from its mind. Neither the truism nor Piaget's explanation may be quite right, but they help make my general point: the young mind is overwhelmingly geared to the outside world, as it is concurrently perceived and acted upon (Piaget 1964; also Bjorklund 2005; Perner 1991). Even though young children remember past events and experiences, and continuously update their representations of the world, their mental focus is nevertheless on a scene of current perceptuomotor or affectuomotor interest—the here and now of concrete, spatiotemporally determined things, events and people that can be emotionally and behaviorally engaged. This is what I mean by the pull of the outside world, whether it be social (other people), biological (other organisms), physical or cultural.

Besides ordinary observations and psychological data that confirm this pull of the outside world, recent research also points to clusters of innate predispositions or biases, manifested since infancy, which form a sort of intuitive expertise that operates in thematically distinct areas of the world surrounding young children. These forms of expertise have become known as naive physics, naive biology, naive arithmetic, naive psychology (or theory of mind), and other such (Gopnik and Meltzoff 1997). Naive physics and arithmetic, for example, enable youngsters to recognize the permanence of objects, their causal relations and their perceived numerosity, respectively, among other accomplishments (Carey 1985). In the social domain, naive psychology enables children to recognize the visible expressions of other people's agency, emotions, attention, and gaze (Perner 1991; Tomasello 1999; Wellman 1990).

Such predispositions suggest an evolutionary history of selection for abilities that kick in early to shape the infants' adaptive responses and provide a platform and matrix for the development of successor abilities in these areas of intuitive expertise. This pattern of development makes sense because the challenges faced by infants are mostly external, and fairly specific at this early period of life.

Ordinary observation and psychological data also reveal key features of young mentation that confirm the overwhelming pull of the outside world. I will briefly describe them and then anticipate why they do not afford an understanding and conscious sense of one's own thoughts and attitudes. One such feature is the *spatiotemporal concreteness* of the targets of young children's mentation, whether these targets are physical things or events, facial expressions or vocalizations or the gazing of other people, or cultural gadgets and routines. Another feature is that these concrete targets are represented in a *here-and-now* frame of mind, which is generated by dominant perceptuomotor or affectuomotor schemes and constantly updated sensory representations (Perner 1991; Piaget 1964).

Even when, after the age of one-and-a-half, young children are supposed to operate with multiple mental models, some departing from a here-and-now situation (for example, in means-ends reasoning, inferring the location of an invisibly displaced object or pretend play), it is still the initial perception of targets that remains the dominant model, motivating and driving the alternative ones (Perner 1991). The pull of the outside world, as perceived and/or acted on, is still there but at a further representational remove.

How-To Minds

That young minds are stimulus-driven and world-bound dovetails with how they represent information and handle the resulting representations. As we shall see, the dominant modalities in which infants first engage the world (and are extrovertly conscious, on my analysis) are communicational, affectuomotor and perceptuomotor. In all three, the *motor* connection is essential: infant mentation, like animal mentation, is a how-to sort of mentation that maps input discriminations onto action schemes— behavioral categorizations, as I called them elsewhere (Bogdan 1994, 1997). The results are modally specific *procedural representations* that are processed as indecomposable units. In other words, procedural representations do not interact in virtue of their *internal* composition *and* what the components represent separately—in the way in which, say, the specific meaning and even word order of an utterance one hears may influence where one looks or how one reacts. The latter is a data structure in the literal sense: it encodes and conveys information in virtue of what its components represent and how they are related.

Procedural or how-to cognition, based on behavioral categories, does not operate with and on data structures, except for sensory or memory inputs. The information contained in procedural representations remains implicit and generally unavailable to higher-level processing. The inde-composability, autarchy and implicitness of procedural representations are features that are adaptive and effective for specialized and quick behavioral responses to sensory inputs, but are inimical to a flexible, creative, reflective and cross-domains commerce among thoughts as data structures, which is the hallmark of children's minds after 4 (Karmiloff-Smith 1992, chapter 1).

After 4

The mind that develops after the age of 4 begins to move away from the limitations of its precursor: it is no longer simply stimulus-driven and mostly limited to the here-and-now of concurrent perception and motivation; it can imagine possible or fictional scenarios, plan ahead, deliberate and mix representations from various domains. Most importantly, the internal structure of its inputs as well as imagined or mind-constructed representations become explicit and available to higher-level processing and intermodal interactions. All of these novelties, as we shall see, are necessary for the emergence of self-understanding and introvert self-consciousness.

2.2 Memory

Two kinds of memory play a major role in the development of self-under-standing—long-term and short-term memory. The former stores past information and enables the mind to compare its current contents with past ones. The latter, when sufficiently developed after 4, encodes currently represented contents, as many as it can encode, and in so doing, handles a complex and multidimensional mentation. Young children's long-term memory lacks a key element—a representation of the past self in relation to various mental contents, which is required for understanding one's own thoughts and attitudes.

Past without Self

That memory is a sort of passive playback in early childhood, and not yet under mental initiative and control, can be ascertained from the forms in which it appears to operate at that age. The psychological literature distinguishes three forms of memory—semantic, episodic and autobiographical—even though many researchers run the last two together (a mistake, I think).

Short-term or working memory is where serious thinking takes place, where thoughts and attitudes are not only formed and processed but also examined and evaluated reflexively. It is also the place for interface and active and controlled interaction among various modalities, such as long-term memory, perception, language, imagination and others. This is why working memory is necessary (though not sufficient) for developing a sense of one's own thoughts and attitudes, as they relate to inputs from other modalities and to targets in the world or in the mind. Young children's working memory is underdeveloped until about 4 or 5 (Bjorklund 2005; Nelson 1996), and is thus limited in what it can do for the children's self-understanding.

Before 4: Only Semantic and Episodic Memory

Young children have good memory for things, events and situations. This is *semantic* memory. It retrieves the content of what was once seen or heard or touched, without the actual experience. My semantic memory reminds me that Ankara is the capital of Turkey and that Istanbul was once called Constantinople, but I have no recollection of the initial contexts and experiences that introduced me to these items of information. Many if not most of our beliefs, prejudices, preferences, standardized speech formulae ('Have a nice day!' 'May I help you?') are stored in semantic memory and lack definite experiential associations.

Another sort of memory, called *episodic*, stores and retrieves experiential details of and associations with past contents, and links them to spatio-temporal contexts and also to once-vivid reactions and emotions. Episodic memory also operates in young children, and probably in some non-human species (Clayton, Griffiths, Emery and Dickenson 2002). Two facts indicate a close link between perceptual experience and episodic memory. One is that episodic memories are represented in the same areas of the brain as actual perceptual (and particularly visual) experiences. The other fact is that young children's episodic memories evoke relatively short-lived experiences and the access to such memories tends to degrade rather quickly (Conway 2002). These facts suggest that the task of episodic memory is to *reenact* the initial perceptual experience and its associated reactions with all its virtues, such as immediacy and vividness, but also with its limitations, such as lack of initiative, control and autobiographical reconstruction.

There is also the famous infantile amnesia: people do not normally remember events from their first three years of life. This is an intriguing phenomenon to which I will return, because it opens a revealing window on early mentation and its later changes. It suffices to say, for now, that the end of the period covered by infantile amnesia marks roughly the beginning of the period covered by autobiographical memory. The contrast, I suggest, is due to the ability of the latter, and the inability of early semantic and episodic memory, to project in the past a self represented explicitly as *related* to the items remembered. Early long-term memory is thus a memory without a past self, so to speak, that is, a memory of facts and experiences unrelated to the past self who registered those facts and lived those experiences in the first place.

After 4: Autobiographical Memory

Missing from early childhood memory is thus an autobiographical memory capable of consciously and deliberately projecting a self in the past and relating it to a remembered content. This new sort of memory develops during the interval between 4 and 5 (Bjorklund 2005, 264; Nelson 1996, 162). Somehow, autobiographical memory seems to fix durably the otherwise short-lived episodic memories. To remember autobiographically is to initiate and control a mental reconstruction that relies on inference, imagination, introspection, often narration and certainly the ability to guide and control one's mental activities (Dennett 1991; Nelson 1996). The deployment of these resources, in turn, depends on a capacious and efficient working memory. The resources for all these new mental endeavors develop only after 4 (Conway 2002). Recent research shows that the development of autobiographical memory is actually work in progress throughout childhood and adolescence, with best performance and full reconstructive abilities being reached between the ages of 18 and 21 (Ofen et al. 2007).

The relations among the three forms of memory distinguished here may be schematized as follows:

semantic memory [of facts and events] + [recreation of experiences in terms of perceptual vividness, spatiotemporal framing and affective associations] = episodic memory

episodic memory + [introspection + imagination + inference + etc.] = autobiographical memory?

Despite appearances, retrieving past experiences introspectively, imaginatively and inferentially may not be enough for autobiographical memory. One may recall episodically, through imagery or inference, the passing show of past events without necessarily representing one's past self and one's past attitudes. What is needed, in addition, is a central piece of auto-biographical memory, and of self-understanding, which is the sense of one's own self-to-target relatedness. This enables one's self to be projected in the past as related, in some modality and attitude, to what is remembered. How does one get this explicit sense of past self-relatedness? Josef Perner's answer (1991, 163–169; 2000) is *metarepresentation*. It explains why episodic memory turns autobiographical and why (on my analysis) auto-biographical memory can represent one's past self in relation to remembered things and situations.

The idea of metarepresentation at the heart of autobiographical memory is plausible for at least two reasons. In recalling our own past attitudes, we *represent* ourselves some time ago as past selves *representing* the contents of past attitudes. This is what metarepresentation does—represent represent-ing relations. The idea is also plausible because, as noted earlier, metarep-resentation in general develops around the age of 4, in tandem with autobiographical memory and the other abilities involved in its operation. The sort of metarepresentation Perner has in mind originates exclusively in children's naive psychology and develops a year earlier—as evidenced, according to Perner, by the recognition of false belief—and is symmetri-cally shared by self- and other-ascriptions.

I think that Perner's story is nearly but not entirely right. For one thing, the recognition of false belief need not be metarepresentational and sym-metric with respect to self and others (Bogdan 2003). More to the point, though, the metarepresentations that animate autobiographical memory emerge in a later, commonsense psychology which differs significantly from the naive psychology of earlier years. That naive psychology can handle false belief without metarepresentation is argued in section 2.5, below. It is the later commonsense psychology that generates the self-ascriptive thoughts that animate autobiographical memory; these ideas will be elaborated in chapters 6 and 7. For now, we retain the idea that semantic and episodic memory, developed and active before 4, store con-tents issued by extrovert modalities, whereas autobiographical memory, which relies on introvert self-ascriptions of thoughts and attitudes, devel-ops only after 4. Autobiographical memory is the memory of an 'offline' thinker, which—as seen next—the young child is not.

2.3 Thinking

When it comes to thinking, the others-before-self asymmetry thesis is best analyzed in terms of the contrast between online and offline thinking.

Informally, online thinking is about, and generated by, what one perceives in various modalities or remembers semantically or episodically. Online thinking is mostly input-driven thinking. Offline thinking can be input- and even world-independent—that is, it can take the form of counterfactual or hypothetical imagination, abstraction, fictionalizing and the like. The task now is to show that offline thinking, which is necessary for self-understanding and hence for introvert self-consciousness, develops only after 4. I propose to check the developmental transition from online to offline thinking in terms of *pretending*, which is the earliest and behaviorally most visible form of imaginative thinking, and quite possibly its incubator. In my view, pretending—and imaginative thinking in general—develops primarily under sociocultural pressures (Bogdan 2005a).

Pretend Play

For a working definition, we can say that *pretending* is an ability to (a) generate mentally, (b) infer from, and (c) deliberately act upon, imaginary scenarios (Carruthers 2002; Harris 2000; Lillard 1994; Perner 1991). Absent these features, it would be hard to distinguish pretending from daydreaming or playing. Lacking one or more of those defining features, the minds of playful animals cannot be in the pretending business.

What about human children? In the earliest years, they are mentally capable of more than play but less than full pretense. This interim exercise is *pretend play* or acting as-if. It deliberately takes things, actions or persons for what they are not, or emulates with exaggeration roles and scripts observed in the adult world. Pretend play is most frequently undertaken in three kinds of activities—playing with functional objects and gadgets, role play and play according to shared behavioral scripts. In all these versions, pretend play operates in social and cultural contexts. This is no accident, for the evolutionary pressures for pretend play emerge most strongly in these contexts (Bogdan 2005a; Harris 2000).

Pretend play is anchored in and motivated by the perceptual and motivational here-and-now, and is unable to deploy the resources needed for genuine offline imaginative thinking and hence for self-understanding. It is only after 4 that children develop genuine pretense, as a manifestation of offline thinking.

What does it take to engage in pretend play? Paul Harris's comprehensive investigation of pretend play posits four conditions: (a) a make-believe stipulation or stance that fixes the abnormal identity of an object or action (e.g., banana as telephone); (b) suspension of truth; (c) insertion of the pretend item into a causal sequence; and (d) a narrative unfolding, which unpacks imaginatively or inferentially the causal consequences of the initial stipulation (Harris 2000, chapter 2).

What mental resources would the young children need to meet these conditions? Pretend play produces a deliberate but limited modification of a normal behavioral pattern or object use. Thus, using a banana as a telephone involves a physical object that is held near the mouth or ear and listened to or talked into—which is the normal behavioral script; but the object is different from normal telephones—which is the limited modification. Imagination is needed to represent such a modified situation and to unpack mentally what would or could follow from such a representation. Think of *imagination* as the ability to represent some thing or situation that is partly or totally different from what one perceives or remembers. This is a very rough characterization, but sufficient for our purposes.

Two forms of imagination may be at work in pretend play (Bogdan 2000, 58–59). *Simple imagination* operates online, is driven by current goals, and projects situations that are anchored in and resemble a currently perceived (or remembered) situation but differ through the permutation, omission or addition of some of its elements. For these reasons, simple imagination is a *situated* form of imagination. Although able to deploy multiple representations of currently perceived situations, simple and situated imaginers do not have the mental freedom to envisage entirely non-actual or never-witnessed situations, which are completely divorced from their perception or memory. That mental freedom is the mark of pretense.

Since pretend play is a deliberate effort intended to simulate reaching a goal by unusual means, the pretending usually concerns the means. This is why pretend play may call for an *instrumental imagination*. Think of it this way: to bring about a goal-situation, one injects in one's imaginative projection a representation of an object, organism or behavioral pattern that is embedded as an implement or tool in an otherwise normal action (Bogdan 2000, chapter 2). Play-pretending that the cat is a pillow (a favorite of my childhood) involves knowingly imagining conflicting states of affairs—that one normally sleeps on pillows, that cats are not pillows yet can be acted upon as such, with counterfactual delight. The same is true in role play of the children who pretend to be doctors by giving pills to other children as their patients, or children pretending to be mailmen delivering letters and packages or the like.

Both simple and instrumental imaginers are creative but not recreative (Currie and Ravenscroft 2002). They can combine representations in novel, unprecedented ways to create situations that differ from reality (creativity), but cannot shift perspectives, and represent and reason about things entirely from the perspective of what is imagined (recreativity). A child who imagines a house with a big apple on the top, instead of the roof, is creative in her simple imagining. Imagining being a vampire, and thinking and behaving like one, is being imaginative recreatively. Pretense is generally recreative. But the pretend play of young children (and possibly of human-raised apes) is merely creative, usually in a limited and situated way.

To use a metaphor to which I return in later chapters, we can think of the pretend stance of the young mind as a sort of little screen or box that opens in a corner of the larger mental screen dominated by current motivation, perception and/or memory. Foregrounding and partially adopting the stance of this little screen, while backgrounding the larger one, the young mind can imaginatively improvise new behaviors and playfully explore their consequences. What it cannot do is considerably magnify this little pretend screen, dramatically miniaturize the larger reality screen and relegate *it* to a corner of the mental workspace, and then, totally offline—through various inferential and imaginative moves—open a nested succession of further screens from inside of the pretend screen, all the while explicitly keeping track of the diverse attitudes to the various contents displayed on the many screens. All of this would be involved in (recreative) pretense, and comes later, after 4.

To sum up: the limitations in the imagination of young children explain why their pretend play is still play and not pretense, as an exclusively offline mental undertaking. What pretend play shows is that young minds can imagine beyond the inputs of perception or memory, although those inputs initiate, constrain and shape what is imagined.

Pretense

The offline mind can represent targets that need not be actual or remembered and need not be acted upon. This ability underpins a new (third) form of imagination, *suppositional imagination*, which consists in imagining-otherwise, solely for the sake of some further mental activity. This is the basis of pretense. Suppositional imagination requires an explicitly hypothetical stance toward what is pretended. I construe it as a stance that requires metarepresenting one's own hypothetical attitude toward what is pretended. It is at this point in development, after 4, that pretense involves not just metarepresentation but also a concept of pretense. It also requires self-ascriptions of thoughts and attitudes.

To pretend, therefore, one must (a) imagine facts and situations entirely divorced from reality, (b) know the difference between what is imagined and what is real, (c) know that one merely entertains or has a suppositional attitude toward what is imagined (self-ascription), and (d) know that one's representations are directed at imagined targets (metarepresentation). Young (pretend-playing) children can represent real and imaginary contents, are aware of and distinguish among the modalities in which they represent, such as perception or imagination. What they cannot do is metarepresent and self-ascribe attitudes. In particular, they cannot metarepresent the suppositional attitude toward what they imagine and the target-relatedness and affordances of that attitude.

The development of pretense is thus intertwined with that of the intuitive psychology needed for self-ascriptions of attitudes. If pretense is a form of offline thinking, as I think it is, then the 4 to 5 interval marks the transition from an outward-oriented and perceptually situated online thinking to an imaginative and offline thinking.

2.4   Self-Control

Two key neuropsychological abilities responsible for self-control have a decisive role in the development of self-understanding and self-consciousness—inhibition and self-regulation. As I read the evidence, both show the same developmental asymmetry as the other competencies examined in this chapter.

Inhibition

There is solid psychological and neurological evidence that inhibition develops after the age of 4 (Bjorklund 2005; Diamond 2001; Houdé 1995; Leslie 2000). Dominated by perceptual or memory inputs, young children have a hard time inhibiting their speech or forgetting useless or irrelevant information, and have an equally hard time resisting the interference of novel stimuli and maintaining a steady focus of attention.

Neurologically, inhibition is associated with a massive growth of the prefrontal cortex in the 4 to 6 interval. Significantly, adults with frontal lobe damage show many of the same limitations in inhibition and resistance to interference as do young children. Equally significant and relevant to the argument of this chapter is Frank Dempster's hypothesis about three forms of inhibition and resistance to interference manifested differentially in early and late childhood, in tune with distinct phases in the development of frontal lobes (Dempster 1992; also Bjorklund 2005, 148–149). The forms in question are motor, perceptual and linguistic. Each form shows maximal responsiveness to interference, and hence lack of inhibition, during the period in which it dominates the children's mind and behavior. Thus, the motor form of sensitivity to interference is the highest of the three in early childhood, and declines gradually as children mature. The perceptual form has the highest vulnerability to interference in the first five years of childhood, confirming once again the situatedness of very young minds and the massive control over them exercised by perceptual inputs. The linguistic vulnerability to interference is minimal in the first 3 to 4 years, indicating a relatively low-grade role of language in children's mental life, but shoots up significantly after 4, indicating a diminution of the control role of perceptual stimuli and an increased role for language.

The increased control role of language—first externally driven, whence the high sensitivity to linguistic interference, and only later under voluntary mental control, with a decrease in such sensitivity—presages the development of mental self-control, which is increasingly exercised over attitudes after 4. We often talk ourselves, almost literally, into *not* doing something we feel an urge doing, or desiring or even believing something we shouldn't. And we also often talk ourselves into doing things we feel like not doing (eating tofu, in my case, or watching boxing) or believing things just because a memorable phrase says so (e.g., an apple a day keeps the doctor away; really?).

Why do we do that? One basic reason is that language is effective in enabling us to represent and control the target-relatedness and affordances of our attitudes. This is what, more basically, self-regulation does. Language, in this respect, becomes children's (and adults') best self-regulator, an idea convincingly and influentially articulated by Lev Vygotsky many decades ago (1934/1962) and also developed by Dan Dennett in his account of consciousness (Dennett 1991, chaps. 7 and 8).

Self-Regulation

Self-regulation, in various forms, will become the fulcrum of my constructive argument, beginning in chapter 4. For now it suffices to note its teleological connection with a sense of target-relatedness and its developmental phases before and after 4.

It is because organisms are goal-directed that they are bound to engage the world, where most of their goals reside, and to evolve effective strategies of registering, monitoring, controlling and doing something about their *relations* to goal-relevant targets in the world. These are the strategies of self-regulation. Organisms evolve a variety of forms of self-regulating their target-relatedness, including their actions directed at targets, from the simplest feedback and feedforward versions of motor cognition to complex simulations of means-ends sequences in social and communicational interactions with other people and physical actions with tools and cultural gadgets.

The dominant modalities in which young children actively engage the world and the format of such engagements suggest the scope of their self-regulatory capacities, and therefore the presence and scope of their self-consciousness. As section 2.6 notes, below, the modalities in which young children display self-consciousness are those in which they show intent, means-ends initiative, top-down attention and control, multitasking, intermodal integration of information and contextual flexibility. These, according to later chapters, turn out to be the key executive abilities initially responsible for self-consciousness. In childhood, these abilities are first at work in social modalities directed at other people—affective, communicational and naive-psychological—and later in the perceptuomotor modality. It is only after 4 that the same abilities begin to operate inside the mind and regulate intramental modalities.

With a general sense of the extrovert-before-introvert orientation of children's minds, we turn finally to the two tightly interlocked faculties that dominate the argument of this book—understanding minds, in the form of an intuitive psychology, and self-consciousness. Both show the same pattern of ontogenetic asymmetry noted so far.

2.5 Naive Psychology

This section is going to be rather long and elaborate—for a good reason. On my hypothesis, children's understanding of minds—others' and their own—is the driving force behind the development of self-consciousness. This is why it is important to get things as right as possible about this capacity and the reasons why it is so intimately implicated in the development of self-consciousness.

The capacity to understand—or more modestly, make sense of—minds is variously called intuitive psychology, theory of mind, mindreading or interpretation. There are also the labels of folk or commonsense psychology, but I reserve the latter for a more sophisticated and late-developing version, discussed in chapter 6. In tune with the terminology used for other areas of young children's naive expertise, I prefer the label *naive psychology* for the early version. This label names a largely *procedural* or *know-how* competence that is actually made of several such abilities: to register, recognize, categorize, predict, evaluate and respond to the overtly expressed thoughts, attitudes and actions of others. Naive psychology is dominant during children's first few years and, after 4, is partially and gradually replaced by and partially absorbed into a more complex and explicit commonsense psychology. This overarching competence, with naive and commonsense versions, will be called *intuitive psychology.*

Although they are the main tools of understanding minds, naive psychology and its commonsense successor cannot do the job alone. They need other resources, in particular memory and thinking. As previous sections noted, these resources show a marked developmental asymmetry that favors the outside world and other people over one's own mind. This is evidence enough that young children's naive psychology is more than likely to follow the same pattern and show the same outward orientation. And so it does, for its own good reasons. The minds of others, through their overt expressions, are what infants first interact with, react to and depend on for their survival and well-being. What young children discern in other people are mostly the visible and easily recognizable expressions of their various inner states.

The view I advocate is in minority. Most philosophers in the modern tradition of Descartes thought that we are conscious of and understand our own thoughts and attitudes *before* those of others. Many philosophers and a few psychologists still think this way. But most psychologists nowadays and many philosophers see a *symmetry* between self- and other-ascriptions of attitudes in terms of developmental schedule and mental resources employed.

I disagree with *both* views. I see the asymmetry going the other way, with other minds first on the radar of young children's naive psychology, and their own minds registered and understood only later. I explain later in this section and in the next chapter where I think the majority view goes wrong. Before that, however, we need to survey the evidence and discuss its relevance to the others-before-self asymmetry thesis.

Other Minds First
There are several other-directed abilities, belonging mostly (though not exclusively) to naive psychology, which infants display from the earliest moments of postnatal life, in somewhat chronological order, until about 4: facial imitation; recognition of affect and emotion expressed in facial configurations, vocalizations and movements; recognition and tracking of

gaze; recognition of intent to communicate; recognition of trying to do something; recognition and then sharing of attention; recognition of desire and later belief, to cite just a few landmarks (Gopnik and Meltzoff 1997; Hobson 1993; Perner 1991; Tomasello 1999; Wellman 1990).

It may be objected that only these abilities have overt and behavioral expressions, and can therefore be studied scientifically. The objector may add that until the age of 2 children cannot describe or express how they view their own mental lives, assuming that they view them some way. So, the objection goes, there is no way of knowing. As a result, the self-conscious inner life of infants need not be excluded. There is indeed no way of directly refuting this objection. But there is evidence of various sorts that speaks rather convincingly for the alternative.

Some Data

Although debated, there is some direct evidence for the others-before-self asymmetry in the development of naive psychology. Thus, children appear to understand the desires of others around the age of 2 (Wellman 1990), but do not grasp their own previously unfulfilled or changed desires even a year later (Gopnik 1993). The same seems to be true of false belief: estimates by Astington and Gopnik (1988) place the self-ascription of false belief around 5, but its other-ascription around 3 to 4 (also Flavell et al. 1995; and Frith and Frith 2003, for surveys). Astington and Gopnik (1988) also report that, for young children, self-ascribing a false belief is more difficult than recognizing the false belief of another person. This asymmetry becomes even more pronounced when we consider data showing that children younger than 3 seem to recognize, implicitly and preverbally, the false beliefs of others (Clements and Perner 1994). I will return to the complex saga of false belief later in this section.

There is also indirect evidence for others-before-self asymmetry, which I find (if anything) even more robust and convincing. It indicates the absence in early childhood of abilities that either make self-ascriptions of attitudes possible or rely on such self-ascriptions. Thus, young children's *metacognition* that monitors intramental (as opposed to cognitive-motor) processing develops only after 4 and takes time to mature (Bjorklund 2005). Likewise *introspection*, which makes one's own thoughts manifest to oneself and their explicitly reflexive self-ascription possible, is estimated to emerge several years later, perhaps around 7 and 8 (Flavell et al. 1995; Nelson 1996). Before 7 to 8 children often fail to identify their own past thoughts, even when those thoughts were recently entertained (Flavell et al. 1995, 80–81). And as noted earlier, until 4, children lack autobiographical memory (Conway 2002; Nelson 1996). This advanced and in-control form of memory, which also develops gradually, is needed in—and is also symptomatic of—self-ascriptions of past thoughts and attitudes.

If, according to the majority views, young children master self-ascriptions of attitudes either earlier than or as soon as they master other-ascriptions; and if, as seems likely, they master the basics of ascribing attitudes to other people before 4, and some as early as infancy: why these significant delays in metacognition, introspection and autobiographical memory? Wouldn't this show that self-ascriptions of attitudes actually develop late and rather slowly? Furthermore—and as importantly—metacognition, introspection, autobiographical memory and self-ascriptions, particularly of past attitudes, require the *inhibition* of one's current cognition and often motivation. In a deliberate mode, one needs to quarantine or at least background the latter in order to run the former—and our inhibition has been shown to develop after 4 (Diamond 2001; Houdé 1995; Leslie 2000).

There is also fairly good *neurological* evidence for the others-before-self asymmetry. The early recognition of face, gaze and agency is handled mostly by the *left* hemisphere of the brain (Baron-Cohen 1995). The essentially procedural left hemisphere excels at routine and script-like employments of naive-psychological schemes which are typical of the recognition of face, gaze and agency, and also excels at selecting and processing a single, dominant mode of representation, and blocking out all the others— which is how the other-ascriptions of the first 3 to 4 years work. In contrast, the concept- and inference-based self-ascriptions of attitudes, which also require shifts in perspective through interactions with other-ascriptions, rely heavily on the frontal lobes and the work of the right hemisphere—both of which develop massively after 4 (Brownell et al. 2000; Stone 2000).

The *clinical* evidence seems to lend its support, too. Damage to the left hemisphere and some frontal areas of the brain, manifested in certain forms of autism, compromises the ability to handle joint attention and other-ascriptions of false belief—all failures of early naive psychology. In contrast, damage to the frontal cortex or right hemisphere, seen in some forms of schizophrenia, prevents complex (and second-order) self- and other-ascriptions—while leaving simple (first-order) other-ascriptions intact (Baron-Cohen 1995; Brownell et al. 2000; Corcoran 2000; Frith 1992; Stone 2000). As noted in chapter 6, the integrative work of the right hemisphere and the prefrontal cortex develops particularly after 4. Significantly for my asymmetry thesis, autism sets in at an early age and impairs the naive psychology of other minds, whereas schizophrenia usually emerges much later in adolescence and affects primarily self-ascriptions of thoughts and attitudes.

Both autism and schizophrenia are of course complex deficits with many forms and probably many causes, and both receive diverse explanations. I return to schizophrenia in chapter 7. For now, it suffices to add these clinical estimates to the story of asymmetry developed in this chapter.

Ascribing Attitudes

Having cited data, direct and indirect, for the others-before-self asymmetry, we need to focus on those specifics that explain the data and also explain why the early naive psychology cannot generate self-ascriptions of attitudes and hence (on my analysis) cannot underpin the development of introvert self-consciousness. It would help to begin with a conceptual sense of what it takes to ascribe an attitude and the different ways of doing it. Three conditions stand out.

Evidence
the evidence for other-ascriptions of attitudes is mostly visual and behavioral, whereas the evidence for self-ascriptions comes from inner experiences—a sense of mental activity, introspection, memories and more

Right Categories
having appropriate ways of recognizing, categorizing and eventually forming concepts of attitudes (desires, beliefs, etc.)

A Sense of Target-Relatedness and Its Affordances
understanding attitudes as related to targets and in the case of self-ascriptions, having a sense of one's *own* attitudes being related to targets and their affordances

These conditions can be met by several strategies, with different mental resources and different results. I will focus on those that matter to our inquiry. I discern three major strategies in the ontogeny (and possibly phylogeny) of naive psychology. One is based on one's ongoing perception, mostly visual, of someone else's observable relations to concrete and easily identifiable targets in a shared environment. I call this strategy *metarelational*, because it focuses on the observable target-relatedness of another mind. A second, mostly self-directed strategy (but with possible third-person applications in imaginative simulation) is based on one's inner experience of one's own attitudes and their contents. I call it a *metaexperiential* sense of self-attitudes. The third strategy is the *metarepresentation* of propositional attitudes, so called because children explicitly represent the target-relatedness of the mental representations of others or themselves. The first two strategies dominate the first four years; the third emerges only after 4.

Metarelatedness

Young children (and possibly chimpanzees) interpret the attitudes of others targeted on spatiotemporally concrete items in a shared environment, from an egocentric perspective defined by their current perception, motivation and action. I group these parameters under the notion of *situated* naive psychology (inspired by Perner's 1991 notion of a situation theory of mind). This is to say that situated naive psychologists represent observable other-to-target relations, such as seeing, or relations easily read from behavioral symptoms, such as wanting, emoting or attending. The situated recognition of another person's target-related attitude consists in categorizing and tracking three elements—the attitude's purposive *relatedness* to a target, the *direction* of that relatedness, and the *target* itself as a concrete, spatiotemporally defined item. In short:

metarelational category of attitude = purposive relatedness $\rightarrow$ visible direction $\rightarrow$ concrete target

Thus, for example, when young naive psychologists represent—perceptually, here and now, or in visual memory—another person looking at some object, they detect in the person's eyes and bodily posture a mental intent (e.g., curiosity, attention or interest) that is oriented in a visible direction to the targeted object. What they cannot do is imagine or infer someone else's attitude from nonvisual evidence, explicitly represent the other person's representations in relation to their targets, and factor in how the other person would represent the target. The latter scheme, which is metarepresentational, develops only after 4.

The main reasons for these limitations of the metarelational naive psychology are, roughly, the following (Bogdan 1997, chapter 5; also Bogdan 2003). As an evolved competence, naive psychology is essentially a perceptuomotor, *procedural* or how-to sort of expertise and practice, whose categories consist of *conditional rules*, activated by sensory or memory inputs (usually visual) and feeding into some action. Consider, for example, the behavioral category of gaze, construed as a set of such rules. On my analysis, this category tells the naive psychologist that

a. IF (someone's eyes are open), THEN (expect alertness and propensity for behavior), SO (affordance: be ready or do something)

b. IF (someone's eyes are open and looking in some direction), THEN (expect his interest or goal in that direction), SO (affordance: watch carefully or get involved)

On this analysis, naive psychologists understand gaze implicitly, in terms of such input–output rules, rather than explicitly, in terms of data structures formed by concepts that activate memories, mental images and other concepts inferentially or imaginatively. The same analysis works for other categories, such as desire, attention, and—as noted in a moment—belief as well (Bogdan 1997). This procedural and implicit grasp of the (rather simple) attitudes of others is quite distinct from the later explicit understanding of (more complex) propositional attitudes within the matrix of the successor, commonsense psychology.

There is further evidence of the procedural format of the early naive psychology. First, this format is consonant with how young children operate in the affectuomotor and perceptuomotor domains of social interaction. Second, there is a high likelihood that the earliest naive-psychological skills are innate, whether construed as modules (Baron-Cohen 1995; Leslie 2000) or weaker predispositions or biases (Karmiloff-Smith 1992; Meltzoff and Gopnik 1993). They are all likely to operate procedurally in a how-to format. When it comes to adaptations, evolution tends to install procedural skills rather than explicit bodies of knowledge, and the naive-psychological skills that young children need to do well in their earliest helpless and adult-dependent period are very critical adaptations indeed.

The instinctive and implicit procedurality of early naive psychology and its metarelational design has several important implications: (a) naive psychology is different from its commonsense successor and unable to represent propositional attitudes; (b) it is designed to represent and track other people's overt relations to visible and concrete targets; and (c) it cannot turn toward self and its introvertly accessible attitudes.

This analysis may be disrupted and thrown off its path by two zones of turbulence in the area of the study of intuitive psychology. Flying safely through them is essential to the cogency of our project.

False Belief and the Experiential Fallacy
One zone of strong turbulence is created by the fabled category of false belief. The other, less noticed but no less consequential, is created by the notion that the experience of one's own attitudes delivers a

metarepresentation of their target-relatedness. The former encourages the view that the recognition of false belief amounts to an understanding of propositional attitudes before 4 in terms that apply to both self and others. The latter suggests that self-understanding and introvert self-consciousness develop early, also before 4.

Both views, particularly when conjoined, undermine the asymmetry thesis and the general project defended in this book. This is because the recognition of false belief, in others and in oneself, is widely thought to distinguish conclusively between what is in the mind and what is in the world, thus providing an understanding of mental states as such; and because, in one's own case, if the experience of attitudes, and in particular of false belief, delivers a sense of target-relatedness, then children must possess self-understanding since infancy, in tandem with their experience of attitudes.

Fortunately, these views do not seem very plausible. But (the reader is forewarned) it will take some elaboration to show this. I begin with false belief and analyze it in two stages. In the first, I show that young children's recognition of false beliefs in others need not be metarepresentational, and can be handled by their early naive psychology. I then show that the experience of an attitude does not deliver a sense of its target-relatedness. Finally, I return to the story of first-person false belief and argue that, if young children seem to recognize their own false beliefs as easily and early as they recognize those of others, it is because the standard experiments measure, and their theories explain, only the children's *experience* of their beliefs—not the target-relatedness of the beliefs and hence their falsity. This is the experiential fallacy.

False Belief: Metarelationally Represented

There is a wide consensus in the developmental literature that young children can metarepresent, thus having a grasp of attitudes as related to propositional contents, and therefore are able to perform other-ascriptions and self-ascriptions of attitudes at the same time and with the same mental resources, roughly in the interval between 3 and 4. The critical test thought to confirm this accomplishment is the recognition of false belief.

I beg to differ.

One reason for my dissent has been anticipated: on some (admittedly small and debated) evidence, the recognition of one's own false belief emerges later than that of the false belief of others, suggesting a difference in the resources employed (Astington and Gopnik 1988). There is, however, a deeper reason for the asymmetry of resources. It is the distinct possibility that the recognition of false belief in other people, significant as it may be, may be within the procedural powers of children's *metarelational* naive psychology, with its egocentric stance and its bias toward the visible evidence of someone else's manifest relations to concrete (i.e., nonpropositional) targets in the world. Here are some highlights of this analysis (Bogdan 2003, 2005b).

For starters, there is an older dissident view that children younger than 3 might recognize false belief (Chandler 1988; C. Lewis 1994). There is more recent corroborating evidence that children younger than 3 are implicitly and preverbally aware of the false belief of another person by looking at the correct location where the other person believes an object is, before they answer questions about that location (Clements and Perner 1994). Some experiments push this recognition even earlier into infancy (Onishi and Baillargeon 2005). There are debates over these results. But if the estimates are right, then surely young children are bound to represent the false beliefs of others in metarelational and procedural terms. And if they do it at earlier ages, then they can surely do it with the same metarelational and procedural resources in the 3 to 4 interval.

Another argument is that recognizing false belief amounts to recognizing a *cognitive mismatch*. Yet cognitive mismatch is not the only sort of mismatch that young children recognize early in metarelational terms. Andrew Meltzoff (1995) has shown that 18-month-olds recognize *conative* mismatch as well, in the form of failed intentions or (more precisely) failed attempts by others to reach some visible goal. In the same conative mode, children younger than 3 also appear to recognize the misaimed desires of others (Wellman 1990, chaps. 8 and 10). With the help of alternative representations of actual and imagined situations, of which young children are capable (Perner 1991, chapter 3), failed trying, misaimed desires and false beliefs could all be represented by young children as another person's manifest relations to concrete targets: in the conative case of trying and desires (to put it graphically), as arrows coming from the inside out but failing to reach their targets; and in the cognitive case of false belief, as a present arrow going from outside in but failing to reach the person's mind and affect his behavior, because of an earlier arrow that did reach his mind (actually his eyes and then memory). In short, the fact that children younger than 3 or 4 recognize mismatch generally in metarelational terms suggests that they can do so without resort to metarepresentation. This recognition could apply to belief as well.

Still, one may wonder, could young children recognize belief at all without metarepresenting attitudes to propositions? I think they could.

First of all, the children's lean category of belief may be modeled on earlier categories of simple desire and perception or informational access (Wellman 1990). The latter *are* situated and metarelational. Mental development is likely to be conservative and resort to old tricks whenever possible, before venturing in new directions.

More convincing may be a different reading of the famous experiment (Wimmer and Perner 1983) that put false belief on the psychological map. The young naive psychologist, Sam, watches a room where Maxi, his friend, places some chocolate in a blue drawer and then leaves the room; mother enters, opens the blue drawer, takes the chocolate and puts it in a green drawer nearby; Maxi comes back to get his chocolate. Sam, the observer, is asked where Maxi will look for the chocolate. A Sam younger than 3 to 4 will say that Maxi will look for the chocolate in the green drawer (where it actually is); an older Sam will indicate the initial blue drawer (where Maxi actually thinks the chocolate is).

My reading of what the older Sam is able to do is (a) *inhibit* his current perceptual knowledge of where the chocolate is (green drawer), also (b) inhibit his propensity to relate Maxi to the chocolate in the green drawer, and (c) interpret Maxi's past perception of the chocolate at the old location (the blue drawer) as what Maxi remembers and thus causes his behavior. This last interpretation may take the form of a conditional rule, linking perception and memory, of the form, IF (someone has seen object X at location A), THEN (someone would remember X being at A).

Neurological evidence concurs. It turns out that false-belief tasks place strong demands on inhibitory control, sequencing and working memory—all represented in the frontal lobes and develop significantly around the age of 4 (Stone 2000).

Sam's representation of the whole story, in perceptual and memory terms, need not be more than metarelational. Sam recognizes only implicitly that there is something in Maxi's head (some visual memory) that does not fit the current facts. This recognition is implicit in Sam's mental moves made to ascertain Maxi's false belief. I do not think that the 3-to-4-year-old Sam, let alone his younger versions, could have an explicit and concept-driven representation of Maxi's false belief—or in general of what it is for somebody to have a mental representation that does not fit the facts. Sam's category of belief and his grasp of the word 'believe' are likely to draw implicitly on conditional rules like the one just suggested.

The point of this somewhat detailed analysis is not to contribute to an already huge literature on false belief. The point is to note the metarelational bias of young naive psychology, which extends to the grasp of false belief. The implication, against a wide consensus, is that this early naive psychology is not yet metarepresentational, and cannot be symmetrically deployed in self-ascriptions of attitudes. The procedural categories of metarelational naive psychology, evolved specifically to recognize third-person mind–world relations, cannot be turned to self and yield the same results. (Chapter 6 will expand on this limitation.) The contrary impression, which fuels the symmetry consensus and even the simulation asymmetry view, is also and largely due to a misreading of the second strategy of young naive psychologists: the metaexperiential one.

Experiencing Attitudes

Having an attitude, such as desire or hope, is usually accompanied by an experience—some longing or compulsion in the case of desire, resoluteness or excitement in the case of hope, and so on. The experience signals the presence of the attitude and may also identify it under some experience-driven category. This experiential evidence is one of the key conditions, noted earlier, for attitude ascriptions. (The other two are having the right category of attitude and a sense of its target-relatedness and affordances.)

The majority views—and in particular the theory-theory that advocates an other–self symmetry and the simulation theory that advocates a self-before-other asymmetry—often treat young children's experiences of attitudes and of their contents as *sufficient* for self-ascriptions of attitudes. For lack of a better term, I call these views *experientialist*. Since young children can easily recognize and linguistically describe the experiences associated with their various mental states and attitudes, the experientialist view seems to vindicate the theory-theory symmetry or the simulation asymmetry. The experientialist approach can be summarized as follows.

It starts from this assumption: if young children know the type of experience involved (say, a desire) and its content (what is experienced as desired), and also know that a particular sort of experienced desire and a particular sort of content are always associated, then they know *that* the desire is target-directed. So: they have the concept of desire as genuine attitude.

Suppose, for example, that we ask young Alice what she desires, and she says an orange. And suppose that, under further questioning, we determine that her answer draws on her recognition of a past experience (say, the taste) of oranges. Doesn't this show that Alice recognizes her desire *as* an attitude *directed* at oranges? If Alice recognizes that she has a desire *for* oranges, isn't this *ipso facto* a recognition of the desire being *related to* oranges (Josef Perner, personal communication)?

A related point can be made about memory (or any other experience associated with some attitude): isn't a child's memory of an event X an experience the child recognizes as representing X in a relational sense (Bertram Malle, personal communication)? If the answer is yes, then children can be credited with an experience-based recognition of the target-relatedness of a self-attitude, such as desire or memory.

I beg to differ.

Children may recognize their own attitudes and their targets as a result of how they are experienced, without thereby recognizing the *relations* between attitudes and their targets and affordances. Many observations and influential experiments misdiagnose children's self-ascriptions by measuring only their experiences of attitudes and experience-based categorizations of the attitudes, while missing the sense of their target-relatedness and affordances. Let me explain why.

I begin with a conceptual point. Having an experience of X, associated with an attitude about X, need not entail the recognition *that* the experienced attitude is related to X. The experience may signal the attitude type (desire or memory) as well as its target, but not the target-directed relation between the two. The target of the attitude is transparent *in* its experience, but not necessarily *in relation to* the experience. Experiences can be and often are autarchic or self-contained.

This is why consciously experiencing an attitude and its target is not yet having the *concept* of the attitude, which necessarily factors in the attitude's relation to the target and its affordances. Young children have thoughts, beliefs and memories, distinguish them experientially from other mental kinds (such as desires or perceptions), and know what their contents are (what they think, believe or remember) but do not, until a few years later, develop the concepts of attitudes as target-related and having affordances.

This analysis also invites a *reductio*: if the experiences of an attitude and of its content suffice for having the concept of attitude, why don't infants have the concepts of various attitudes, such as desire or belief? After all, infants *do* have beliefs and desires directed at targets of interest, and also experience them. Yet almost every student of naive psychology would agree that infants have not yet developed the pertinent concepts. Experiences are simply not enough.

Even regular associations between kinds of experiences and kinds of targets would not do. An analogy with language should help. Animals—particularly dogs and parrots—learn to associate experiences of sounds or gestures with targets in the world. If such learned associations yielded a sense of the target-relatedness of the experiences involved, these animals ought to understand word or gesture reference as a relation. But they don't. Children learn their first words, around six months, by association, *without* a sense that the words are intended to refer to their targets. That early understanding of words is radically different from, and significantly inferior to, the words learned ten or so months later through attention shared with adults. Only the latter reveals to the children the intended referentiality of words (Bates 1976; Bogdan 2009; Tomasello 1999, 2003). If naive psychology were acquired by learning regular associations between how conspecifics react or what they do and relevant targets in the world, then most animal species should be naive psychologists. But they aren't.

The same analysis works for self-ascriptions of attitudes. If regular associations between one's own experienced attitudes and their targets provided a sense of the target-relatedness of the attitudes, then animals and very young children, who can associate experiences and targets and get used to their regularity, ought to be able to *self-ascribe* attitudes in some form. But they don't.

If young children have any conscious sense of the target-relatedness of their mental states, it would most likely be at the level and in the modality in which they experience the target and engage it. In the earlier example of desiring an orange, young Alice would have a conscious sense of her visual and perhaps gustatory-motor orange-relatedness of her experienced desire (i.e., of what she sees and is poised to feel and do, given the anticipated taste), rather than a sense of her desire as a genuine propositional attitude.

This analysis of the experientialist fallacy invites a reexamination of the standard view of children's recognition of their *own* false beliefs. The theory-theory and simulation views take this recognition to be contemporary with that of false belief in others, and effected with the same mental resources. Again, I disagree.

One's Own False Belief: Only Metaexperienced

Suppose one once believed that the house on the corner was ugly, and now remembers that belief. How does one do it? There are two usual ways (though not the only ones) in which one may remember a past belief. Some clues may help one retrieve the initial *experience* associated with that past belief. (One sees another ugly house on some other corner and is reminded, by association, of that past belief.) Or alternatively, one may initiate a mental search by recalling and comparing notes with memories of one's past *self* as it mentally or behaviorally related to some other pertinent events, drawing some inferences, confabulating a bit and the like. The former strategy draws on episodic memory, which was said to be driven by past experience; whereas the latter strategy draws on autobiographical memory, which is less vivid, more abstract, and driven by imagination and inference.

It turns out that experience-driven, episodic memory cannot retrieve a past belief *qua belief*, that is, recognized as an attitude related to some fact. Episodic memory registers and retains the impact of the belief on the mind, the experience itself, but not its target-relatedness. Episodically, one just remembers the ugly house, and not the belief being *related to* the ugly house, even though one takes the remembered experience to be a sign of that past belief. It is only in the autobiographical mode that one remembers that one *believed that* the house on the corner was ugly, in the explicit sense that one was in that past mental relation to the house.

The moral of the story is this. If one has only an episodic memory of past experiences, one would remember one's own past beliefs only *as experiences*, and not as target-*related* beliefs. The memory of young children *is* episodic—and semantic as well—but not autobiographical. So the young memory cannot remember past beliefs *as* target-related attitudes, and hence as genuine beliefs. But if a young mind could not recognize beliefs as beliefs in the past, it would not recognize them in the present either. For, if anything, it is easier for a young mind to detach itself from a past experience than from a current one, and check on its past relation to the source of a given experience. If one cannot do it with the experience of a past fact, one is much less likely to do it with a current experience. In short, it seems that a mind exclusively driven by experience, present and past—call it, for our purposes, an *experiential mind*—cannot have a sense, let alone an understanding of its own attitudes as target-related, even though it has the experience of an attitude and can remember that experience. Young children may understand (metarelationally) the beliefs of others as beliefs, by registering their target-relatedness; but they do not understand their own beliefs as target-related beliefs.

This conclusion is confirmed by a much-discussed experiment, which I read along the lines just suggested. Young children were shown a vividly colored and easily recognizable box of Smarties (candies), and asked to guess what was inside the box. The children naturally guessed Smarties. Then they were shown that the box actually contained pencils. A bit later, the children were asked what they had first *believed* was in the box. If the experimental setup was such that the children could appeal to memories of their recent visual experience and of the questions asked (which were about Smarties), then they were able to recognize their own past false belief (that there were Smarties in the box) as early as 3 to 4, which is also the age at which they recognize false beliefs in others. But if the experimental setup was such that the children could not appeal to memories of what they had seen and what had been said, and had to reconstruct inferentially their past belief from indirect questions, then the 3- to 4-year-olds would say (wrongly) that they had believed there were pencils in the box, and only 5-year-olds would say (rightly) that they had believed there were Smarties in the box (Astington and Gopnik 1988).

The reader will recognize here the contrast between two types of memory. The first experiment actually tested the children's *episodic* memory of a past belief *as experience*, and not really their sense of a target-related (and hence false) belief. The second experiment tested the children's *autobiographical* memory of a past belief as an attitude *related to* a past target, confirming the fact that this sort of memory requires inference and sensitivity to context. This reading of the Smarties/pencils experiment speaks against the symmetry view of the theory-theory and the self-before-others asymmetry view of the simulation theory.

There is something else, quite important, about the Smarties experiment concerning one's own false beliefs in relation to the Maxi experiment concerning the false beliefs of others. In both experiments children are asked to figure out inferentially, or *reason* about, the beliefs involved. In the Maxi experiment, Sam, the young naive psychologist, is asked where Maxi would *look* for the chocolate, and the answer is taken to indicate *implicitly* the possession of the concept of third-person belief, or the lack thereof. In the Smarties experiment, the young naive psychologist is asked what she first *believed* or *thought* was in the box (pencils or Smarties), and the answer is taken to indicate *explicitly* the possession of first-person concept of belief or the lack thereof.

These are *distinct* questions whose vocabularies point to distinct abilities being investigated. It is much easier for Sam to figure out where Maxi would *look* than where Maxi *thought* or *believed* the chocolate was. And even if Sam could correctly answer the second question, my guess is that he would interpret it much like the first—in the visual terms of looking. The fact that children younger than 3 may recognize false beliefs in others by *looking* where the others should look confirms their predisposition to frame the false-belief task in visual terms. Likewise, the Smarties experiment is easier to pass, and at an earlier age, if framed in terms of visual or episodic memory but harder to pass, and at a later age, if framed in the more abstract terms of thought or belief, which are the terms of autobiographical memory.

These differences reflect the contrast between the early naive psychology, which is procedural, spontaneous, instinctive, largely noninferential, extrovert, other-directed and indebted to visual observation, and the later commonsense psychology, which is more descriptive, reflective, reconstructive and inferential, often introvert and self-directed. As naive psychologists, young children are not in the habit of 'reasoning' when detecting the gaze, attention, ignorance, pointing or simple desires of others; they seem to *do* it simply by deploying the right procedural abilities. Young children do 'reason' about visible other minds–world relations, such as beliefs, *when asked* by experimenters and occasionally adults around them. But then, it isn't always clear—at least, not to me—what exactly is being analyzed and evaluated by such questions. Is it the adult concepts and the extent to which these concepts are mastered by young children, or the language in which such concepts are described, or finally, the young naive-psychological abilities themselves? The semantics of young children's talk is likely to track their own abilities rather than the adult concepts and the adult language use.

The Larger Picture

In addition to what has been said so far, there are more general reasons for the others-before-self asymmetry.

I begin on an *evolutionary* note. A strong case can be made that young children's survival and well-being depend on adults. What young children need most is the interaction with and cooperation of adults in order to regulate their basic physiological, mental and behavioral processes, secure protection, and later assimilate the ways of adult society and culture, including language. Many of these priorities require the deployment of naive-psychological skills. In contrast, it is not a developmental priority at this early stage to understand oneself or even be conscious of one's own mind. In early childhood, most of the mental resources for these latter jobs are not available anyway. As noted in the second part of the book, the turn of intuitive psychology to one's own mind has its specific evolutionary reasons, concerning mental self-regulation, which are vastly different from the reasons involved earlier in the naive psychology of other minds.

The next, narrower point concerns the role of *vision* in naive psychology. The toughest challenge for young children's self-directed naive psychology is registering and conceptualizing the target-relatedness of their own attitudes. The *evidence* children have for the target-relatedness of the attitudes of others is not the same as in their own case. The target-relatedness of other-attitudes is detectible in the visible bodily features and behaviors of others, whereas the target-relatedness of self-attitudes is not visible in one's own behavior or mental activity. This evidential asymmetry is a matter of commonsense observation, and is confirmed by psychological research (Barresi and Moore 1996; Olson and Kamewar 1999). Congenitally blind children are delayed in developing a naive psychology (Hobson 1993).

Having said that, I think that the evidential role of vision is less consequential than it may seem. Children do not simply *learn* from visual experience to recognize the target-relatedness of attitudes in general. If that were the case, many animal species would be capable of naive psychology—but again, they aren't. All that an observer registers visually is the various spatiotemporal relations between movements, expressions or reactions of others and targets. The attitudinal directedness of those relations is neither visible nor obvious in any other way (Barresi and Moore 1996).

The real issue is the *wider matrix* in which the visual evidence fits and makes sense. To find out what that matrix is, one must ask what sort of evidence is needed for what sort of recognitional and conceptual abilities, handling what tasks and for what reasons. The analysis, in other words, should go in the other direction, from reasons to tasks to abilities to evidence—the standard and fruitful top-down method in cognitive science, which works for naive psychology as it does for other areas of cognition (Bogdan 1994, 1997). From this angle, the asymmetry in the evidence for other-ascriptions versus self-ascriptions reflects an asymmetry of reasons, tasks, and hence recognitional and conceptual abilities.

The reason young children *first* recognize *visually* the affects and emotions of others in their facial expressions, their gaze and its direction in their eyes and movements, and so forth, is that these are *precisely* the features of others that young children need first to react and adjust to, and also to manipulate and control, if they are to be adapted at this early stage in life. Furthermore, young children's adaptive responses to others (as forms of recognition, cooperation, communication, control, manipulation) need to be quickly, reliably and distally—hence visually—accessible to others in order to be effective.

So, before language, vision happens to be the most efficient, reliable and direct form of evidence for handling the recognition tasks generated by the challenges just noted. That vision cannot be directed at one's own attitudinal mind, to detect its target-relatedness and its affordances, is a trivial limitation in this early context of adaptation. For even if it could be self-directed—say, by imagining the visual perspective of another toward oneself, as is sometimes suggested (Barresi and Moore 1996; Tomasello 1999)—such visual detection would have *other* adaptive implications—say, for social intersubjectivity, interpersonal agreement, collaboration or establishing conventions—but would still not yield self-understanding, if the analysis of the next few chapters is right.

This concludes the argument for the outward orientation of the early naive psychology and its blindness to young children's own minds. It is an orientation matched by the young children's self-consciousness. This is the message of the next section. The second part of the book will argue that, far from being accidental, this match reflects a causal relation—from naive psychology to self-consciousness.

2.6 Self-Consciousness

The fuller story of self-consciousness will be told in the second part of the book. The narrower question now is how conscious are young children of their own thoughts and attitudes. Not much, if at all. This is the answer I find most plausible. Before I explain this answer, however, a competing and more radical answer must be addressed and disposed of.

Unconscious Infancy?

Some psychologists speculate that young children may lack consciousness altogether (Foulkes 1999), as do some philosophers who advocate a higher-order-thought theory of consciousness (Carruthers 1996, 2005). David Foulkes' argument is based mainly on infantile amnesia. His claim is that people don't remember events from the first three years of life *because* the original experiences themselves were not conscious. A dream expert, Foulkes also thinks that young children do not dream or dream very poorly for the same reason: to be dreamt, according to him, an event must be first consciously experienced, which is not the case in early childhood. On his view, amnesia about early childhood and the lack of dreaming during early childhood both suggest a lack of consciousness during that period. Peter Carruthers (1996; 2005, 49–53) bases his argument on the notion (which I greatly simplify here) that to be conscious is to have the capacity of forming thoughts about thoughts, which in turn requires having a meta-representational sort of naive psychology, which young children do not yet possess. So, the conclusion goes, young children (as well as animals) must be unconscious.

Leaving its plausibility aside—though not for long—this radical idea has the salutary effect of encouraging us to think of consciousness not as a brute given of the human mind, fully formed at birth and permanent, but rather as a gradual development that proceeds, possibly unevenly, along several (possibly independent) tracks, enabled by various abilities.

I concur. Instead of being a monolithic phenomenon, as often assumed, consciousness is more likely to develop in diverse modalities and forms that emerge out of a variety of resources, each having its own developmental schedule and rationale. It is in this spirit, that I propose to look at the ontogeny of self-consciousness.

The first step in this direction is to make the right distinctions. The radical idea that infants are totally unconscious implies that they manage their mental and behavioral affairs much like blindsighters in their blind field. Yet blindsighters manage visuomotor tasks without intent or means-ends initiative toward the targets of their visuomotor engagements (unless prompted), do not react to or reason and emote about their visual inputs, do not integrate those inputs with other sorts of available information from other modalities, and so on. As argued in chapter 5, these are among the vital executive abilities that install extrovert self-consciousness. Unlike blindsighters, young children do possess some of these abilities, judging from their steady advances in interpersonal interactions, prelinguistic communication and language acquisition.

To the extent that such advances point to abilities involved in self-consciousness (as I argue they do, in chapter 5), and also become springboards for later acquisitions, it is hard to see how young minds could initiate and manage these acquisitions unconsciously. And if they could, it is not clear what would prompt these minds to become conscious later on, when other acquisitions require similar abilities. Differently said: if young children are initially and for quite a while unconscious, while acquiring competencies that suggest the presence of intent, multitasking, top-down attention and the like, it is hard to explain how and why there could be a radical and brusque change from unconsciousness to consciousness later on, when other competencies are acquired under similar conditions.

What is possible, nevertheless, and indeed likely, is that young children are self-conscious only in the modalities subject to the executive abilities responsible for self-consciousness, whose range is exclusively extrovert, and possibly, at least in the early stages, only when those abilities are active. In other words, this could initially be a sort of intermittent, on-and-off consciousness that is not yet fully and durably installed as a permanent competence. Be this as it may, what seems plausible and consistent with the argument of this chapter is that young minds lack the *introvert* self-consciousness of their own offline thoughts and attitudes.

Missing: Introvert Self-Consciousness

Even though converging data from metacognition, introspection, autobiographical memory and intuitive psychology suggest that children younger than 4 are not conscious of their own offline thoughts, they may yet be aware, perhaps sporadically, of their *online* thoughts. Over many years, extensive research by John Flavell and collaborators has shown that young children have some conscious sense of thinking as mental activity and of thoughts as private mental states and events, distinct from external things and events (Flavell, Green and Flavell 1995; Flavell, Green and Flavell 1998; Flavell 2000). Also, young children's pretend play draws on an ability to distinguish pretend thoughts from actual perceptions or memories. Yet, as noted, these partly offline pretend thoughts seem largely continuous with, while introducing limited departures from, their current online perceptions, desires and memories.

At the same time, young children seem unaware of several key dimensions of their online thoughts, which are relevant to our discussion. The research by Flavell and collaborators indicates that young children do not register the temporal as well as thematic continuity of their online thoughts. They register thoughts as isolated and unconnected events, whose contents do not necessarily fit each other or a larger and continuous theme. Young children also fail to distinguish clearly between thoughts they initiate and thoughts that just happen to pop up in their heads, just as they do not see much of a difference between thinking and being distracted and losing one's train of thought. Further research by the Flavell team also shows that before 4 children are not much aware of their inner speech and do not practice it as much as older children and adults do (Flavell, Green, Flavell and Grossman 1997).

Besides giving some credibility to the earlier-noted idea of an on-and-off consciousness in young children, all this adds up to the following conjecture: before 4, children are aware only of the bare act of thinking, its experience, and of thoughts as isolated experiences, somehow popping up in their heads. To the minimal extent that they show up, their offline thoughts are not intended, controlled and actively pursued in light of what they represent and of the effects they can have, which is why (on my analysis) these children do not exhibit self-understanding and introvert self-consciousness.

Summing Up

The conclusion of this long, laborious but important chapter is that before 4 young minds are not yet ready to understand their own thoughts and attitudes. The needed resources are not yet in place or not sufficiently developed. Their naive psychology is oriented only toward other minds. As a result (as argued in chapter 5), young self-consciousness is extrovert. In support of this conclusion, our analysis also showed that other resources involved in or symptomatic of the development of self-ascriptions of attitudes—in particular, autobiographical memory, imaginative thinking and self-control—are not yet sufficiently developed for self-understanding to emerge.

This diagnosis poses a serious challenge to the most popular theories of naive psychology, at least as far as the self-ascriptions of attitudes are concerned. Making this critical and polemical case, in the next chapter, will add further weight to the conclusions of the present chapter; it will also bring in further details, consider other explanatory options, answer several objections, and consolidate the ground for the constructive arguments made in the second part of this book.

3 Theories of Self-Understanding

For most of the long history of philosophy and short history of psychology the question of self-understanding was largely a nonquestion. It was widely assumed that, somehow, the mind is always aware of its own thoughts and attitudes, and—if needed, with some disciplined effort—that it can focus on them introspectively. Easy and immediate access to one's own thoughts and attitudes was taken for granted, and their categorization into desires, beliefs and so on, was treated as more or less self-evident. Citations from Descartes, Locke, Hume, William James and phenomenology could easily prove the point. (I will have more to say about the Cartesian tradition below, and in chapters 7 and 8.) It is only within the last few decades that philosophers of mind and developmental psychologists have turned their attention to intuitive psychology as a specialized mental competence that is dedicated to the detection, categorization and interpretation of mental states—others' and one's own. In this chapter, I examine (rather briefly) the theories of self-understanding that dominate the field and have generated the most empirical data as well as heated debate.

The main accounts of self-ascriptions of attitudes are the theory-theory view and the simulation view. I locate my own position relative to them by reversing the predictions of failure that each makes against the other. The theory-theory predicts that simulation theory, by positing that self-ascriptions are prior to and easier to make than other-ascriptions, would be invalidated by evidence of temporal and cognitive symmetries between the two sorts of ascriptions. Simulation theory predicts that the theory-theory, by positing such symmetries, would be invalidated by evidence of asymmetries favoring self-ascriptions as earlier and easier than other-ascriptions.

I take the argument of the previous chapter to invalidate both theories: against the theory-theory, it suggested a temporal and cognitive asymmetry; but against simulation theory, it found other-ascriptions to be earlier and easier than self-ascriptions. Both theories share the assumption that other- and self-ascriptions draw on the same mental resources. In the next chapters I will also argue against this assumption and thus, again, against both theories.

A third account of naive psychology, which posits modular mechanisms of other-ascriptions, is very unlikely to apply to self-ascriptions of attitudes. Two other sorts of accounts are on my critical radar. One posits internal mechanisms that scan one's own mind and thereby deliver representations of one's own attitudes; the other considers mechanisms that render one's own attitudes and those of others shareable. Whatever their other merits, neither account explains the asymmetries analyzed in the previous chapter.

3.1   Naive Theorizing

This is the view that naive psychology operates almost literally like a theory, with specialized concepts that animate generalizations that in turn are employed in explanation and prediction. (Since naive psychology is most often called 'theory of mind' or ToM, this particular view of naive psychology, as naive theorizing, has been labeled 'theory-theory,' meaning the *theory* view of ToM. An inelegant and rather implausible label, but let this pass.)

What counts here is that the theory-theory view is committed to the developmental and conceptual symmetry between other- and self-ascriptions of attitudes (Gopnik 1993; Gopnik and Meltzoff 1997; Gopnik and Wellman 1992; Perner 1991; Wellman 1990; to cite just a few landmark works). I take the fairly comprehensive case made for the other-before-self asymmetry in chapter 2, to count against this position. But I have more specific arguments as well. The theory-theorist may agree that there are differences between self-ascriptions and other-ascriptions with respect to evidence and some supporting cognitive resources, such as inhibition and memory, yet still insist that they need not entail a difference in the *concepts* utilized, and that these concepts are what really matters in such ascriptions. The sameness of the ascription concepts would then appear to invalidate the asymmetry thesis. Actually, it doesn't—for several good reasons.

Let us recall first that the others-before-self asymmetry is *developmental*. At this point, the issue is not what sort of intuitive psychology the mature mind *ends up* with (a commonsense psychology, I will argue), but rather how the intuitive psychology begins and progresses in distinct phases of childhood. If, according to chapter 2, young children do *not* register the target-relatedness of their own attitudes, and that target-relatedness is an essential part of the concept of attitudes, while they register the target-relatedness of other-attitudes, then, during early childhood, children do not have the *same* concepts for other- and self-attitudes. Indeed, they do not have any concepts whatsoever for the latter. The fact, itself to be explained, that after several years the same concepts end up being applied in both types of ascriptions, does not invalidate the developmental point I am making.

Several points made in chapter 2 can be telegraphically recalled insofar as they weigh against the same-concepts position. One was the *evolutionary* point about the functions of intuitive psychology at different developmental stages. The early function of naive psychology is to deal with conspecifics, not with selves. The turn to self, as noted in chapter 6, is a late development that reflects new functions for the new commonsense psychology.

Another point concerned the different formats in which children represent attitudes before and after 4: the formats are based only on observable evidence and geared to visible relations of other people to concrete targets, before 4, and based on more complex, often linguistic evidence and geared to propositional attitudes, after 4. The concepts involved could not be same in the two stages, even though they become the same later on. Here is the main reason why.

Theory-theorists think that the child's naive-psychological concepts are formed and revised *in response to* perceptually accessible facts and regularities (Gopnik 1993; Gopnik and Meltzoff 1997; Gopnik and Wellman 1992). If so, it is hard to see how the concepts of other-attitudes could *initially* be the same as those about one's own attitudes, when what is perceived in others (eyes, bodily posture, actions) is so different from what one registers internally about oneself (various experiences). Unless, as the behaviorist joke has it, one needs to observe one's own body and behavior in order to infer one's own attitudes. And even when, later in childhood, the same concepts begin to operate in both types of ascriptions, it will not be because the evidence for naive theorizing becomes similar—for it doesn't. This is why I do not think that the theory-theory view has an explanation for this later process, any more than it does for the others-before-self asymmetry in early childhood.

3.2 Modules

Encouraged by Jerry Fodor's (1983) influential account of modularity, a few psychologists proposed that the basic resources of naive psychology are modular. The evidence for this proposal is that early naive psychology is species-wide and probably innate at its basic joints; is subject to well-sequenced developmental patterns; operates spontaneously, unreflectively, quickly and successfully; has its own specific domain; apparently draws on a proprietary database, not shared with other faculties; is immune to the influence of other mental traits, such as talent, motivation or intelligence; and, as autism shows, is subject to brain impairments, possibly of genetic origins. Among child psychologists, Alan Leslie (1991, 1994), Simon Baron-Cohen (1995) and Baron-Cohen and Ring (1994) argue for the strong modularity of naive psychology, as does Fodor himself (1992).

Baron-Cohen (1995) and Baron-Cohen and Ring (1994) distinguish several modules, which are independent but cooperative: an intentionality detector, an eye-direction detector, a shared attention module, and the theory-of-mind module that handles attitude ascriptions. This view allocates the functions of naive psychology to distinct mechanisms dedicated to a specific job, assumes fixed and unchanging architectural constraints on the form taken by the naive-psychological competence, and connects these constraints with definite brain locations with specific functions.

Despite massive disagreements in the literature, I think there are fairly good evolutionary and neuropsychological reasons for accepting that the young children's naive psychology may begin on a modular note, either with its own modules or by exploiting modules from the wider competence of social cognition (Bogdan 1997; Frith and Frith 2003). Modularity theorists agree that a modular naive psychology is directed at *other* minds only, and evolved for this very job. It is hard to see how the same modules, mostly sensitive to the visible features of other people (such as eyes, gaze, movements, and bodily aspects) can be redirected toward one's own (rather invisible) attitudes.

A problem for the modularity view is that by the time children begin to engage in self-ascriptions of attitudes, after 4, the role of the modules seems to diminish, making room for the flexible and open-ended strategies of a more elaborate, more powerful, more inferential and less instinctive commonsense psychology. This later development further vindicates the notion that naive-psychological modules are for other minds, not one's own, and only for early stages in ontogeny (Bogdan 1997). This very limitation of modularity thus confirms the others-before-self asymmetry in the development of naive psychology.

3.3   Simulating Others

According to the simulation view, one uses one's own mind to figure out another mind and predict or explain the latter's thoughts and actions.

There are two ways of doing this, the lean and the rich way. The lean way consists in using one's own practical-reasoning mechanisms (which one uses in making decisions and planning) to figure out how someone else would think and act, *without* employing naive-psychological concepts, anymore than one does in one's own thinking and acting (Gordon 1986, 2007). The rich way consists in introspecting one's own attitudes, which enables one to categorize them intuitively into appropriate kinds (desires, beliefs and so on), and then project the result onto someone else's mind (Goldman 1993, 2006; Harris 1992, 2000). Both the lean and the rich simulation strategies operate offline, in a pretend mode: one takes oneself to be in the shoes of another by imagining how one would think and act were one in the other's situation.

To begin with a generalization, I think simulation is somewhat problematic in the first few years of childhood, whether it applies to other minds or one's own. If that is so, then simulation theory is not really competing with other views as an account of early naive psychology. Consider other minds first. Young children's minds do not operate fully offline and therefore cannot engage in genuine imaginative pretense. They cannot simulate other minds in a reflective way. Nor, lacking inhibition, can they fully quarantine their ongoing mental activities in order to handle only the simulation tasks. Nor do young children really plan or reason practically in any full sense (Bjorklund 2005). It is therefore hard to see how effective they can be in using their practical-reasoning machinery to simulate what others would think, plan and do.

True, as in pretend play, young children can imagine limited alternatives to a current situation. They may therefore playfully pretend to be *in* the other's situation but cannot pretend to *be* the other and see the situation from the other's perspective. Taking the mental (as opposed to merely visual) perspective of another person is a late acquisition, maturing slowly after 4 (Flavell et al. 1995; Taylor 1988). All young simulators can do is me-in-the-other's-situation (something simulation theorists do not want). But then again, all the limitations of the young *me*, of my own mental life and imagination, would carry over to how *I* (young child) simulate the other. And we saw in the last chapter what those limitations are. They do not seem to enable simulative access, lean or rich, to other minds.

Notice the alternative: if naive psychology were a specialized theory or a set of modules, then the limitations of the young mind would be less consequential (less than in simulation, that is), because those specialized resources, no matter how limited, would be in the business of figuring out other minds. By avoiding specialization, simulation opens itself up to the possibility that young minds are not yet ready for naive psychology. But even if the simulation view could successfully explain third-person ascriptions, I do not think it has a coherent account of self-ascriptions, certainly not in young children.

Consider first the lean, practical-reasoning version of Robert Gordon (1986, 1993, 2007), which does not require ascription concepts. It has two options. One is an *ascent routine* that habituates the child to the link between a content in mind and first-person locutions, such as 'I believe that . . .' As noted in chapter 2.4, this habituation can at best link a content and an experience without necessarily delivering the target-relatedness of the experienced attitude. Furthermore, I do not see how the ascent routine works for 'I falsely believe that . . .' and particularly for the past-tense self-ascription, 'I believed falsely that . . .' without begging the question at issue, which is how one's own past (doxastic) target-relatedness is represented. As Gordon notes, the ascent routine cannot deliver that relatedness (1993, 45). The routine provides at best a head start for counterfactual and imaginative simulation, which is the other option. How would this option work, assuming (quite counterfactually) that it could work in early childhood?

According to Paul Harris (1992), in the test of one's own past false belief, the child must imagine the proposition she originally entertained and took to be true (Smarties in the box, according to the experiment discussed in chapter 2.4) and, inhibiting her current knowledge (of pencils), report that original proposition. Before 4, children have the same difficulty representing their own past false beliefs as they do those of others, for (according to Harris) they do not have enough counterfactual imagination. But even if they had enough such imagination, how would that imagination track the target-relatedness of their own past belief? Young children imagine mostly in visual terms and those, I have argued, are not the right terms for discerning one's own *past* target-relatedness.

How about the rich, introspective simulation based on ascription *concepts* (Harris 1992; Goldman 1993, 2006)? This view advocates an asymmetry in the opposite direction from mine: self-ascriptions develop earlier and are easier to make than other-ascriptions. One problem, already noted in chapter 2, is that the introspection that classifies attitudes need not reach beyond experience, current or remembered. As Alvin Goldman notes (1993, 105), introspection can identify the type and content of a self-attitude but not its target-relatedness and hence truth value. As he puts it, "the cognitive system [must] use . . . information about the *intrinsic* (nonrelational) and *categorical* (nondispositional) properties of the target state. . . . The best candidates . . . are the so-called *qualitative properties* of mental states—their phenomenological or subjective feelings" (1993, 87). Quite so. As Goldman acknowledges, such qualitative properties are less central to propositional attitudes, such as beliefs or intentions. But the critical point has to do with the target-relatedness of one's own attitudes, which the introspective information cannot reveal, not by itself.

Another problem is that introspection looks like a fairly late development, perhaps as late as 7 or 8 (Flavell et al. 1995), which is even later than the onset of self-ascriptions. Like Harris, Goldman (1993, 43) thinks that the key obstacle for young introspectors attempting to recognize their own past false beliefs is the sorting out and dating of conflicting representations. This is right, but even when the representations of current and past contents are sorted out and dated, young introspectors still have no idea of their former self being representationally related to and actually misrepresenting a past content. They just recall—episodically but not autobiographically—a past content, as experienced, that is different from a current one. That, I have argued, is not good enough for understanding attitudes.

Naive psychology by simulation may be a viable strategy for figuring out *other* minds, but only after the age of 4, when the right resources are in place and the child's mind benefits from various other acquisitions as well. Yet, given the reasons cited throughout this book, I doubt that, simply in its own terms and with its own resources, introspective simulation can deliver a sense of the target-relatedness of one's own thoughts and attitudes.

3.4   The Inner Metamind

The introspective simulation view follows in the footsteps of the influential Cartesian tradition, according to which our own mental states, and in particular our own thoughts and attitudes, are immediately or noninferentially accessible to us in content and type. When I desire that p, both the desiring and its content (p) instantly enter my consciousness, without further ado. It is as if a special center or capacity of the mind—which I will call, generically, the metamind (tipping my hat to Keith Lehrer 1997)—starts scanning the mind as soon as the latter is 'turned on,' and detects and classifies the basic units of the passing mental show and grasps what they represent. Since Descartes, the job of the metamind and the immediately or noninferentially accessible mental states it spontaneously illuminates have played a major role in analyses of phenomenal consciousness, self-knowledge and epistemic justification. These topics, however, are not of concern here. The concern is with how children develop an understanding and consciousness of their own thoughts and attitudes and in particular of their target-relatedness and affordances.

Philosophers have proposed mechanisms that run the metamind, such as inner perception (Armstrong 1968; Lycan 1996) or introspection (e.g., the rich simulation view noted earlier). A version of the inner perception view, sensitive to naive psychology and developmental data, has been proposed by Shaun Nichols and Stephen Stich (2003). They posit a self-monitoring mechanism—actually a module—that detects and recognizes one's own mental states. This mechanism is held to be active from the age of 2. It works like this: "when activated, [it] takes the representation *p* in the Belief Box as input and produces the representation *I believe that p* as output . . . To produce representations of one's own beliefs, the monitoring mechanism merely has to copy representations from the Belief Box, embed the copies in a representation schema of the form *I believe that* ____, and then place the new representations back in the Belief Box" (Nichols and Stich 2003, 160–161).

Nichols and Stich talk of the self-awareness of one's own attitudes that is generated by the work of the monitoring module. As I see it, the major problem here is that such self-awareness is likely to be absent in young minds. As noted in chapter 2, young children are aware of their affects, emotions, perceptions, perceptuomotor intents and perceptual memories, and are extrovertly conscious of these experiences being related to targets and having affordances. But young children do not seem to be aware of their more sophisticated attitudes, such as beliefs and intentions, in the same target-related and affordance terms. They cannot perform the belief-box trick described by Nichols and Stich until later—indeed, until they reach 4, on my reckoning.

In a footnote, Nichols and Stich write that "the monitor is just a rather simple information-processing mechanism that generates explicit representations about the representations in various components of the mind and inserts these new representations in the Belief Box" (loc. cit.). To my mind, this description is compatible with young children's lack of understanding and consciousness of their own thoughts and attitudes. As noted in the next chapter, no mind—human or animal, young or mature—can operate successfully without internally monitoring its representations. But such monitoring need not generate *conscious* representations of what is monitored, and in general it doesn't; it can operate unconsciously and subpersonally (so to speak), unless the conditions for introvert self-consciousness are met, which (in my view) are met only in human minds and only after the age of 4.

Nichols and Stich's proposal does not directly address the crucial question of the monitoring of the target-relatedness and affordances of one's own attitudes. The parameters monitored are the attitude type (e.g., belief) and the content (what is believed). This, again, is close to young children's metaexperiential strategy (discussed in chapter 2.4), and also to the introspective simulation and inner perception views noted earlier. These two experiential parameters—attitude type and content—need not reveal the *relation* between the representation involved and its target or the affordances of the relation. But then, it is not clear that young children can be plausibly said to be introvertly conscious of those mental states *as* genuine attitudes.

Nichols and Stich draw a careful and useful distinction between detecting mental states, which is the job the monitoring mechanism, and reasoning about mental states, which is the job of naive psychology. Looking ahead, I will also honor this distinction in later chapters, but on somewhat different grounds and in different terms. One difference is that the monitoring mechanism posited by Nichols and Stich is, in my later analysis, part of a more complex self-regulation that reaches beyond one's inner experience (which is what the monitoring proposed by Nichols and Stich ranges over) and involves its target-relatedness and affordances. This self-regulation remains introvertly unconscious of the thoughts and attitudes it handles until 4 or thereabouts.

Another difference is this. Young children recognize their own experiences—affectuomotor, emotional, perceptual and memorial in particular—as they relate to targets and have affordances. But this recognition, I suggest in chapter 5, is more complicated than that delivered by a simple monitoring mechanism and does not reach one's own attitudes in an introvertly conscious way until several years later.

3.5 Shared Minds

A potential and promising approach to self-understanding exploits a cluster of recent discoveries and hypotheses that may be subsumed, rather eclectically, under the label of 'shared minds.' The overarching idea is that young minds either come equipped with or develop capacities to resonate directly to and thus to share in the experiences, actions, perceptions and attitudes of others, without the mediation of representation, imagination or inference. I will call these capacities for *mental sharing*. They come in two categories, depending on the targets at the end of the sharing relation.

In the first category, with minds at both ends, we find such well known phenomena as bilateral exchanges of facial expressions, the unmediated sharing of feelings (in the form of empathy, emotional contagion), the direct expression and reception of some experience or state of mind (such as anger or fear), and also facial and behavioral imitation. These are the first interactions of human infants, and are entirely interpersonal. To the extent that infants relate to specific mental states of others as targets, relative to which they exercise intent, top-down attention, means-ends initiative and other appropriate executive abilities, infants may develop their earliest conscious sense, in a communicational or affectuomotor modality, of a self-to-a-mental-target-in-another-person relatedness. It is a conscious sense bearing on the relatedness of the infants' experiences, not really attitudes, and they are exclusively extrovert and others-oriented.

In the second category, we find the worldly targets to which children and other persons are related. Of interest here are those forms of mental sharing that require or produce a conscious sense of target-relatedness both in others and self. In this category we find several candidates. One candidate, recently discovered and the most discussed, is *neural mirroring*. The mirror neurons involved do double duty: they fire when a primate (monkey, ape or human) observes the action of a conspecific and when he, himself, performs a similar action (Rizzolatti et al. 1996). Mirror neurons in turn may be a platform, but not the only resource, for the imitation of target-related actions (Meltzoff and Decety 2003).

There is another candidate as well. To explain imitation, particularly of target-related actions, Andrew Meltzoff and collaborators have developed the idea of a mapping of young children's motor plans and experiences, monitored internally, onto the observed actions, postures and attitudes of others, resulting in a *'like-me' intersubjective equivalence* (Meltzoff and Moore 1977; Meltzoff and Gopnik 1993; Meltzoff and Decety 2003).

Finally, John Barresi and Chris Moore (1996) advanced the hypothesis of an "intentional schema" that integrates in a common format first-person experiential information about an attitude and third-person information about an other-attitude to a target. The resulting common representation can be applied to the mental states and activities of both self and others. The intentional schema is intermodal, since it integrates first-person kinesthetic and proprioceptive information with visual information about third-person behavior, and preserves the quality of both sorts of information. Thus, for example, through the use of the intentional schema, the observer of another person who looks in a certain direction could generate a representation of an attitude that could be applied equally to self or the other. In more mature minds, imagination can replace current kinesthetic information about self and perception of someone else's body and action, and feed the intentional schema with information from memory.

Finally, somehow echoing the Meltzoff proposal, Olson and Kamawar (1999) suggest an alternative version, without the mediation of an intentional schema, in which the internal experience of a feeling is directly associated with the observation of the attitude of another person.

All these proposals are variations on the larger theme of mental sharing. As far as our discussion goes, mental sharing can be seen as a bridge between abilities to detect and represent self-to-target and other-to-target relatedness. In principle, the transfer could go in either direction. Simulation theorists could argue that a sense of self-to-target relatedness may be projected through mirror neurons onto the actions and experiences of another person. In the other direction, a theory-theorist might argue that 'like-me' equivalencies enable young children to transfer the detection of others' perceptual and behavioral relatedness to their own experienced attitudes. The intentional schema and the simplified version of Olson and Kamawar would also go in this direction, from the perception of the target-related other to the experience of the self.

Whatever the direction, the question is whether this transfer idea is plausible. Let me begin by recalling that our inquiry is about attitudes. All these versions of mental sharing concern early childhood, which has already been identified as a period during which young minds are largely limited to the here-and-now of perception and motivation, and register and recognize mostly perception- and action-bound relations in others. Young children also register their own experiences of perception, motivation, intent to act, feelings, simple desires and so on. But their own target-related attitudes are beyond the reach of their minds, for a while at least—so transfer by mental sharing is not going to help on this score. It is not clear to me that mental sharing of attitudes (as opposed to feelings, emotions, imitations and the like) by the mechanisms just surveyed operates in later childhood and maturity. Even if it does, it must interact with a rich panoply of other acquisitions in ways that make the transfer much more mediated.

Having said that, I think the transfer idea may be less plausible even on its narrower domain of perception and action during early childhood. It is not clear that *by themselves* mirror neurons or 'like-me' equivalencies or even the intentional schema can detect and represent the target-relatedness of perception and action—of another or of oneself. If young children's minds merely register *associations* between the other's behavioral expressions or actions and targets out there, or, in their own case, between proprioceptive or kinesthetic or other sorts of experiences and targets acted upon, then the mental-sharing mechanisms would simply transfer representations of such associations. The question, therefore, is what *other* mechanisms are engaged in such mental sharing, which could deliver a robust and possibly transferable sense of target-relatedness and its affordances. But then we are back to the points made critically in chapter 2. It should be noted that mirror neurons and 'like-me' equivalence mechanisms operate most of the time unconsciously, which is not conducive to a conscious sense of the target-relatedness of one's own attitudes—not unless one's conscious experiences are appropriately engaged, as seems to be the case only with the intentional schema.

Despite my skepticism as to whether the mental-sharing mechanisms examined here can sponsor the later and more complex self-ascriptions of attitudes—that is, attitudes other than communicational, perceptuomotor and affectuomotor, which dominate early childhood—I think that the general idea of mental sharing is promising and worth pursuing if construed as a form of *coregulation* (Bogdan 2000, 2001, 2007, 2009). In early childhood it may take one or more of the forms just surveyed. In late childhood, as I note in chapter 6, it involves an alignment of one's own self-regulatory abilities and experiences to the public concepts, rules and practices of a commonsense psychology, with self-understanding as a result.

Transition
The main point of this critical chapter was to show that the most influential accounts of early naive psychology do not explain the developmental asymmetry noted in chapter 2, and in particular the absence of self-understanding in early childhood. The empirical data and the larger picture of what young minds can and cannot do in various modalities, surveyed in the preceding chapter, as well as the objections to alternative accounts made in this chapter, suggest that children become able to self-ascribe attitudes, thereby manifesting self-understanding, and become introvertly self-conscious of them, only after the age of 4.

If this is a fact, what explains it? Why does self-understanding develop later than the understanding of other minds, at least with respect to the target-relatedness and affordances of the attitudes involved? And why, as a result, does children's self-consciousness develop first in an extrovert direction and only later in an introvert direction? These are questions that will occupy our attention in the second part of this book.

II Toward an Explanation

4 Premises

This chapter marks the limits of the territory to be explored in what follows and identifies the main landmarks that will guide our inquiry. To start things off with a clear sense of what is *not* explained in this second part of the book, section 1 will signal major departures from standard accounts of consciousness. One departure is to quarantine phenomenal consciousness and focus solely on the functional format of self-consciousness. The other departure is to reject the essentialist notion that consciousness is innately constitutive of the human mind and generated by dedicated mechanisms.

The next two sections jointly make the case for the intrinsically relational format of self-consciousness, on intuitive and conceptual grounds (section 2) and empirically through the work of self-regulatory mechanisms that demarcate the self from the world and supervise its relations to the world and their affordances (section 3). These self-regulatory mechanisms, found in practically all animal minds, point to the executive premises of self-consciousness. The question, then, is for what reasons and in what conditions the executive mechanisms install self-consciousness.

The remainder of this chapter and the next two chapters gradually articulate an explanation. Section 4 introduces the first piece of the eventual answer. It is the self-regulatory role of the children's intuitive psychology. The latter guides and controls the assimilation and mastery of sociocultural activities and practices, and does so in a means-ends format that recruits and assembles the executive abilities whose joint operation installs self-consciousness in its two versions, first extrovert and then introvert.

4.1 The Paths Not Taken

Philosophizing about consciousness is like walking on nails. I hope to avoid the philosophical wounds these nails inflict, for a simple reason: I will not propose an account of consciousness in general, nor will I tackle the difficult and elusive phenomenal side of consciousness, where most of the nails are. My narrow aim is to sketch a functional profile of self-consciousness as uncontroversially as possible, in order to explain its roots and asymmetric development. At this stage of the inquiry, the main dimensions of this profile are the relational format and the self-regulatory origins of self-consciousness.

Before proceeding, it may preempt misunderstandings and further clarify my explanatory strategy if I say a few words about how my take on self-consciousness relates to some intensely debated topics in the study of consciousness.

Self-Consciousness versus Phenomenality

Even though phenomenal consciousness is not on the agenda of this book, an assumption about it is. The assumption is that the normal *manifestation* of phenomenal consciousness in fully developed human minds is made possible by the executive machinery responsible for self-consciousness. This is to say that there would be no normal phenomenal consciousness without self-consciousness grounded in self-regulation. As noted later, there may be phenomenal pulsations, of the on-and-off sort, in some animal or semi-vegetative or infant minds, suggesting that the self-regulation responsible for self-consciousness is limited or impaired or, in the case of children, not yet fully developed.

The foregoing being merely an assumption, there will be no argument for it in what follows. Nevertheless, this and later chapters do produce some intuitive as well as experimental evidence that *phenomenal* consciousness depends on executive mechanisms and their functional interactions. At the same time, there is a strong possibility, intuitively plausible, that consciousness also has *nonphenomenal* manifestations—as, for example, in abstract thinking or when entertaining so-called cold attitudes, such as suppositions or conjectures. Paradoxical as this may sound, it may turn out that phenomenality is not the essence of consciousness but rather a potent and biologically useful way of manifesting it. I will not press this point here but will add a few remarks in the concluding chapter.

Essentialisms

It is fair to anticipate that my take on self-consciousness disagrees with theories which, for lack of a better word, I will call *essentialist*. These are theories that assume that consciousness is somehow intrinsic and congenital to the human mind, either as its essence or mode of existence (the strong Cartesian view) or as the output of specialized and dedicated mechanisms of introspection or inner perception or, metaphorically, as the experience of an 'inner eye' (a variety of recent views).

There are good reasons to be skeptical of such essentialist views. One well-known reason is that most of the cognitive work of the human mind, including the work of uniquely human capacities, such as grammar, is done unconsciously. Another reason, unintuitive but steadily gaining acceptance, is the experimental evidence that a good deal of deliberate mentation—in intending, decision making, problem solving and planning—is also carried out unconsciously, allowing consciousness only a limited role of vetoing the result or changing tack. These two reasons raise the question of what exactly is the (apparently rather limited) function of consciousness. I do not have an answer to this question, but the argument of the next chapters points to an initially self-regulatory function exercised first in sociocultural tasks and practices.

Still another reason to doubt the essentialist wisdom about consciousness can be derived from the developmental analysis proposed here. Suppose, as I hope to convince you below, that there are two major forms of consciousness, extrovert and introvert, distinguished by major neuro-executive differences in the growth and work of the prefrontal cortex, and that these two forms develop at distinct stages of ontogeny, in close conjunction with intuitive psychology and its regulatory operation. The latter in turn activates a suite of executive abilities that are reliably associated, both intuitively and neuropsychologically, with manifestations of consciousness. It is hard then to see how consciousness, particularly its introvert version assumed by the Cartesian tradition, could be essential to or constitutive of the mind, and equally hard to see how innately specialized and dedicated monitoring or introspective mechanisms could be responsible for the developmental pattern outlined in previous chapters and further elaborated later.

Finally, consciousness has this much in common with language, construed as a cocktail of capacities with distinct functions (for phonetics, morphology, grammar, semantics, discourse): like language, consciousness does not *self-install* in development as a general disposition (as does irritability, for example, or facial imitation) or as a specialized mechanism (such as attention), and it actually requires the assembly and orchestration of many distinct abilities in order to be installed as a durable capacity. And like the development of language, that of consciousness takes a good number of years to reach normal maturity, shows different degrees of proficiency along the way, and its normal exercise can be impaired by a variety of deficits and injuries affecting the contributing abilities. Mindful of these shared features, if one is not essentialist about language, then one should not be about consciousness, either.

The Apparent Priority of Consciousness

There is a long tradition in philosophy, at least since Descartes and resiliently surviving to this very day, which holds that our own thoughts and attitudes consciously appear to us directly, effortlessly and immediately or noninferentially; they just stare at us from inside, as it were, with their contents transparent and their functional profile, as thoughts and sundry attitudes (desires, beliefs and so on), identified in virtue of being consciously accessible. I argued in chapter 3, against both the introvert simulation view and the inner monitoring view (sections 4.3 and 4.4), that their position is implausible for three main reasons: first, young children do not possess an introvert consciousness; second, even if they did, they as well as older children could at best recognize experiences associated with attitudes, but not their target-relatedness; and third, as simulation theorists admit, bootstrapping a sense of its target-relatedness out of experiencing an attitude is close to an impossible task.

Nevertheless, these positions and Cartesianism in general may object that, recognition of target-relatedness aside, it must still be the case that one should first be conscious of the states of one's mind *before* recognizing them (by whatever means) as being of one attitudinal sort or another. This objection aims at my argument in chapter 7, to the effect that it is self-ascriptions of attitudes and hence self-understanding that install introvert self-consciousness by recruiting and assembling the right executive abilities. This objection occasions a number of apparently plausible questions that suggest that my argument may be heading in the wrong direction. Let us begin by framing the questions intuitively.

Doesn't one first need to illuminate one's mind and register what is there before—and in order to—recognize, classify and make use of what is there? Don't we first turn on the lights before seeing and recognizing what is in the room? And isn't consciousness this light that illuminates the mind, before anything else is figured out there? Isn't it the case that in the morning, when awakening, the brain first turns on the consciousness switch before we become aware—and in order to become aware—of what is going on around us and inside our minds? And when consciousness weakens or is switched off, so is the mind worth talking about. In short, mustn't one become introvertly conscious of one's own thoughts *before* determining their attitudinal profile?

Turning to empirical data, isn't there even a well-documented developmental instance that supports the Cartesian insight: in the older children studied by John Flavell and collaborators (1995)? These children, we recall, are conscious of some free-floating and almost pulsative thoughts, which they cannot yet anchor as stable attitudes and relate to other thoughts and possible actions. Don't these children fit the Cartesian idea that introvert consciousness of thoughts develops before the functional profile of thoughts, as attitudes, take over?

In sum, the challenge in this Cartesian line of argument is that consciousness in general and its introvert version in particular are the *primary* phenomena, in the literal Greek sense of what appears to us from inside, and that everything else follows from and is dependent on it. In particular, if one can spontaneously have introvertly conscious thoughts, why would self-ascriptions of attitudes be prior to and necessary for introvert self-consciousness, as chapter 7 will argue?

There is an intuitive basis for this Cartesian challenge. Neither young children nor adults need to activate their intuitive psychology in order to perceive and believe something consciously. Nor do older children and adults need to self-ascribe attitudes in order to be introvertly conscious of their offline thoughts. And yet, the very intuitiveness of the Cartesian challenge points to what I think is fallacious about it, when looked at *developmentally*.

Competence versus Performance
The Cartesian angle on consciousness is a *performance* angle. It is the angle on how things work mentally, once all the necessary conditions and resources are in place and operational. It is *not* the angle adopted in this book. Explored here is the *development of a competence*, not its normal exercise afterwards. In other words, the issue here is how children *become* self-conscious in the first place, and not how their self-consciousness operates later. Driving, as a competence, is initially learned by explicit instruction, most of it verbal, and by explicit motor imitation, but it ends up as an instinctive and nonverbal how-to routine in performance. One cannot use the result to figure out the emergence of a competence; in general, one cannot use performance to figure out the acquisition of a competence.

Besides being unfathomable from the perspective of its exercise, the competence for self-consciousness has further intriguing features. On my analysis, self-consciousness as a competence develops out of several executive abilities that have little to do with its eventual exercise. Yet it is only its exercise in performance and what it applies to that we register in general and intuit introspectively in particular. Many mental competencies develop for reasons and in ways that have little if anything in common with their later exercise. For example, in its early stages, the major mechanism for word acquisition is shared attention, even though words are later acquired and used without sharing attention with others. Likewise, the competence for predication draws on shared attention and socially enabled word acquisition, even though its later exercise no longer presupposes either (Bogdan 2009). Grammar may be activated only in contexts of early communication, yet later it does not need communication anymore and often structures solitary thinking. And so on.

I think the same is true of self-consciousness in both its extrovert and introvert versions. Intuitions about the mind in general and consciousness in particular, including the potent and durable Cartesian intuitions, draw on and are shaped by our mental performances—by how things consciously appear to us when we perceive, think, believe, imagine, remember, introspect, and so on. Even with analytic discipline, this is just the phenomenological surface. Neither developmental history nor mental software nor the neuropsychological springs of our mental design are visible or even intelligible from this performance angle, yet all three are critical to this inquiry, concerned as it is with what *installs* the competence for self-consciousness in the first place and why.

Needless to say, once this installation has taken place, self-consciousness in both versions acquires a life of its own, with ever new contents and applications, many of which are outside intuitive psychology and sociocultural activities. But then, such is the case with so many competencies, from walking to speaking: the initial domains of selection or development—call them the *installation domains*—are enriched, changed and sometime even replaced by new and unrelated domains of use. Yet the reason for and often the design of the competence involved would be unintelligible without attending to the installation domain, with its specific selection pressures and resulting adaptations.

Transition

This first section has been about which central features of consciousness will not be discussed in this book—primarily its phenomenal character—and which takes on consciousness my inquiry finds implausible—the performance perspective just described and, earlier, the essentialist views that consciousness is innately constitutive of the human mind or is the output of a dedicated mechanism, and that therefore it self-installs, much like bodily organs, out of dedicated genetic bases. Having thus cleared the ground and limited the territory to be covered, we now turn to the constructive story. The first task is to show that self-consciousness operates in a relational format.

4.2 Relational Consciousness

From the intuitive angle of its exercise, consciousness may not appear relational. Conscious experiences of various sorts, both introvert and extrovert, usually appear as merely conscious of some content (full stop) rather than conscious of being related to some target and conscious of the affordances of such a relation. From the same intuitive angle on performance, mental states appear to be conscious in and by themselves. A vast literature, motivated mostly by the puzzle of phenomenal consciousness, has been built on the angle of performance, of how things appear to us intuitively. Phenomenal consciousness is easy to intuit, as the accessible output of an underlying competence, but is hard if not impossible to explain reductively, because any such explanation must focus on the competence, and the latter (*pace* Leibniz) is neither phenomenal at its basic joints nor phenomenally accessible.

In short, the exclusive preoccupation with phenomenal consciousness and the intuitive angle on its exercise have led to a nonrelational view on autarchically conscious mental states. This, I think, is not how things look from the perspective of consciousness as competence. On closer inspection, though, things do not look that way even conceptually and intuitively.

Eminently Relational

The reader would recall that the present notion of self-consciousness is understood *relationally* as consciousness of self-to-target relatedness and of its affordances. This is not just extrovert consciousness *of* a target, as in being conscious of an apple on the table. It is the consciousness of seeing, or being visually related to, the apple. Drawing on memory, motor schemes, habits, and so on, it is also the consciousness of what apples are for, or of what can be done with them. The latter is consciousness of the affordances of target-relatedness. Likewise, introvertly, self-consciousness is not just the consciousness of a thought but rather of being related to what the thought is about and affords.

Furthermore, self-consciousness is not consciousness of one's target-relatedness in a disembodied and atemporal sense but rather consciousness of *being*—most often actively—related to or interacting in some modality with a target. So construed, self-consciousness amounts to catching oneself consciously in the act of interacting with a target, to paraphrase Antonio Damasio's apt metaphor (Damasio 1999).

To recast this idea more precisely, I submit that, construed as a competence, consciousness is relational in two major respects. First, it is consciousness-of a target *in some modality*, whether perception, memory or thinking. And this consciousness-of in turn cannot fail to be consciousness of *a self-related-modally-to-a-target*, hence cannot fail to be self-consciousness, on my analysis. It follows that consciousness is *necessarily* self-consciousness. The *exercise* of the competence may occasionally fail to have a target (e.g., thinking of nothing in particular, as we often say) or may fail to factor in the relatedness to a target. But that does not undermine the relational *design* of the competence. We sometimes output nonsensical sentences but that is not how the language competence ordinarily works, nor is this a feature of its design.

The second major respect in which consciousness is modally relational concerns the *affordances* of its target-relatedness. One is conscious not only of a knife, say, but also of what one can *do* with that knife; or one is conscious not only of a bear in front of one, but also of what one *knows* about bears and what one is disposed to do, as a result. Being conscious of a target thus amounts also to being conscious of what one can do about or with the target or expect from a target or else what a target can do to one. This is what the notion of affordances is all about. (It was first introduced by James Gibson (1979) in his analysis of visual perception.) The implication here is that the consciousness of being related to a target has the function of making one also conscious of the mental and behavioral affordances of being related to that target.

The notion proposed here can therefore be summarized as follows:

for one *to be self-conscious of X*—where X is a target represented in some modality—is for one to be aware or sentient of being *modally related* to X, and also aware or sentient of the *affordances* of that relatedness, when the relevant executive abilities are jointly exercised

So much for a philosophical case on behalf of the relational format of self-consciousness. Closer inspection reveals a relational format even in the ordinary notion of consciousness, but I leave this task to a later discussion on the consciousness of target-relatedness and its affordances (see notes). The empirical story of the executive abilities involved in self-consciousness will be told in chapters 5 and 7. Right now, I want to tighten the anticipated link between the relational format of consciousness and its self-regulatory grounds by introducing a further important distinction.

Directedness versus Aboutness

Philosophers intend the (rather misnamed) notion of *intentionality* to capture the target-relatedness of mental states—whether the targets are concrete or abstract, present or past, future or fictional. Intentionality is occasionally construed, more naturalistically, as an organism-world relatedness, whereby processes and states of the organism, internal as well as behavioral, relate to targets outside and inside the organism. Since the notion of intentionality hosts two meanings and the ordinary one (of having an intention) is more potent and widespread, I will stick with my stipulated label of target-relatedness.

There are two sides to target-relatedness. One is *internal* or mind-driven and often mind-initiated. We may call it mental *directedness*. This is the mental relation made famous by Franz Brentano (the re-inventor of the medieval notion of intentionality) with his notion of "intentional inexistence"—roughly, the idea that, uniquely in the world, minds can represent something that does not exist (world peace or arctic wine) or cannot possibly exist (square circle). There is also an *external* or target-dependent and most often target-caused side, which, for lack of a better word, we may call *aboutness*.

If, out of the blue, I think of the tallest pink joke, my mind is deliberately *directed* to a nonexisting entity, as I have mischievously initiated this thought and thereby created its target. But if, here and now, I perceive a cat, my perception is *about* the cat, as it was caused by the cat. On this analysis, thoughts can be directed at nonexistent targets but cannot be about nonexistent targets. Thoughts can also be directed to targets without being about anything but, as noted in the next section, cannot be about a target without first being directed at it.

Mental directedness has received much attention in the phenomenological literature initiated by Brentano and continued by Husserl and his followers. The aboutness relation has received increased attention in recent decades in a more naturalistic philosophical literature, and has been analyzed in various terms—causal, nomological, covariational, informational, teleological and evolutionary. Such an analysis is intended to reveal and explain the conditions in which a mental state hooks up successfully with its target. The analysis also establishes that mental states must be structured and processed in certain ways, as in vision, or have a specific qualitative character, as in various forms of sensation, in order to engage and successfully track their targets. This brief description suggests that the aboutness relation depends not only on the mind but also on actual targets and their causal or informational impact on the mind, in addition to environmental, historical or evolutionary facts.

Yet an analysis of aboutness is only half of the story, because, by itself, it cannot explain the contents of higher mental states, such as thoughts and intentions, which are most often mind-initiated rather than target-caused. Even more basically, that analysis cannot explain why a mind would engage the world in aboutness relations, to begin with, and represent these relations as it does. I do not intend to develop the first point here, but for those who would like a defense of it I mention that—following Quine's seminal *Word and Object* (1960)—there is an ample philosophical literature on the indeterminacy of reference, the causal analysis of thoughts and attitudes, and the (so-called) intensionality or opacity of mental states. It turns out that an analysis of aboutness fails to account for how even the simplest perceptual and motor states hook up with external targets. The next section begins to explain why this is so. Furthermore, an analysis of aboutness is also unable to explain why mental contents are consciously represented (McGinn 1991a; 1991b).

As for the second question—why minds engage the world in aboutness relations to begin with—the answer I favor is that organisms represent targets because they are designed to engage the world cognitively and behaviorally, and are so designed because they are goal-directed. Stones and grass have states that are about nothing, even though they constantly interact causally with elements of their surroundings. A specific configuration of a stone may even specify—or carry information about—what sort of object in the environment caused it. Yet this fact does not make the latter a target that the former is (literally) about. Mental and behavioral states are about targets *because* they are internally *directed* at targets in the first place, and that is because organisms have goals to be reached by way of those states. The target-relatedness of organisms is purposive because it is so designed by evolution (Bogdan 1994).

An organism's purposive target-relatedness is initiated by its internal directedness. And internal directedness is the component of target-relatedness that matters in the analysis of self-consciousness. Several philosophers have suggested an intrinsic link between—or inseparability of—mental directedness and phenomenal consciousness (e.g., Graham, Horgan and Tienson 2007; McGinn 1991a, 1991b; Searle 1992). Some—most notably McGinn—have also conjectured that the mystery of phenomenal consciousness may also affect the explanation of mental directedness.

I am less pessimistic, for two reasons. First, I think that the intrinsic link is between mental directedness and self-consciousness—defined functionally, not phenomenally. As a result, the mystery of phenomenal consciousness need not affect the relation between mental directedness and self-consciousness. Second, mental directedness can be plausibly grounded in and explained by the machinery of self-regulation, as the next section shows. Most of the work of that machinery is premental, subpersonal and unconscious, yet is target-directed. There is target-directedness *without* consciousness. This is not the conscious directedness envisaged by Brentano and the philosophers (some just cited) who find phenomenal consciousness and intentionality inseparable. But it is, I think, its neuropsychological platform. If that is so, then the question is what it takes to bring self-consciousness and directedness together. My executive take on self-consciousness is meant to build an explanatory bridge between the two. In order for this bridging to succeed, there is another critical question that had better be answered first and as plausibly as possible.

Framing Consciousness

What exactly is conscious? Is it a mental state, such as a thought or emotion, a set of such, an entire mind or even an entire person? I call this the *framing* question. Answering this question is particularly important for an approach, like the present one, that finds self-regulation at the functional heart of consciousness. For such an approach holds that what is self-regulated in certain conditions—the range of the competence—*is* what is functionally conscious and a fortiori phenomenally conscious. This implication is at variance with some popular views, found particularly in the philosophical literature.

There are two framing notions that I find implausible, except as a manner of speaking about the presence of consciousness. One is the notion of *creature consciousness* (Rosenthal 2005). This notion is used to distinguish, say, between a human, who is conscious, and a rock (or perhaps a shrimp), which is not; or between a human who is awake and conscious, and one who is asleep and unconscious. What I think we do, in using this notion, is mark the presence of consciousness as a global disposition and bracket out its actual exercise, which is specific and relational. Creature consciousness is not really a notion of a *distinct* form of consciousness, but rather a manner of indicating the mere presence of or disposition for consciousness. Again, one cannot be just conscious, full stop, or conscious of nothing whatsoever. Even in the first moments of wakefulness, in the morning or immediately after a serious accident, when the mind is groggy, unfocused and targetless, consciousness is dispositionally relational and alert to affordances, although the disposition is not fully actuated.

The same diagnosis applies to a more popular notion that holds that a mental state is conscious for reasons that have nothing to do with its target-relatedness and affordances. I call this the notion of the *autarchic mental-state consciousness*. It comes in several versions. One version focuses on emblematically qualitative states, such as pains and feelings, and argues that they are conscious intrinsically, just by being what they are. This does not make much sense. A pain is in the brain, while the damaged tissue is in (say) a leg—so there must be a relation between the two; a feeling, such as fatigue, signals bodily and mental conditions, so again there must be a relation between signal and the signaled conditions; and both pain and fatigue, when consciously registered, generate mental and behavioral affordances. Pains, feelings and other such states seem autarchic when one adopts only the intuitive angle on how their consciousness is manifested——a position criticized in the previous section.

It is also often said that target-related states, such as thoughts and attitudes, are nevertheless conscious nonrelationally. In one version of this view, such states are conscious just by being brain states of a certain sort. On this view, phenomenal consciousness is an intrinsic property of the neurochemistry of the brain (e.g., Searle 1992). The phenomenal aspect may well be neurochemically grounded but the consciousness itself, as I analyze it here, is not.

Still another version, somewhat less autarchic, is constituted by a cluster of otherwise different views that have this much in common: mental states are conscious in virtue of their relations to *other* mental states, including themselves, but *not* in relation to (a) their targets, (b) their affordances and (c) the (executive) conditions in which relation and affordances are managed (which is my position). Two of these views can be grouped under the label of *higher-order monitoring* theories. Both suggest that mental states are conscious whenever they are monitored by and or at least related to higher-order states, in one case higher-order thoughts (Carruthers 2005; Rosenthal 2005), in the other higher-order introspective perceptions (Armstrong 1968; Lycan 1996). These views have been much debated in the literature (e.g., Block et al. 1997 for a survey; also Carruthers 2005). My narrow point here is that these views have an upstream take (as it were) on the relational character of mental-state consciousness: mental states are conscious because they have relations to higher-level monitoring states; but the targets of mental states and their affordances are not factored into the analysis.

Another relational view—quite autarchic, initiated by Brentano—is that mental states are conscious in virtue of *representing themselves* or their occurrence, in a sort of reflexive loop (Kriegel 2004; Lehrer 1997). This reflexive relation is not concerned with the target or content or affordances of the mental state it renders conscious. Whatever the possible merits of this view, it removes and isolates consciousness from any causal interaction, and therefore makes it hard to find the underlying mechanisms of or indeed reasons for consciousness.

Finally, a diversity of functionalist views defines mental-state consciousness in terms of the *access* or *interaction relations* that a mental state has to other mental states (e.g., Baars 1988; Block 1995; Dennett 1991). These views, which are closer to mine in important respects, posit a horizontal and distributed sort of relatedness that may account for the affordances of consciousness and the conditions in which they are realized but, as far as I can see, do not factor explicitly the target-relatedness of mental states in the equation.

There is also the *representationalist* view that does factor in the target-relatedness of consciousness. This view aims to explain the phenomenal character of conscious states in terms of their contents (Dretske 1995; Tye 1995). The basic insight is that mental states are phenomenally conscious by making us conscious of targets to which they relate in some modality. I think this is the right insight, but it cannot be plausibly grounded just in the fact that mental states have content. A range of mental states represent targets unconsciously, so something else must render them conscious.

Aside from their many and often radical differences, these views about mental-state consciousness have a common denominator that looks suspect to me. It is the idea that consciousness is—or can be—limited to and instantiated only by a *single* mental state. This idea seems suspect even when what makes a mental state conscious is its relation to other mental states—be that upstream, as in higher-order theories; or horizontally, as in functionalist theories; or downstream, as in representationalist theories. I find this the wrong way to frame what is conscious, a much too narrow and autarchic approach to be intuitively or neuropsychologically plausible.

At any given time a normal human mind consciously operates with and integrates a multiplicity of mental states. Even if the focus of attention is narrowly directed at a single target, many other related and unrelated states make us peripherally conscious of other targets, including internal ones, such as pains, feelings or thoughts. Attention is not consciousness, as noted in the next chapter, and what one is conscious of is not exhausted by attention. Intuitive observation matches what Kant called the 'unity of apperception'—an ability consciously to apprehend a manifold of thoughts and other states at any given moment. Apperception is exercised not atomically, over isolated mental states (that might be the job of attention), but globally and synthetically. There are plausible ways to relate the Kantian notion of apperception to current theories of consciousness (Nelkin 1996, chapter 8). For our purposes, I note that it is only through a synthesizing apperception that the mind can effectively be conscious of targets, relations to them, and especially the resulting affordances. There are also—and importantly—executive reasons why consciousness is distributed and ranges over extended manifolds of mental states. These reasons reflect the executive abilities that make consciousness possible. The story of this executive possibility debuts next.

4.3   Executive Grounds for Self-Consciousness

What Lies Ahead
Having made a largely intuitive and conceptual case for the relational format of consciousness, with respect to its targets and affordances, it is time to switch gears and inquire into its *internal* springs, thus strengthening the case empirically. We want to know what sort of resources underpin self-consciousness and also explain its asymmetric ontogenesis. For this, I suggest, we should turn to the neuropsychology of self-regulation. The syllogism behind this suggestion can be parsed as follows:

a. self-consciousness is doubly relational, as a conscious sense of being related to targets and to their affordances (section 1, above)

b. an organism's relatedness to targets and its affordances are subject to self-regulation (biological idea, explicated below)

c. key parameters of self-consciousness, such as means-ends initiative, top-down attention, control, multitasking, intermodal integration of information and intendingness, reflect executive abilities involved in self-regulation (explained below, and in chapters 5 and 7)

d. the self-regulation of target-relatedness and its affordances operates by simulative anticipation (as explained below)

e. all good reasons, then, to think of simulative self-regulation, exercised through the suite of abilities noted at (c), as executive grounds for self-consciousness

The conclusion (e) sums up the central hypothesis that this section aims to unpack, explicate, document and defend. If plausibly demonstrated, this hypothesis establishes the *executive* roots of self-consciousness. Chapters 5 and 7 will show how the executive abilities underpinning self-consciousness are recruited and assembled by a developing intuitive psychology, when children have to engage in and master *sociocultural* tasks and practices. This regulatory role of intuitive psychology will be elaborated in the next section.

The notion of simulation, just evoked, will play two roles here. First, it identifies the specific mechanism through which self-regulation is exercised over the mind's target-relatedness and its affordances. This is a rather well established empirical hypothesis, at least for cognitive-motor processes. Second, given the hypothesis about the executive roots of self-consciousness, it is likely that self-regulatory simulation is implicated in what makes a mind conscious functionally and—through the biochemistry of the brain—phenomenally as well.

To avoid terminological confusion, it should be stressed that regulative simulation is distinct from and much more basic than the imaginative simulation of other minds as part of intuitive psychology. This latter notion was discussed earlier (in chapter 3.3).

One last preliminary word about how I intend to proceed. If, deep down, self-consciousness results from self-regulation, which is a basic and universal biological phenomenon, it makes sense to look for precursors of self-consciousness in simpler forms of the self-regulation of target-relatedness and its affordances. These precursors can explain the reasons for and origins of simulative self-regulation, and throw some contrasting light on the conditions that led to self-consciousness. So let us first look, briefly, at some such precursors.

Sentience

Sentience can be thought of as a neural precursor of consciousness. Since our intuitions depend on what we are conscious of, sentience is not itself intuitable. Our best approximation is the notion of unconscious awareness—an oxymoron until recently, but no longer, thanks to the study of blindsight and other relevant phenomena. Of consciousness, we can at least say that we intuit what it is like to have it from inside and phenomenally. But of unconscious sentience, we cannot say anything of the sort. The best we can say is that sentience is a basic property of living creatures endowed with a nervous system. For more details, we turn to science. For the human forms of sentience in particular, we must defer to neuropsychology. As noted in the beginning of this book, blindsight is a case of visual but unconscious sentience in the blind field. The dorsal stream registers, processes and reacts functionally to visual stimuli—hence, senses the stimuli. I use the verb "to sense" to indicate that sentience, as neural sensitivity or awareness, is exercised unconsciously. The blindsighter senses, but is not conscious of, visual stimuli in the blind field. Absent-mindedness also suggests unconscious sentience in the relevant modality—perceptuomotor, in the case of the absent-minded driver. Both cases will be further discussed in chapter 5.

Antonio Damasio describes cases in which the basic self-consciousness—what he calls "core consciousness"—is severely impaired or even absent, and yet a state of wakefulness and even minimal attention is present (Damasio 1999, 94–106, 260–264). I take this to indicate sentience. One such case is epileptic automatism, in which, during the seizure, the patient remains awake, minimally attentive and able to register objects and events, and even navigate the environment successfully, but shows no sign of normal consciousness. Another case is akinetic mutism, which is a lack of movement and speech, again associated with minimal attention and reaction but with little or no sign of consciousness. Damasio speculates that some people with advanced Alzheimer's tend to gravitate toward the same condition.

One reading of these cases is that the patients may be like blindsighters in their blind field, lacking self-consciousness, yet minimally aware and able to operate, cognitively and behaviorally, under the exclusive impact of external stimuli. Damasio writes that "even without consciousness, the brain can process sensory signals across varied neural stations and cause activation of at least some of the areas usually involved in the process of perception" (1999, 99). Sentience, in short, is an ability to sense, process and react attentively yet unconsciously to stimuli in various modalities, and as a result, to guide behavior appropriately.

Attention and the cognitive guidance of behavior could not operate in a sentient creature without *self-regulatory mechanisms* that track and control the creature's modal relations to the targets revealed by stimuli and engaged behaviorally. The operation of these mechanisms produces some sense—a sentient sense—of the organism's target-relatedness and its affordances. Although this is not a conscious sense, it is nonetheless relational to the extent that it registers whether or not the creature's cognitive states and behaviors are on target or how close they are to target, and what behavioral implications may follow as a result. This point is elaborated next.

Self-Regulation

There is no need to stress the biological importance of self-regulation. Life could not exist without it. Self-regulation operates internally in a variety of forms that manage basic processes such as metabolism, homeostasis, temperature, immunological protection and more. It also operates externally, as it guides, controls and optimizes an organism's ability to pursue and reach its goals. It is this external form that matters in our story. The reason is the following.

Organisms are goal-directed: they engage in internal processes and external behaviors aimed at reaching their goals. I construe *goals* as states of affairs that an organism's activities are programmed or habituated to bring about. So construed, goals are distinct from—being the targets of—their internal markers, such as urges, desires, intents and so on. Organisms are target-related and recognize affordances *because* they are goal-directed. They evolve abilities to track and often explicitly represent their external targets in order to reach their goals. To be successful in this enterprise, organisms register, monitor and control—that is, self-regulate—the cognitive and behavioral means by which they reach their goals. Whereas goal-directedness is the biological source of and reason for an organism's target-relatedness and its affordances, the self-regulation of both is the source of and reason for the organism's *sense*—initially, merely sentient—of its target-relatedness and its affordances in a dominant modality.

Self-Regulatory Tasks

To exercise self-regulation, an organism faces two major tasks. I call them the 'selfhood task' and the 'guidance task.' The *selfhood* task consists in distinguishing what belongs to, happens inside of or is caused by the organism, from what belongs to, happens within or is caused by the outside world. The *guidance* task consists in registering, monitoring and controlling an organism's relations to targets in the world. The means evolved to handle these two tasks have taken the forms of specialized mechanisms, which I will call *self-mechanisms* and *guidance mechanisms*. The interactive work of these two kinds of mechanisms provides an organism with a *sense* of self-to-target relatedness and its affordances. What philosophers mean by an ownership sense of self is, on this analysis, the result of the work of self-mechanisms; and what they mean by an agency sense of self is the result of the work of both mechanisms. A few words about the self-mechanisms first.

Self-Determination

The regulation of one's self-to-action-to-target cannot work unless the self is distinguished from its surroundings. There are many sorts of self-mechanisms in an organism, commensurate with the domains of entities and processes that need to be distinguished and regulated. For example, the immunological mechanisms can tell which cells belong to one's body and which don't. There are also cognitive self-mechanisms that distinguish informational processes and states initiated by the organism from those caused by the outside world (Dennett 1991, chapter 7; Gallagher 2005, chapter 3).

Consider the classical example of the perception of movement. The movement of an object results in a movement of the image of the object on the retina. The latter is perceived by the brain as an actual movement of the object. But when the eyes are moved voluntarily, there is also a movement of the image on the retina—which is not perceived as the movement of an external object. Why not? The classical answer has been known since the 1950s, variously, as *efference copy* or *feedforward copy* or *corollary discharge* (Sperry 1950; von Holst and Mittelstaed 1950). In anticipation of their successor I will lump these notions under the rubric of (self-regulative) *simulation*.

The basic idea is that the brain makes a *copy* of its instructions to the eye muscles. This 'feedforward' copy corresponds to the expected or predicted input from the sensory processes that monitor the limb movements of the organism. It is a simulation of what may or will happen. The brain then compares the simulation with actual incoming information about the limb movements. If it finds no difference between the two, it "concludes" that its instructions have been carried out successfully. But if the comparison shows a discrepancy between the simulation and the input, or if the latter is absent, then the brain "concludes" that either the instructions have not been carried out, due to some effector malfunction, or else that the input originates at the sensory gates. In other words, if the movement on the retinal image has no counterpart in the simulation, it will be perceived as the movement of an external object.

Things, of course, are not so simple (they rarely are), and there are debates about how to construe the whole process (Poulet and Hedwig 2006) and there are various approaches to its explanation (with references below). But this rough picture will do, for now, to establish three major themes of our analysis: (a) that a basic sense of the biological self is essential to self-regulation and hence, eventually, to self-consciousness; (b) that at the appropriate cognitive-behavioral level, this sense of self is generated mechanistically, by a structural match between feedforward simulations and sensory inputs; and (c) more speculatively, that feedforward simulation or something functionally like it, together with internal models of action and visual memories, may have gradually evolved into higher (thinking) forms of mental simulation.

The first two themes should make it clear that, and why, an organism cannot self-regulate its ways in the world without having a sense of its distinct selfhood; and that, therefore, if the organism is conscious of targets in the world, it must *necessarily* be conscious of itself as distinct from, yet related to, those targets. And if it turns out—as it will, on my analysis—that self-regulation also operates on the organism's conative, cognitive and behavioral *relations* to targets and their affordances, and generates self-consciousness when its operation activates executive abilities under the tutelage of intuitive psychology, then the organism's conscious sense of targets is *necessarily* a conscious sense of its self *because*—and *to the extent that*—it modally relates to targets and their affordances.

I develop briefly the first two themes below, beginning with selfhood. It is important to do so in order to avoid any philosophically inflationary expectations about the basic and minimal notion of selfhood at work in this inquiry. The third theme will be developed later in the discussion of self-guidance.

Executive Self

The simulation gambit is thought to generate a sentient but unconscious *sense* of a self that is distinct from the outside world. This sense was said to result from a comparison between simulations and sensory inputs. Both simulations and inputs are neural configurations that carry information from and to the brain (respectively) in virtue of their *structures*. The brain's comparison consists in determining a match or mismatch between the structure of a simulation and that of a sensory input.

In all self-identification tasks, from immunological to sensorimotor to mental, *structural match* is all that matters, as far as the brain is concerned, in order to distinguish self from world. As a result, it is structural match that generates a sentient or conscious sense of self—whether a bodily, sensorimotor or mental self. Structural match is a physical event, not unlike that of the thermostat setting that activates the refrigerator when it is matched by a certain temperature-related motion of air molecules, and not unlike the way in which a computer activates an operation when the symbol typed on its keyboard matches a pattern in its memory. Neither the thermostat nor the computer is a sentient organism—neither has the task of distinguishing self from nonself, and neither has the further task of tracking its relation to some aspect of nonself—which is why neither has a *sense* of anything, as a result of such a structural match or mismatch.

This emphasis on the structural match as solely responsible for a sense of selfhood in organisms should dispose of the temptation to posit some homunculus or inner perceptions or thoughts directed at an entity called 'self.' There is no such entity. In sentient but unconscious organisms, the sense of self that results from structural-match processes reflects what specialized mechanisms tell each other and how they react as a result. More complex senses of selfhood, of various kinds of selves actually, result from more complex forms of structural match. Even a comparator, as a special organ or faculty, may not be needed; it may often suffice that a structural match generate some kind of follow-up processes and a mismatch another kind.

As discussed so far, the ownership sense of self, as distinctness from the world, is likely to be nonlocal, contrastive, implicit and procedural— nonlocal, because it does not single out any specific carrier or seat of self-hood; contrastive, because it delineates the scope of selfhood only by opposing events inside to those outside the organism; and implicit and procedural, because it is embodied in the operation of a self-identification machinery and not in any specific representation, such as an image or some other sort of data structure. In most organisms and also in humans, this sense of self is normally unconscious. And normally again, the work of the self-mechanisms is integrated with that of guidance mechanisms.

The self, normally, is both owner and agent. One may become aware of the ownership sense of self when the operation of the self-mechanisms is disrupted, as it is in some cases of schizophrenia or in some clever experiments when, for example, one does not know whose hand one is moving (Frith 1992; Gallagher 2005; Jeannerod 2006). In short, for an organism to have a sense of self as owner of its mental and behavioral states and activities is for its self-identification machinery to do its work correctly: it is an *executive* sense of self.

Although simple, basic and primitive, the mechanism of simulation anticipates how the ownership sense of selfhood originates and how it works. Many of the same mechanisms are thought to be also (though not alone) implicated in guidance and to have been at the origin of sensorimotor and even perceptual simulation (Poulet and Hedwig 2006). That is our next topic.

Self-Guidance

Self-identification does not provide an organism with a sense of self-to-target relatedness and its affordances. The target-relatedness results from having goals and being mentally and behaviorally related to them. The affordances result from how an organism goes about reaching its goals, what it knows or expects about the means employed and about the implications of the goals being or not being reached. The self-regulation exercised over an organism's target-relatedness and its affordances amounts to *self-guidance*.

Both in evolution and development, self-guidance begins with, and for most species is dominated by, input–motor action–target relations, and their innately reflex or habituated effects. It is a vital priority for all mobile organisms to register and track their targets, activate expectations about the effects of their actions, and move toward or away from them in order to reach their goals. Likewise, the first modalities in which young children consciously self-regulate their relations with the social and physical world involve motor actions. So I propose to treat *all* these modalities as *mind-to-motor* modalities and their outputs as *motor actions*, broadly construed. Thus, children's intentful facial imitation or smile or goal-directed vocalization count here as motor actions, and so do their looking in a direction to attract mother's attention to the cat or pointing at the cat. This proposal is Piagetian in spirit but not in the letter, as it sides with the Vygotskian alternative in taking the earliest and most important mind-to-motor modalities and actions to be other-directed and social rather than object-oriented and mechanical.

The *motor connection* is central to my argument, for several reasons. First, it grounds the relational format of self-guidance mechanisms. Second, motor mentation is the earliest in evolution and, in its social version, the earliest in human ontogeny as well. So, if advances in self-regulation explain the path from self-sentience to self-consciousness, then the self-regulation of motor mentation should leave its imprint on the development of self-consciousness, particularly in its early, extrovert version. And so it does.

Recent research has made progress in explaining and modeling simulative versions of mind-to-motor-action-to-target self-regulation, particularly in the perceptuomotor modality (Frith 1992; Gallagher 2005; Grush 2004; Hurley 1999; Jeannerod 1997, 2006; Wolpert et al. 1998). A few models extend these insights to self-consciousness in a spirit which is close to that of the present inquiry (Damasio 1999; Gallagher 2005; Metzinger 2003;

Vosgerau and Newen 2007; on which, more in chapter 8). But the extension, promising as it is, is not yet fully explained and documented. The tough question still awaiting an answer is what it takes to graduate from a motor self-sentience to self-consciousness.

Not surprisingly, I do not have an answer to this question. But, following a *divide et impera* strategy, the question can be parsed into two further and more manageable questions. The first question is concerned with the conditions that explain, through their mental impact, *why* the self-regulation of sentient target-relatedness and its affordances turns into self-consciousness. I propose an answer to this question in chapter 5 for extrovert self-consciousness, and in chapter 7 for the introvert version. This answer points to sociocultural tasks and practices of childhood, as external conditions, and internally to the executive abilities involved in these activities and initially assembled and run by the children's intuitive psychology. This answer tells us (very broadly) *why* children's minds develop self-consciousness. But it does not tell us *how* self-sentience actually morphs into self-consciousness. That is, it does not tell us what the internal mechanics of this metamorphosis are. This is the second question, and is a killer.

As far as I can determine, no one knows the answer. Phylogenetic and ontogenetic comparisons as well as insights from neuropsychology suggest that the simulative self-regulation of motor cognition and action somehow bootstraps itself into simulative self-regulation of thinking and other higher mental processes. It is possible that this 'bootstrapping' proceeded gradually in various species through a spectrum of self-regulatory abilities ranging over complex navigational, locomotor and social behaviors (an idea suggested by a reviewer of the manuscript). Some of these acquisitions may have entered the self-regulatory repertory of the primate lineage and been redesigned in the human mind by the novel developments of language, intuitive psychology and various executive abilities of the frontal lobes.

The neuropsychology of this bootstrapping is still very much in the dark. Leading neuropsychologists and neurophilosophers admit that very little is known and empirically documented about how this bootstrapping might work and in particular about how the simulative machinery of self-regulation might operate on thinking and other high-level mental processes (Daniel Dennett, Pierre Jacob, Marc Jeannerod and Wolfgang Prinz, personal communications). This theoretical predicament leaves no choice but to focus on the first answer. That answer assumes that human thoughts are simulatively self-regulated, and aims to show that during ontogeny the predominantly sociocultural thoughts of children are self-regulated by means of an intuitive psychology that recruits and integrates the executive abilities that install self-consciousness. This explanation debuts in the next section. Before we get there, however, there is one more fundamental question that needs to be asked at the end of this quick foray into the territory of self-regulation.

Why Target-Relatedness and Why Affordances

Self-regulation was said to operate at all levels of life, from immunological and circulatory to motor and cognitive. At many of these levels, target-relatedness and affordances are absent. Furthermore, closer to overt behavior, there may be conscious self-regulation of bodily posture and motor action that involves no computation of affordances. The same may be true of the self-regulation of some higher mental states, such as affordance-free thoughts or targetless feelings. So why would target-relatedness and affordances necessarily enter the explanation of why and how self-regulation begets self-consciousness?

A first answer returns to the earlier distinctions between competence and performance and between domains of installation and domains of use. The target-relatedness and affordances of mental states are part of the *installation* domain of self-consciousness and explain its emergence as a durable competence. In later applications of the self-regulation of mental states, the registration of target-relatedness or the computation of affordances is not obligatory for the presence of self-consciousness. If self-consciousness is present, it is because of its initial installation as a competence, and not because of the particular act of self-regulation.

Going deeper, however: why target-relatedness and affordances in the installation domain and period? I can think of two reasons. First, if consciousness is necessarily relational, as consciousness of a target and of being related to a target, as shown earlier, then the self-regulation of target-relatedness appears as its most plausible incubator. One could also throw in the claim that, to play an adaptive role, consciousness must sharpen or modulate or enhance our (sentient) sense of targets in the world and of our own minds and bodies in relation to such targets (Damasio 1999). The very transparency of consciousness, reflected in the fact that we are modally conscious of targets but not of the underlying processes and states, many of them targetless, suggests that the function of consciousness is relational.

Second, the regulation of target-relatedness, from its registration and tracking to its evaluation and correction, and the computation of the affordances of target-relatedness are bound to require a wider spectrum of executive abilities and to solicit these abilities much more intensely than can targetless and affordance-free forms of self-regulation. It takes such a wide spectrum of executive abilities, acting jointly, to install self-consciousness, and it takes a very demanding and complex competence, such as intuitive psychology, to call these executive abilities to duty to respond to the strongest challenges posed by the sociocultural tasks and practices encountered by growing human children. How intuitive psychology accomplishes this will be explained next.

4.4   Representing Minds as Means to Ends

It will help to begin by placing the argument that follows in a wider perspective before proceeding with the narrower explanation.

Evolutionary Background

The anthropological and psychological research of the past decades has fairly conclusively shown that the species deemed most sophisticated mentally—primates, dolphins, elephants—have the most prolonged, immature and adult-dependent childhood and are also intensely engaged in communicational, collaborative and competitive interactions. Since Nicholas Humphrey's pioneering insight about sociopolitical roots of primate intelligence (Humphrey 1976/1988), the supporting phylogenetic and ontogenetic evidence has been accumulating at a fast pace (Bjorklund and Pellegrini 2002; Byrne and Whiten 1988; de Waal 1982; Donald 1991; Tomasello 1999, 2008; Tomasello and Call 1997; Whiten 1991).

The human species stands out as the only one that generates, transmits and continuously modifies its culture, in the form of language, artifacts, norms, institutions and practices. The engagement with culture is bound to call for radically new mental abilities (Boyd and Silk 1997; Donald 1991, 2001; Tomasello 1999). Consciousness, I am arguing here, is a byproduct of these new abilities. Indispensably and centrally involved in sociocultural activities, the human intuitive psychology is at the heart of this developmental process.

The evolutionary equation just sketched can be (very roughly) schematized as follows:

very immature and adult-dependent childhood → intense sociopolitical and cultural life → intuitive psychology → self-conscious mind

This equation will be amplified in later chapters, as we examine how children's intuitive psychology discharges its vital role in the development of self-consciousness. The question to ask at this point is what enables intuitive psychology to play this role in the first place. This is not a question about the reasons for its role: the evolutionary equation is clear about the reasons (Bogdan 1997). And the question is not how the young intuitive psychology installs self-consciousness—namely, by recruiting and joining executive abilities in a self-regulatory mode: this question will be tackled in the next chapters. The question, at this point, is about the design and modus operandi of intuitive psychology that enables it to operate in ways that are conducive to the installation of self-consciousness.

The Basic Idea

As a helpful metaphor, think of a versatile tool with many components for diverse utilizations. The Swiss Army knife comes to mind. Unlike the latter, however, our metaphorical tool operates with several components at once, or in very quick succession, in different, fast-changing and inter-related applications. Such a multifaceted and dynamic operation requires expert knowledge of the properties and dispositions of the tool's components and equally expert knowledge of how to utilize the components to reach one's ends. Also and as importantly, because of its many simultaneous or quickly unfolding, and often related applications, the knowledge of the tool's multifaceted operation recruits and integrates a host of other abilities in the tool user's mind.

I suggest that the human mind is more like the metaphorical tool just sketched, while human intuitive psychology is more like the expert knowledge of such a mind. To represent and effectively handle such a tool-like mind, intuitive psychologists must recruit and integrate in their own minds a large variety of abilities. A select group of the latter turns out to be made of the executive abilities that install self-consciousness.

This is the general idea, elaborated below and in the remainder of this book. It backs the claim that self-consciousness may be a unique human trait, because of the uniqueness of an intuitive psychology that has a decisive impact on a unique mental ontogeny.

The Means-Ends Stance

Since organisms are intrinsically goal-directed, they are genetically primed to process information and act on it in a means-ends format (Bogdan 1994). In humans, the sociopolitical interactions and cultural practices call for an intuitive psychology that can effectively service their goal-directed strategies and actions. So construed, intuitive psychology has a *means-ends* or *instrumental* stance on conspecifics and their world-relations as well as on interpersonal relations (Bogdan 1997, 2000). For our purposes, we can lump these kinds of relations under the label of *attitude*. We can then say that intuitive psychology has a means-ends stance on attitudes, which means that it represents and treats attitudes, others' and one's own, as means to ends. It is from this instrumental stance on attitudes that young children's intuitive psychology makes a decisive difference to the development of their consciousness.

This hypothesis makes two claims:

a. conspecific interactions and sociocultural activities call for an intuitive psychology that represents and treats attitudes as means to ends

b. in doing so, intuitive psychologists employ ascriptions of attitudes for self-regulation and the pursuit of goal strategies, thus recruiting and assembling executive abilities that install a conscious sense of one's modal target-relatedness and its affordances

There is ample behavioral evidence for the first claim in both nonhuman and young human primates. Chimpanzees and other nonhuman primates represent and use conspecifics as means to ends. Chimpanzees are known to use conspecifics as shields in conflicts or sexual encounters. They also track inter-chimps relations, such as friendship or enmity, in anticipating sociopolitical actions, and are likely to represent such relations as means to ends. Chimpanzees also use the world-bound relations of others, such as gaze, to distract attention or deceive in order to obtain some result. They learn by imitating others in certain culturally transmitted activities (washing potatoes, for example) and, particularly in captivity, they manage to imitate some new and rather unusual means-ends actions of humans (Tomasello and Call 1997).

Chapter 2 noted that young human children represent and use the attitudes of others in coregulation and also as means to ends. Their communication, both nonverbal and verbal, is mostly a way of regulating their social behavior and getting others, as means, to help with their goals. Their imitation is sensitive to the means-ends pattern of the attitudes and actions to be imitated. And so on (Adamson 1995; Bruner 1983; Perner 1991; Tomasello 1999).

Given their means-ends use of conspecific relations to the world and each other, should we conclude that chimpanzees, like humans, are likely to develop self-consciousness, at least in its extrovert version? I think there are good reasons to be cautious, if not skeptical. Identifying these reasons would require a brief but instructive detour meant to explain further the mind-design potency of human intuitive psychology.

Tools versus Implements

It may help to start in the technological domain, before attending to the mental domain. A longstanding consensus in anthropology holds that the unique potency and originality of the human mind can be traced to the tool-making and tool-using abilities of modern humans. The suspected mental sophistication of a few other species, such as nonhuman primates (and perhaps beavers, crows, and others) is also credited to their (alleged) tool use. As noted, a recent consensus has shifted the burden of explanation to primate sociopolitical life. It is therefore worth looking at minds operating in the technological and sociopolitical domains.

Animals act on the world causally in order to reach their goals and, in the relatively few 'tool-using' species, act causally with physical *implements as extensions* of their bodies and action routines. Implement use is genetically programmed for, or learned in, specific and typically routine sorts of actions (building nests, fishing for termites and breaking nuts, to name just a few notable examples), and are repeatedly and uncreatively applied in the same sorts of contexts.

It is tempting to think, as many students of animal behavior do, that the implement-using species are genuine tool users, if not tool makers. I disagree, and have argued this point elsewhere (Bogdan 2000, chapter 2). For our purposes here, I note that a tool user satisfies two conditions that an implement user does not. A tool user causally intervenes in the world, in order to reach goals, by

a. deliberately and often improvisationally initiating actions (often without prior genetic or learned programming) on

b. objects, other organisms or situations whose *intrinsic* properties and dispositions are known *generally* and often *creatively*, across a variety of contexts, and also known *separately* from the user's bodily parts and routine action patterns

Schematically, we can say that organisms that merely act causally on the world follow the first script (where '→' stands for causation):

(1) agent acts → desired outcome

Implement-using organisms follow a different script:

(2) agent acts with implement → desired outcome

Finally, the script for tool-using organisms is:

(3) agent acts on → [tool → desired outcome]

Scripts (1) and (2) represent action in a simple causation format: action by itself or with an implement (as extension) causes an outcome. Stimulated by an insight of Jean Piaget (1964, 1974; developed also by Tomasello 1999 and Tomasello and Call 1997), I suggested that script (3) represents action in a *cause/causation format*: the agent acts causally on a tool in order for *it* to cause a desired effect—whence the idea of *double* causation (Bogdan 2000, 42–56). Thus script (3) alone requires *causal knowledge* of the tool in the sense of condition (b) above. It is the sort of knowledge that defines a genuine tool user.

The square brackets in script (3) indicate that the causal knowledge and the action it guides are employed by the tool user to represent and cause a distinct and separate causation, whereby a tool causes an outcome. This means that the tool user not only knows the intrinsic causal powers of the tool, in a variety of contexts and separately from the user's own propensities and actions; the tool user also knows how the causal powers and other properties of the tool *relate to the targets* to which the tool is applied, and to the *affordances* thus occasioned, and factors all these pieces of knowledge into a goal strategy.

Thus, for example, one uses a knife as a tool by knowing what it can causally do (cut or carve things) in virtue of its intrinsic causal powers (being sharp, graded, hard, etc.) which can be exercised in a variety of contexts (on foods or textiles, in defense, etc.). Having this causal knowledge, one can also improvise new applications of the knife, such as unscrewing a very tiny screw with its tip or extracting some object from a narrow slit. This is the sort of causal knowledge of tools, with standard and new affordances, that implement-using species do not possess.

Various animal species use physical objects as means to their goals, but the means are only implements—simple and uncreative extensions of their bodies or action patterns. This limitation is visible, for example, in the chimpanzees' privileged use of tree branches to fish for termites, without any (documented) attempt to use branches in other, equally vital contexts, such as fighting with others or defending themselves against predators (Tomasello and Call 1997; Tomasello 1999). The same can be said about crows using branches or beavers working on their dams: implement use only leads to a minimal culture, one which is unlikely to evolve.

But knives, branches or other physical objects are not what human infants *first* encounter or much care about. It is other people and their attitudes that matter most. This is when and where attitudes, represented and handled by children as tools, enter the explanatory picture.

Attitudes as Tools

The first tools infants encounter are other people and specifically their postures, reactions and attitudes—toward the infants themselves and the surrounding world. In the first months of life, infants are poor at locomotion and manual handling of objects. It is not just the underdevelopment of their limbs but also the lack of proprioception, as a form of control of and feedback on the movements of their bodies. As a result, infants have a poor sense, if any, of a perceptuomotor self, hence little or no sense of being intently and controllably related to the world in the perceptuomotor mode, and (on my analysis) may lack perceptuomotor self-consciousness. It is only around 14 months that children become fully fledged perceptuomotor agents capable of engaging in tool-like actions with physical objects and their cultural uses (Butterworth 1991; Russell 1996).

Yet during all this early period infants spend countless hours interacting with adults, first bilaterally and then trilaterally, triangulating objects and events in a shared world. They gradually develop the abilities to read emotions expressed facially, vocally and behaviorally, to follow gaze, bodily posture and pointing, to understand intended actions, simple desires, to engage in shared attention and joint action, to detect beliefs and more. From this platform, young children also begin to read various attitudes behind social conventions, ritualized behaviors, the use of cultural gadgets and a variety of cultural practices. It is in this ontogenetic framework that young children begin to represent and use the attitudes of others as tools for self-regulation and in the pursuit of their goals.

Apes and possibly other intensely social species seem to have a rather limited repertoire of others-as-means strategies, rarely if ever applied flexibly and creatively to novel contexts. As noted, chimpanzees use gaze to distract attention or deceive. They also seem to calculate various relations among individuals as means to their ends. On my analysis, they use such relations as implements, not as tools; they act causally on the relations to bring about desired effects (script (2), above). Furthermore, chimpanzees represent those relations *egocentrically*, as they respond to their own interests and action routines, without an awareness that such relations have their own causal powers that can be acted upon and manipulated in virtue of how they engage targets and their affordances (as in script (3) above). This is a recipe for mental and behavioral conservatism, which is challenged only in rare situations and particularly in cultural captivity among humans.

In contrast, to reach their goals, young children are under pressure, and gradually manage, to treat other people, their attitudes and actions, as well as cultural practices, *on their terms* and not merely as egocentric extensions of the children's own mental states, bodies and actions. Although infants' intuitive-psychological stance on others begins egocentrically, by the middle of their second year it shifts to an increasingly other-centered stance, as it handles a variety of new communicational and behavioral interactions, and new cultural acquisitions, from a shared, public and increasingly conventional perspective. That cannot be done with a strictly egocentric take on the attitudes of others.

Consider, for example, a young child who engages his mother in shared-attention communication in order to get mother to attend to something or do something for the child. To manage the required interpersonal and behavioral choreography (described in more detail in the next chapter), the child represents mother's gaze, the gaze-action link and the bilateral child-mother exchanges of looks, facial and vocal expressions in general terms that work for a variety of other contexts. Not only are the terms general; they are also flexible and often creative, in the sense that in other contexts they can be combined in different patterns and with new components (such as representations of desire or emotion), and are revisable, according to context.

I think that the distinction between egocentric implement use and other-centered tool use makes a mighty difference to the design of the minds involved, and in particular to their potential for developing self-consciousness. To put it intuitively, the reason for the difference, turning mostly on the presence or absence of cause/causation knowledge, is that egocentric implement use is mentally much less demanding and involves far fewer mental abilities in fewer applications and combinations than does other-centered tool use. And among tools, during development, none is as mentally demanding in mastering and using as are the attitudes—first others' and then one's own. It is by treating the attitudes of others as tools that young children's intuitive psychology activates and orchestrates a suite of executive abilities that install extrovert self-consciousness. How this comes about is the topic of the next chapter.

Recapitulating

This chapter has laid out the key premises for the demonstration that will be undertaken in the next few chapters. Preemptively, a first premise sidelined the phenomenal aspect of consciousness, leaving the functional aspect at the center of our attention. It further specified what should be avoided on this functional side, namely, the notion that consciousness is innately constitutive of the mind or the output of a dedicated mechanism, the indistinction between competence and performance, and the focus on isolated and targetless mental states as units of consciousness. A second premise held that consciousness is intrinsically relational, always having a target-related content, which reflects the goal-directed design of minds. A third premise held that the target-relatedness of minds is subject to self-regulation, as both self-determination and self-guidance. Finally, the fourth premise portrayed intuitive psychology as having a means-ends stance on attitudes, treating them as tools, in its job of guiding and regulating children's immersion in and management of sociocultural activities.

5 Becoming Self-Conscious

The first order of business, in section 1, is to introduce the phenomenon to be explained, which is extrovert self-consciousness. I will approach it from two directions, which I aim to bring into a sort of reflective equilibrium. First, starting from empirical findings, I return to blindsight and also bring in absent-mindedness in order to characterize extrovert self-consciousness indirectly, linking its absence to the absence of several executive abilities, such as intending, deliberate anticipation, top-down attention, means-ends initiative and multitasking. This is the most vivid and best documented connection, intuitively and experimentally, between the relevant executive abilities and extrovert self-consciousness. Second, starting from theory, I note that a respectable plurality of functionalist accounts identify those very same executive abilities as the key parameters of consciousness in general.

By way of contrast with blindsight and absent-mindedness, section 2 surveys those juvenile activities that are the least likely to be reflex, habituated or input-driven, and hence most likely to be extrovertly self-conscious precisely because they draw on the executive abilities that are missing in blindsight and absent-mindedness. These activities, which are most critical in the early years, include communication by shared meaning, shared attention, joint action, pretend play and imitation. All of them involve other people and sociocultural practices. The proposed analysis suggests a tight correlation in early ontogeny between sociocultural activities and the executive abilities underpinning extrovert self-consciousness.

The question is, what explains this correlation? The answer in section 3 points to young children's intuitive psychology in its first, naive version. For young children, assimilating, mastering and practicing sociocultural activities requires interacting and communicating with adults, learning from them, imitating them, and so on, which in turn requires figuring out what adults see, emote about, want and do. That is the job of naive psychology. No less importantly, naive psychology is also an instrument of social coregulation, given infants' dependence on adults, and it retains this role in older children's sociocultural activities. The link between naive psychology and the onset and growth of extrovert self-consciousness is the means-ends format in which the young naive psychologists represent and use the attitudes of others as tools that service their goals. This section shows how the young naive psychology, by managing the children's sociocultural activities, jointly activates the executive abilities suspected to generate extrovert self-consciousness. Section 4 looks forward to the developments that presage self-understanding and the emergence of introvert self-consciousness.

5.1   Extrovert Self-Consciousness

The task of this section is twofold—first, to show that extrovert self-consciousness is present in minds that engage, and absent in minds that do not engage, in purposive activities governed by a specific set of executive abilities; and second, to identify the executive abilities associated with the manifestation of extrovert self-consciousness, and show that they overlap with the parameters of consciousness posited by functionalist theories. I begin with two paradigmatic examples that are much discussed in the neurophilosophical literature, one clinical (blindsight) and another ordinary (absent-mindedness).

Blindsight

We discussed blindsight earlier: it is a case of unconscious vision in the blind field. Both the scene in the blind field and the seeing of it are unconscious. On his own, a blindsighter has no intent, means-ends initiative, top-down attention and control—and hence no conscious self-regulation, on my analysis—in perceiving, thinking about, remembering, planning or acting on what is registered unconsciously in the blind field.

Blindsight illustrates a critical distinction between unconscious visual awareness of, and unconscious attention to, a target, on the one hand, and perceptual and attentive consciousness of a target, on the other. The blindsighter is visually but not consciously aware of targets in the blind field, and can focus on and track the movement of the targets attentively but again not consciously. This means that the blindsighter's unconscious vision *is* target-related. When prompted (or trained, as in the case of a blindsighted ape), blindsighters can navigate the space in the blind field, avoid obstacles, recognize and handle objects, and more (Milner and

Goodale 1995). So they must be able to *self-regulate* their visual relatedness to targets in the blind field, and hence must have an unconscious sense of their visual self-to-target relatedness. Yet, again, they lack the consciousness of the targets they register visually and of being perceptually related to these targets. Blindsighters also lack any spontaneous sense of the affordances of the targets they recognize and manipulate. This, I will argue, is because the self-regulation of their visual relatedness to targets fails to activate the executive abilities that generate self-consciousness.

The research on blindsight separates one's sense of relatedness to targets in unconscious vision and attention from their conscious counterparts in perception. Generalized beyond blindsight, the main implication of this distinction is that an organism can engage its environment successfully, get useful information about its targets, self-regulate its information processing and its actions, and thus reach its goals, *without* being conscious of the targets it registers in some dominant modality (vision in the case of blindsight) and, importantly, *without* being conscious of its relatedness to the targets it registers and of the affordances of such relatedness.

Blindsight also suggests that self-consciousness is modality-specific and that therefore modalities lacking self-consciousness can coexist with others that have it. A blindsighter can think and be self-conscious of his thoughts and what they are about, as can a totally blind person. *Mutatis mutandis*, young children can be self-conscious in some extrovert but not introvert modalities, as previously suggested and further argued later.

It may be thought that the lack of visual consciousness in blindsight is caused exclusively by the damage to the ventral path of vision. This was the initial account of blindsight. The assumption was that the job of the ventral path is to service the conscious perception of objects and properties, whereas the job of the dorsal path is to service fast and unconscious motor action (Milner and Goodale 1995). Even though the ventral path produces more complex representations—and hence activates more executive abilities for its processing and follow-up, which is support for the line taken in this book—the dorsal path should not be underestimated. More recent experimental and clinical evidence suggests that the dorsal path can also exhibit as much consciousness as the ventral path (Jacob and Jeannerod 2003, chapter 3; Jeannerod 2006, chapter 3).

What seems to make the difference is the *speed* of processing visuomotor information. The dorsal processing can be very fast—too fast for consciousness to get its grip on what is being processed. That consciousness needs enough time to materialize is itself evidence that it emerges out of complex processing, which I take to involve extensive executive work.

I leave this idea undeveloped here, but note that the time-consciousness relation is a major theme in Husserl's phenomenology and was plausibly developed, with neuropsychogical support, by Shaun Gallagher (2005, 189–200).

The conclusion I draw is that the lack of consciousness in blindsight is as much due to a ventral impairment as to the lack of the work of the executive abilities associated with extrovert self-consciousness. The executive connection is further supported by absent-mindedness (below) as well by the evidence of lack or diminution of consciousness, including visual consciousness, in normal people who are drowsy or confused or in people who are comatose or vegetative or in still other clinical conditions, such as akinetic mutism (lack of speech and movement) and *petit mal* seizures. In all these cases, the ventral path is normal but it is the executive machinery involved in extrovert self-consciousness that is at fault, often through damage to the prefrontal cortex (Damasio 1999). The implication is that the deepest springs of consciousness may reside in a particular sort of executive self-regulation rather than in conation, cognition, emotion or affect, as often believed.

Generalizing again beyond blindsight, this analysis suggests that many species and many developmental stages in most species may instantiate unconscious versions of blindsight in various modalities. The point is that adaptive behavior need not entail consciousness. Since behavior is our only window on animal minds, it follows that animal behavior, no matter how successful and adaptive, need not reveal whether it is run by conscious mentation. This is why, I think, we need to approach the possibility of consciousness from the angle of the abilities that underpin it and of the environmental pressures for such abilities.

There is also a more mundane experience that provides an intuitive counterpart to the scientific insights about blindsight.

Absent-Mindedness

I have in mind the much-discussed case of the absent-minded (AM) driver. Lost in thought, the AM driver reaches the destination safely but without having been conscious of the road, of having seen the road or of the various affordances of driving on the road. Driving on automatic pilot, as it were, the AM driver has no initiative and deliberate control over driving. Yet the AM driver somehow manages to negotiate the road successfully, which suggests awareness of the road and control over visual relatedness to the road and hence some sense of self-to-road relatedness and its behavioral affordances—all, however, unconscious.

There are various attempts to explain this phenomenon. I will not go into details here [but see note on explanations of absent-mindedness]. What matters now is that the normal adult mind, like that of the blind-sighter, can unconsciously handle cognitive and self-regulatory tasks in a specific modality. It is widely accepted that most information processing in the brain is unconscious. In recent years it has become more evident that unconscious information processing of high complexity can be implicated in motor cognition and control, perception, even thinking and language comprehension. It has also become more evident that there are processing stages that seem to be almost conscious (called preconscious or "vigilance states") or seem conscious for very short periods, in a pulse-like fashion, as in patients in vegetative condition (Damasio 1999; Dehaene et al. 2006; Groopman 2007). Absent-mindedness also shows that one can be conscious in some active modalities, such as thinking, but unconsciously successful in others, such as driving.

This evidence supports the idea that a robust and durable modal exercise of consciousness requires self-regulation that reflects the exercise of executive abilities. It makes evolutionary sense that these abilities should first operate extrovertly in modalities, and in minds, primarily directed at the outside world. If we put together the data about the early ontogeny of consciousness (from chapter 2.6) and about blindsight and absent-mindedness, discussed above, then the parameters proposed below will identify the executive abilities that are most prominent and effective in producing extrovert self-consciousness.

Parameters of Extrovert Self-Consciousness
Thus far, the approach to extrovert self-consciousness has been from below, so to speak, examining the neuropsychological facts of blindsight and the intuitive sense of absent-mindedness. What follows is an approach from the more speculative height inhabited by theory and conceptual analysis. The aim is to bring them in reflective equilibrium.

The theoretical paradigm adopted here is that of functionalism. The reason for this adoption is not the usual one—indifference to hardware and concern for process—but rather an evolutionary one: evolutionary pressures select for adaptive behaviors and the latter in turn reflect what various mechanisms and abilities do and how they discharge their functions. Evolution does not much 'care' what the wings of flying organisms consist of, as long as the wings enable flight. This is why there are so many and so diverse flying species. It is evolution that is functionalist, and not just the philosopher in an armchair. Since the stance of this inquiry is broadly evolutionary, functionalism regarding mental traits, including consciousness, seems a reasonable option.

Functionalist theories of consciousness converge on a spectrum of parameters of consciousness (Baars 1988; Block et al. 1997; Carruthers 2005; Dehaene and Naccache 2001; Dennett 1991; Metzinger 2003; van Gulick 1993). These parameters, I will argue below, reflect the work of executive abilities that I associate with self-consciousness.

To get a feel for my take on the parameters of self-consciousness, I begin with a bit of linguistic archeology. There are two early meanings of the word 'conscious' whose combination nicely approximates what I have in mind. One is the initial meaning of the Latin *conscius* as a *socially shared* (= *con*) knowledge (= *scientia*). This meaning fits into the idea of explaining the ontogeny of self-consciousness in terms of the children's shared sociocultural activities. The other meaning is *psychological* and, according to the *Oxford English Dictionary*, takes "the state or faculty of being conscious, *as a condition and concomitant of all thought, feeling and volition*" (my emphasis). I read the word "concomitant" here (again, notice the *con-*) as suggesting an assembled manifold of abilities, with "volition" in particular suggesting the intent to generate and steer the "thought" about targets of interest and their affordances.

The list of parameters proposed below is far from exhaustive. Its purpose is to identify those executive abilities that, together, are most likely to install extrovert self-consciousness. My conjecture is that these abilities initially develop as ontogenetic adaptations to the sociocultural challenges of childhood, even though, as with many other adaptations, they later operate in other domains.

Two critically important caveats need to be noted from the outset. They also bear on the introvert self-consciousness discussed in chapter 7. First, taken separately, none of the executive abilities involved in extrovert (as well as introvert) self-consciousness need be exercised consciously. (Although this is not a conceptual analysis of consciousness, it is worth noting that there is no circularity in the proposed account.) It is only their *assembly and joint exercise* during early development that, thanks to naive psychology, installs extrovert self-consciousness as a permanent disposition. The idea is that wired together during the installation period in early development, these executive abilities end up creating a new competence.

Second, once installed, extrovert (as well as introvert) self-consciousness is on its own, so to speak, as a durable disposition that can be active without necessarily requiring the interaction of all or most of the contributing executive abilities or needing further help from naive psychology. The same is true of the installation of so many other competencies, mental and behavioral. Shared attention, for example, helps installing a powerful competence for word acquisition but later drops out of the acquisition process (Bogdan 2009; Bruner 1983; Tomasello 1999). Explicit instruction and behavioral imitation install the driving competence but then (in most cases) drop out of the later exercise of the competence.

Yet a major difference must be noted. Unlike the competencies just mentioned and most others, self-consciousness does not *do* anything in particular. It does not seem to have a specific job to perform. It may be more accurate to say that self-consciousness reflects the (simulative) self-regulative readiness of various executive abilities listed below to become active and join forces, as needed. Phrased intuitively, one is self-conscious because and to the extent that one is ready to intend, exercise top-down attention and control, engage in multitasking and so on. Self-consciousness signals this dispositional readiness.

With these general remarks behind us, let us proceed with a brief description of the parameters that, on my analysis, reflect executive abilities involved in the formation of consciousness.

▪ *intendingness*

The term 'intendingness' (or 'intentfulness') is meant to capture the ordinary meaning of thinking or doing something with a simple intent or a more complex intention. Intendingness is one of the mental abilities that is hardest to analyze in general, and in young children in particular. So I will do it, intuitively, by way of contrasts and examples. One telling contrast is with cases in which both intendingness and self-consciousness are absent, which suggests a link between the two. The blindsighter was said to have no intent in the blind field, as was the absent-minded driver as perceptuomotor agent, and neither is self-conscious in those modalities. The same is true of epileptic and akinetic-mute patients (Damasio 1999). If these sorts of people do anything at all, it is by way of mental reflexes, instincts and input-driven acts or under pressures and even guidance from outside. By itself, this link may not look too conclusive but, associated with the other executive abilities, I think it does.

I do not have any special insight into what constitutes intent in young minds, and do not attribute to them any measure of free will or uncaused agency. Rather, I think of intent in young (and older) minds as a capacity to posit goals (most often, means-dependent goals) that can be reached only by activating and coordinating a variety of abilities, categories and representations that respond flexibly and corrigibly to context, past experience, preferences and the like. Unlike preset and reflex mental responses, an intent, no matter how generated, consciously or not, opens up a goal-pursuing process whose self-regulation depends on further executive abilities involved in self-consciousness. The notion of intent is thus forward-looking, being geared to the conditions in which the goal it posits can be satisfied, rather than looking back at the causes that may have triggered the intent.

An intent, like an intention later in development, is not a prime cause of what one is about to do. The prime cause (if there ever is one) is most likely to be some unconscious brain event triggered by some external or internal stimuli. The intent capacity kicks in when the mind has the propensity and equipment to anticipate actions by imagining ahead, considering choices, fine-tuning its response to the changing context, or aborting an action.

- *means-ends initiative*

An intent does not guarantee execution. It is an inclination to do something and at best a plan about how to do it. It takes initiative to carry out an intent and it usually involves some choice of or decision about the means by which to reach the goal posited by the intent and a determination or persistence in carrying it out. At least intuitively, we know of cases, in ourselves and others, when there is an intent to pursue a goal and a decision to use certain means, and yet nothing is being done, for lack of initiative. When the initiative is present, it activates still further abilities.

- *top-down attention*

- *voluntary and sustained supervision of the resources that carry out a means-ends initiative*

These two abilities tend to work together. Carrying out an intent through an initiative to deploy specific means to reach the intended ends requires constant monitoring and also control of the execution of the initiative. Both monitoring and control are effected through top-down attention and require sustained mental effort over a period of time. For example, the young child involved in a protracted shared-attention interaction with an adult and a target would constantly monitor both her own desire to share the target, the means by which she does it (e.g., intently looking or gesturing at it), and the adult's gaze, attitude and reaction. Likewise, the absent-minded driver may consciously monitor his train of thought quite closely and control it when it gets off track but, perhaps as a result, lack similarly conscious—and have, instead, unconscious—monitoring and control in the perceptuomotor modality involved in driving.

• *holding in mind over some period of time a set of related thoughts that are relevant to some intended activity, mental or behavioral*

The intent to engage in some activity, such as looking for something or paying closer attention to something and the initiative to deploy the means of realizing the intent and monitoring its execution require that the relevant representations be durably held in mind, so that stages of execution and eventually the outcome can be compared with the intent and adjusted in case of mismatch or deviation. The contrast here is with an entirely stimulus-driven mentation that reacts to every significant change in the stimuli.

This holding-in-mind ability draws on a stable working memory, which for young children is work in progress. Nevertheless, its rudiments must be in place in order for extended episodes of shared attention or joint actions to succeed. The same is true of lengthy exploration of novel cultural gadgets and their ways of being utilized.

• *purposeful and active intermodal cooperation*

Such cooperation ensures that information processed or available in other modalities is contributed to the dominant modality in executing an intent. Mere interaction among various modalities need not contribute to self-consciousness. Most animals would react to stimuli affecting different modalities—sight, hearing, smell and so on—and integrate the information they supply without doing it actively and purposely. What seems to make a difference (one of many, of course) to self-consciousness in a dominant modality is when other modalities are actively and often deliberately recruited, thanks mostly to top-down initiative and attention, to contribute to the execution of the intent. For a young child, for example, trying to get an adult to play a beloved game requires combining the right memories and the right perceptuomotor schemes with the shared attention patterns and possibly some ritualized gestures and vocalizations.

• *deliberate anticipation or mental rehearsal*

This is the ability to think ahead, somewhat detached from, though usually caused or cued by, some current sensory or memory input, particularly in early childhood. Chimpanzees are credited with some advance planning, when they carry implements, such as stones, for future use, or more often, when they have to figure out tactical alliances and future behaviors in competitive situations by some sort of forward-looking relational thinking

(Tomasello 1999; Tomasello and Call 1997). As noted earlier (chapter 2.3), young children often engage in pretend play by imagining alternative situations and exploring their possible implications.

- *deliberate memory search*

In the opposite direction, this is an ability for backward mental travel. It is unclear whether apes or even young children engage in deliberate memory search but if (or when) they do, it would be a further contributor to self-consciousness, as it engages intent, means-ends initiative (to recruit certain memories for some task), top-down attention, and simultaneously entertaining several thoughts, such as the ones that prompted the memory search and those that are found in such a search. Memory search may seem to require introvert consciousness, but I think (and will argue in chapter 7) that this is true only of autobiographical memory, which young children do not yet have. Searching for facts or experiences in semantic or episodic memory (respectively) is more like attentively checking the scene in front of one's eyes, except that the "mental eyes" (as it were) are turned toward what is stored in memory.

- *multitasking*

Put simply, this is the ability to do several things at once. Multitasking is not simply a matter of attending to several things at once. Many species can do that. Multitasking is about actively and purposely *doing* several mental and behavioral things at once—for example, driving and talking while still actively listening to the music on the radio. Apes, even enculturated ones and even after intense training, cannot multitask (Savage-Rumbaugh 1991). By the time human children master shared attention and joint actions, and later linguistic communication, they are fairly competent multitaskers.

- *online metacognition*

This is the capability to monitor, evaluate and, if necessary, correct or optimize one's cognitive performances. Metacognition is a modal-specific capability: it operates on perception, attention, memory, diverse forms of thinking (planning, problem solving, etc.) and of course behavior. Metacognition can be procedural, concerning which strategies to follow and how to monitor their performance, or declarative, involving explicit knowledge about the tasks to be performed and the strategies to be used. It turns out, not surprisingly, that young children are better at procedural than declarative metacognition, and within the procedural version, better at dealing with such online modalities as perception, attention, online learning and forms of behavior than at offline thinking (Bjorklund 2005, 167–171). Some animal species, and particularly primates, also seem to be capable of certain forms of online metacognition.

Transition

The executive abilities surveyed so far are fairly representative of the extrovert self-consciousness that young children display in their first years, although some may be borderline cases of the extrovert/introvert sort. The question to ask next is what explains the interaction and joint exercise of these abilities in early childhood, which (on my hypothesis) is conducive to the development of extrovert self-consciousness.

My answer will proceed in three steps, from wider to narrower explanations. The widest identifies children's sociocultural tasks and practices as spawning the most likely and potent selection pressures for self-consciousness, first extrovert and later introvert. The next and narrower explanation brings intuitive psychology (in its two versions—naive and later commonsense) as the principal competence involved in and thus responsible for children's mastery and exercise of sociocultural activities. And the final and narrowest explanation brings in the means-ends format in which children deploy their intuitive psychology to self-regulate their management of sociocultural activities and in the process make sense of other minds and their own. It is in this means-ends format of deployment that the children's intuitive psychology recruits, assembles and durably wires in the consciousness-generating executive abilities surveyed above.

5.2   Sociocultural Activities

As the illustrations in chapter 2 have intimated, sociocultural activities occupy most of the time and energy of young children. Some of the most representative and most frequent such activities are:

- communication
- explorative action and play
- shared attention
- joint action
- pretend play
- imitation

These activities involve other people, either actually or virtually (as in self-directed talk, pretend play or imitation), and most also involve or presuppose cultural artifacts and practices. These activities therefore deserve the label of *sociocultural*. They all display the exercise of most if not all of the executive abilities outlined earlier as parameters of extrovert self-consciousness. I begin with a few illustrations and then make a more general point.

Imitation At least since Piaget's pioneering work, there have been disagreements about how to read child imitation (Bjorklund 2005, 235–239). It is not my aim to take sides but rather to recruit imitation as an important sociocultural pointer, in conjunction with others, to the young children's extrovert self-consciousness.

Imitation is different from instinctive mimicry. Significantly for our discussion, the latter lacks intent, means-ends initiative or even awareness of what is going on. Animals mimic, and so do human infants (Chartrand and Bargh 1999; Meltzoff and Moore 1977). Neither form of mimicry needs to be conscious. Male adults watching tennis, boxing or football often mimic as well, most often unconsciously, helped by their mirror neurons (and perhaps stimulated by a beer or two). As a reflex response, mimicry is practiced mostly in infancy, whereas genuine imitation emerges around 18 months or so (Bjorklund 2005). 18 months is an age of great import, when young children share attention with adults in a variety of interpersonal interactions and for a variety of social goals, when words are mastered in novel and powerful ways, when cultural practices begin to be rapidly assimilated, and when communication acquires a genuinely predicative format (Adamson 1995; Bogdan 2009; Hobson 1993; Tomasello 1999).

Unlike mimicry, imitation requires an *intent* to replicate another person's action along several dimensions, such as the recognition of that person's goal, often of the intent or desire behind it, and of the pertinent *means* used to reach the goal (Tomasello 1999). Significantly for the argument of the next chapters, about the means-ends format of intuitive psychology, the young children who do not see the pertinence of a means-ends action do not imitate; for example, they imitate an adult putting a bird, but not a car, to bed (Mandler and McDonough 2000). Furthermore, when infants watch an agent reaching a goal by unusual means (such as activating a light switch with the head) and understand the reason for this (the hands are occupied with something else), they imitate only the goal; but when the infants do not understand the reason, they imitate the whole thing, means and goal (Gergely et al. 2002). I take deferred imitation, extending over longer periods, of which young children are also capable, to suggest some intent and deliberate effort to do it in the absence of the initial stimuli. So much about intent and its means-ends execution. What about the other parameters of extrovert self-consciousness?

Understanding and replicating the pertinent features of somebody else's action (i.e., goal, intent, means, context) requires the imitator to generate actively a *means-ends initiative*, recruit and *integrate* information from several modalities, such as memory, perception, motor routines, naive psychology, and perhaps even engage in some *mental rehearsal*. This gambit also requires *top-down attention*. These are all potential marks of extrovert self-consciousness. There is also neuropsychological evidence indicating *top-down control* on brain centers concerned with the observation of imitated actions (Grezes et al., 1998; Smith and Kosslyn 2007, 464–469).

Pretend Play Pretend play was earlier analyzed (in chapter 2.3) in order to show that young children's imaginative thinking is situated, extrovert and only partly offline. At this point, pretend play is taken as an indicator of intent to switch to imagination, particularly when mentally rehearsing novel means-ends actions or culturally defined forms of behavior or communication (Bogdan 2005a). Though stimulated by something the child sees or remembers, and primed by a predisposition to play and rehearse some typical or new behaviors, children's shift from normal to pretend mentation and behavior is likely to reflect a choice between competing stimuli, impulses and routines rather than a single, overpowering reflex, a learned routine or a passive reaction to stimuli, which are all signs of unconsciousness. To that extent, then, the decision to pretend-play would reflect an intent to reenact playfully a partial alternative to some typically means-ends behavior.

Intent, the means-ends initiative and rehearsal and the ensuing behavior may explain one of the differences between animal play and children's pretend play. On my analysis, animal play need not involve self-consciousness. Some multitasking is also involved in pretend play, as the pretending children must juggle both reality and the imagined departure from it, without losing their sense of the distinction.

Communication by Shared Meaning As a final illustration, consider the communicative acts of young children, preverbal but particularly verbal, which are likely to indicate intent, means-ends initiative and multitasking, especially on the occasions, quite frequent beginning with the second year, when children want to attract the adults' attention to an object or situation of interest or when adults are means to the children's goals.

For a typical example, consider a child engaging her mother in *shared-attention communication*—say, to get mother to bring the cat closer by looking at the cat, then at mother, then at mother looking at the cat, followed by a bilateral exchange of smiles as mutual acknowledgment of their looking at the cat and expecting some action toward it. For this strategy to work, the child's mind must engage in multitasking, activate and coordinate several representation schemes, and link sensory and memory inputs with anticipations or expectations, and with projected actions and often their effects as well. In particular, one would expect the child's online simulations, which anticipate, regulate and monitor this complex array of mental representations and schemes, and the actions they generate, to start from an intent (here, to get the cat closer), and, being steadily guided by it in an attentive, top-down manner, to factor in and coordinate different modalities (e.g., memory, vision, attention), and hold in mind and monitor a well-sequenced manifold of diverse modal and motor representations (e.g., gaze, mother, cat, room, one's own body) and sundry mental schemes connecting them (for extensive discussions, see Bermudez 1998, chapter 9; Tomasello 1999, chapter 3).

Other Species

The sociocultural activities examined in this section as well as others (communication, explorative play, pretend play, imitation, shared attention, joint action, pedagogy, etc.) are among the most consequential for the mental development of human children. Their exercise displays most of the parameters of extrovert self-consciousness indicating the work of the relevant executive abilities. If we consider the ontogeny of our closest (and best studied) primate relatives, chimpanzees and bonobos, we find significant absences on both sides of the equation—activities and parameters of self-consciousness, respectively. Our primate relatives do not communicate by shared meaning (only by imperative signals and emotional responses), do not share attention (but can engage in some joint gazing), do not imitate (but can mimic behaviors), do not play pretendingly (except, possibly, in some captive cases). These limitations suggest that the social understanding of nonhuman primates is confined to observable patterns of sociopolitical behavior and interactions among individuals, including third-party relations, which are useful in political calculations. Their culture and pedagogy are fairly minimal, consisting of only a few transmissible practices, and do not seem to progress across generations (Tomasello 1999; Tomasello and Call 1997).

The other side of the equation, concerning the naive psychology and the executive parameters of self-consciousness, is of course much harder to decipher. There is an ongoing and undecided debate over whether apes possess some rudiments of naive psychology (Hare, Call and Tomasello 2001 versus Povinelli 1996). Most of the debate is about representing the conspecifics' seeing, gazing and the resulting visual knowledge. These visual relations are not very mind revealing, as far as I can tell (Bogdan 2003). Judging from the limitations noted earlier in what the apes and other nonhuman primates do, it is unlikely that their rudiments of naive psychology, if any, would register the mental states of conspecifics.

There are studies of some executive abilities of nonhuman primates—for example, of metacognition in monkeys (Smith, Shields and Washburn 2003). Other abilities, such as top-down attention, may be inferred from complex, usually sociopolitical behaviors. Could the alleged rudiments of ape naive psychology orchestrate some executive abilities into a low-grade extrovert self-consciousness, possibly active in the highly pressured domain of sociopolitical interactions? This is possible, but the issue is empirical and inevitably theory-dependent.

I noted the possibility of on-and-off or pulsative displays of consciousness in almost vegetative patients, suggested by Antonio Damasio (1999). Would this option work for some animal species as well? In humans, self-consciousness develops as a durable and wide-ranging disposition, for the reasons developed in this book. Its impairment may often be less than total, leading to partial and pulsative displays. It is unlikely that the same is true of most animal minds, given the modular design of their minds, their generally standardized behaviors and their fairly stable or predictable environments. The latter, in particular, are unlikely to spawn strong selection pressures for the executive abilities implicated in self-consciousness.

Nevertheless, it is possible that in specific domains of animal behavior that require significant flexibility and contextual improvisation, the selection pressures might call for executive abilities that could sponsor a limited form of self-consciousness. The latter, then, would be domain- and perhaps even tasks-specific, and would be 'on' or active only when such animals handle those specific tasks in those specific domains— otherwise being on some sort of automatic pilot. This may conceivably be the case with sociopolitical interactions among apes and maybe dolphins. The possibility that enough executive abilities could sponsor a low-grade and pulsative self-consciousness in privileged domains of animal activity need not be linked to the work of a high-grade intuitive psychology or any intuitive psychology whatsoever. What an intuitive psychology of the human sort does, is bring and wire together in childhood powerful executive abilities that are jointly able to install a durable, constant, nonpulsative self-consciousness. It is the latter that seems to be a uniquely human acquisition.

What about our direct ancestors in the *homo* lineage? As in chimpanzees, intense sociopolitical life may call for domain-specific executive abilities that light up a limited and extrovert consciousness when active. Steven Mithen evokes the possibility that early humans and Neanderthals in particular may have enjoyed a similarly domain-specific fleeting or ephemeral (nonintrospective, extrovert) consciousness, when engaging in tool-making and foraging, but does not rule out the possibility that they could handle these activities unconsciously (Mithen 1996, 148–149).

Without prejudging the issue of allocating some sort of extrovert self-consciousness across species, my take on self-consciousness sets two specific conditions that can be explored empirically: (a) strong and durable selection pressures for mental abilities and processes that generate self-consciousness; and (b) a plausible evolutionary and/or developmental story for the installation of self-consciousness. (Interspecific sympathy or pet-inspired benevolent readings of animal behaviors would not qualify.) My analysis proposes versions of both conditions. I expect other analyses to propose different versions.

Transition

In sum, there are good intuitive and empirical reasons to infer a robust link between the sociocultural activities of early childhood and key parameters of extrovert self-consciousness. The question to ask next is what explains this link in early childhood. In particular: is there something special about young children's mental handling of sociocultural activities—and different from mentally handling other sorts of activities, and also different from how nonhuman primates handle their sociopolitical and other activities—that could explain the development of extrovert self-consciousness? This question is taken up in the following section.

5.3   Minding Other Minds

Chapter 2.4 presented extensive evidence for the outward orientation, to other minds and the world, of the naive psychology of young children. At this stage in our inquiry, aiming to explain the ontogenetic emergence of extrovert self-consciousness, the focus shifts to the role and modus operandi of naive psychology. The modus operandi is of a means-ends sort (as argued in chapter 4.3); and the role is eminently coregulatory, at least in the early and vital stages of childhood.

Coregulation

Human infants are programmed to be intensely social, much more so than the infants of other species. Their biologically premature birth—which is due, significantly, to a brain growth that might endanger the mother's life beyond nine months of pregnancy—renders them helpless and very adult-dependent for a long period. I insert the qualifier 'significantly' here, because it is children's mental growth that will eventually benefit most from this predicament. In the first weeks and months of life, unable to self-regulate their basic bodily processes, infants need adults, mothers in particular, for proximal coregulation of basic physiological processes. In time, but with many of the same functions, this physiological coregulation is replaced by a more distal psychological coregulation, effected through exchanges of looks, facial movements, smiles, gestures, vocalizations and other forms of behavior that express mostly emotions, communicative and affective states, and are registered by children as such.

The executive predicament of human infancy and the coregulation solutions—physiological and then psychological—that emerge from birth and develop in a well-scheduled pattern, suggest that infants may enter life with an expectation of the *coregulatory other*. In introducing this idea, Colwyn Trevarthen (1993) suggests that human infants are actually born with a dialogical mind based on a sense of a "virtual other." (The idea of the coregulatory other, I note in passing, should be distinguished from that of imprinting, which requires only the identification of a candidate parent, without implying coregulation.)

Initially, the psychological coregulation and the infants' built-in expectation of the coregulatory other are exclusively *bilateral*—mind to mind, and visibly face to face, as it were—as is the infant-adult communication (initially, another form of coregulation). It is an open question whether to include such psychological coregulation into the armamentarium of naive psychology. There are two options. One option is to stick to the notion that the job of naive psychology is to register the mind-world attitudes of others and triangulate shared targets in the world. Then bilateral psychological coregulation can be said to *precede* the development of naive psychology. Yet the acquisitions of the former are likely to be absorbed and retooled into the latter, as will the coregulation function itself.

Still other coregulative acquisitions later become part of the developing naive psychology, using its world orientation for coregulative use. Reading the emotions of others is for young children a way of checking the feasibility of an action or the state of the environment, as in social referencing, or when checking how well they manage some task. Checking the attention of another person is a way of finding out about the world in a way that can modulate one's own desires and reactions, just as registering someone else's desire for something is information that can modulate and regulate one's own desires, beliefs and actions.

The other option is to take a momentous acquisition in psychological coregulation as the very core of naive psychology, as what makes it genuinely about the mind and sets it on a developmental course that is radically different from the rudiments or social cognition found in apes. It is (what may be called) a sense of other minds or, better, a *sense of the mental in others* (Bogdan 2000, 116–128; 2009, 60–63). It is a sense or awareness of the mental invariants and mental directedness of another person's looks, smiles, gestures, vocalizations and other expressions exchanged in bilateral interactions.

By *mental invariant* I mean some inner state, such as emotion, feeling, attention and their various kinds, such as happiness, sorrow, pain, visual focus and intensity, and so on, which are expressed outwardly and variably in facial configurations, gestures, looks, bodily movements, postures, vocalizations and actions. Infants can be said to discern mental invariants if and when they show consistently the *same* reactions, such as emoting at mother's happiness, despite mother's variable expressions (vocal, facial, behavioral) of happiness.

By *mental directedness* I mean the property of emotions, attention, intent and other mental states, outwardly expressed, to relate to and focus on different targets—other people first, then external things and situations. In early bilateral interactions, the first target of the adult's mental directedness, which a child recognizes and acknowledges, is the child himself and his experiences and reactions. It is a strictly interpersonal (I-You and You-Me) sort of mental directedness, which is not yet the world-directedness of the mental states later registered by the child's standard naive psychology (Bogdan 2000, 2009; Gomez 2005; Hobson 1993; Tomasello et al. 2005).

The importance of these acquisitions, due to bilateral psychological coregulation, is that, once absorbed into—if not already part of—naive psychology, they enable young children to become aware of the inner states of other people, in the sense of discerning mental invariants and their directedness in the visible and behavioral relations of others to targets. As a result, those relations to targets begin to be registered by young children as genuinely *mental*, that is, as *attitudes*. This is what makes naive psychology literally *psycho*logical.

The sense of the mental (in others) that emerges in infancy is first of the sort, there-is-something-behind-overt-expressions—something invariant and directed at other people or items in the world. Only after a few years does this sense develop into an awareness that the mental states of others may be misdirected or may have nothing to do with the outside world. In philosophical parlance (as a reviewer suggested), this may be a transition from a *de re* to a *de dicto* sense of the mental (in others). What our analysis will show is that the latter sense poses more challenges and is more demanding for children's intuitive psychology and the executive abilities mobilized to handle it. Children's self-consciousness will track this transition both in increased complexity and outward-to-inward orientation.

Perhaps the most telling illustration in early childhood of the naive-psychological interface between psychological coregulation and attitude representation is shared attention. In mastering shared attention, which is a most critical milestone in mental development, young children develop a sense that someone else's attitudes (mental invariant + directedness) are aimed at some shared target and, at the same time, are intended to steer the children's mental focus toward the same target. The result is the children's conscious sense of the target-relatedness of their own extrovert thoughts involved in attention-registering-and-directing. This is an exercise that requires activating and joining such abilities as intending, means-ends initiative, some control, multitasking and sustained working-memory activity. It is part of the process of installing extrovert self-consciousness. The installation process is significantly enhanced when the shared targets—people, objects, events, activities—are embedded in rich and fast-changing sociocultural contexts that activate and continue to stimulate an even wider plurality of executive abilities.

To sum up so far, it can be said that naive psychology does two major things: (a) in the earliest stages of childhood, it coregulates infants' social interactions, and (b) later, in a self-regulatory mode, it feeds representations of the attitudes of others into children's own goal strategies (Bogdan 1997). So construed, naive psychology has a regulatory role in informing and guiding the children's own attitudes and actions, particularly in sociocultural domains. It is in the format in which naive psychology discharges its coregulatory and later self-regulatory duties that we find the roots and stimulus for the development of self-consciousness. This format, analyzed in chapter 4.3, is of the means-ends sort and draws on the causal knowledge of the attitudes to be represented and dealt with—specifically the attitudes of others in early childhood. Causal knowledge, we recall, requires a grasp of the intrinsic properties of the attitudes of others (as tools, not implements) independently of one's own mental states and action routines. To understand and handle the attitudes of others requires carrying out a suite of tasks, the cumulative outcome of which is the recruitment and assembly of the abilities that install extrovert self-consciousness.

Attitude Tasks

Adults must appear to young children as complex and not easily predictable agents—a challenge compounded by the vast variety of social, cultural and linguistic contexts in which adults operate. Diverse mental resources of young minds must be recruited and assembled to discern what others say, mean, intend, believe, approve of, fear and so on, in this or that sociocultural context. In this learning period, the context itself must be figured out concurrently, most often in terms of still other inferred or assumed attitudes of adults. Call this the *comprehension task*.

The child-adult-culture interactions are also fast-moving and fast-complicating themselves, often in a continuous stream, so that children must engage in mental 'time travel' in order to keep track of what was going on before, remember similar experiences, compute similarities and differences, generate expectations and make predictions. Call this the *temporal tracking task*. Still another variable to be factored into the equation is that, unlike physical tools, other people react, answer back, change their minds, adjust to what others have just said or done, and reveal further attitudes, as various interactions unfold. This may be called the *dynamic interaction task*.

These tasks involve not only the resources of naive psychology but also of memory, inference, problem solving, and later language comprehension and production. Their dynamic aggregation activates the parameters of extrovert self-consciousness that reflect a sort of *horizontal* operation of the executive mind, such as holding a variety of representations in working memory, integrating information across modalities and domains, and a deliberately and closely watched effort to deploy the right thoughts in the right pattern. Yet this is only part of the story, concerned with how children make sense of the attitudes of others and their sociocultural contexts.

The other part is about the young children's *own* sociocultural activities, hence about them as goal-directed agents and means-ends thinkers. It is from this latter stance that children mentally represent and use the attitudes of others as tools in self-regulation and also, within their goal policies, in planning, deciding, pretending, imagining and so on. Consider again the shared-attention interaction whereby the child intently looks at adult, then at a target of interest, gestures toward the latter, then looks again at adult, vocalizes excitedly, and reacts positively when the adult picks up the target. In addition to the "horizontal" parameters mentioned earlier, this interactive game relies on two further abilities contributing to self-consciousness, which operate *vertically*, as it were, in that they involve (higher-order) mental states directed at other (lower-level) mental states. Let me explain.

From the list surveyed in the first section of this chapter, intending, means-ends initiative, top-down attention and deliberate supervision of intentful execution stand out as "vertical" abilities. The means-ends initiative, in particular, is the one that chooses a cause/causation goal strategy, whereby a goal is envisaged through some intent (e.g., bring the cat closer, in our earlier example) and appropriate representations and routines are recruited and aggregated, from memory, current perception, and specialized areas of expertise, such as naive psychology. This intentful exercise results in a set of actions (broadly construed) that are causally directed at the attitudes of an adult and meant to cause the latter to bring about the desired goal. Used regulatively, the top-down attention and mental supervision keep this means-ends initiative on track and control the resources deployed in order to bring it to fruition.

As far as I can see, there is nothing else in young children's experience that would challenge and exercise their minds more—more frequently and more intensely—than dealing with the attitudes of others (broadly construed) in socializing, communicating, collaborating, assimilating and utilizing culture and language, and at the same time—being still adult-dependent yet intrinsically goal-directed—pursuing their own interests and self-regulating such pursuits. The young extrovert self-consciousness develops out of this challenge and reflects the joint work of the executive abilities deployed to meet it.

Transition

Here is what has been argued so far:

• the sociocultural activities of early childhood correlate systematically with executive abilities that install extrovert self-consciousness

▪ following and building on the initial psychological coregulation, the early naive psychology becomes the essential coregulatory link between children and adults, and the essential avenue and guide to the children's mastery and exercise of sociocultural activities

• naive psychology operates in a means-ends format in young children's sociocultural activities and as a result forces their minds to recruit and assemble the suite of executive abilities that jointly install extrovert self-consciousness

• so construed, the early naive psychology best explains the presence and operation of extrovert self-consciousness in young children

Together with the evidence marshaled in chapter 2 and the critical analyses of chapter 3, this chapter has identified naive psychology as the main stimulus and shaper of extrovert self-consciousness. This conclusion, taken together with the absence of self-oriented naive psychology and introvert self-consciousness before the age of 4, supports the asymmetry thesis. The latter holds that children understand and, as a result, are conscious of other minds before they understand and are conscious of their own.

We turn next, but slowly, to the other major objective of this book, which is to explain the later development of understanding one's own attitudes and how it leads to introvert self-consciousness. A word of anticipation is in order.

5.4   Anticipating the Turn

The extrovertly conscious children of our inquiry are about to reach the critical period between 4 and 5. So it is time to ask what mental developments will steer their minds toward self-understanding and hence introvert self-consciousness. The next two chapters aim to answer this question. The basic idea can be previewed as follows. Self-understanding originates in a new kind of thoughts that we ascribe to ourselves. The novelty is that the contents of these thoughts include further self-ascribed thoughts or attitudes. Suppose that

I now think that [I used to worry that p]

The italicized first part is a current thought I ascribe to myself and its content, in square brackets, contains a past attitude of mine (worrying). The content of what I used to worry about (the p in question) could in turn contain a further thought or attitude, and so on. Imagine that p contains an attitude of my father. He actually believed that my going into philosophy was not a very practical idea. (Why don't you do it on weekends? he used to say. Well, father, it so happens that I do it on weekends, too.) I will call such thoughts *self-thoughts* and argue (in chapter 7) that their mastery results in self-understanding. It is the deployment of self-thoughts in sociocultural contexts, managed by a new kind of intuitive psychology, which drives the development of introvert self-consciousness.

This is the general direction the argument will take in chapter 7. What also needs to be previewed is what abilities are required in order to master and deal with self-thoughts. Their story is told in chapter 6.

First of all, a self-thought (like the one above) requires a common understanding of the thoughts and attitudes of oneself and others. Their contents must be represented under the same concepts, for this common understanding to be possible. Second, linking and embedding ascriptions of thoughts and attitudes, as self-thoughts do, requires not only a capacious working memory and logical abilities but also, and critically, an offline imagination and high-power narrative capacities. Finally, to manage all of these new tasks, the new mind must be capable of representing and processing a vast and fast changing plurality of online and offline contents in distinct but connected mental files or 'screens,' as I will call them. Such a new mind emerges only after the age of 4, in the wake of several massive neuropsychological changes, particularly in the executive area of the prefrontal cortex.

Despite the catchy labels I am using to title the book and a chapter—'our own minds' and 'the turn to our own minds' respectively—and despite such expressions as 'mind-directed' or 'mind-oriented,' I do not *mean* that what happens after the age of 4 is a literal turn inward, a sort of look at or inner sense of how the mind works or what it contains. Older children have undoubtedly a higher sensitivity to their own mental states and operations. This, as noted in chapter 7, is part of the reorientation of their metacognition. But self-understanding and introvert self-consciousness are *not* about or directed at one's own mental processes in this metacognitive sense or in any other literal sense, nor are they directed at one's own mind's hardware or software. Self-understanding is about one's own mind's *relatedness* to targets and its affordances and specifically about one's own attitudes to various contents—and so is one's introvert self-consciousness.

What changes after 4 is, first, the children's understanding of their own attitudes under public concepts, and second, their ability to project contents offline under various attitudes. According to a metaphor of the next chapter, the mental screens earlier occupied solely by online perceptual and memory contents are, after 4, joined and often replaced by mental screens that are intently opened from inside and populated by offline imagined or projected contents. Older children's self-consciousness tracks this switch to offline contents and the attitudes toward them, thus acquiring an introvert range.

6 Turning to Our Own Minds

This chapter provides the background and a historical context for the analysis of self-understanding and introvert self-consciousness that will be undertaken in the next chapter. It also examines some key reasons, opportunities and new resources for these developments in childhood after the age of 4. The chapter begins with a historical excursion. The idea that an intuitive psychology, initially aimed at other minds, is later reoriented toward one's own mind, and as a result creates a common conceptual framework for understanding minds in general, is not a new idea—at least not in philosophy—but neither is it very widespread. Most philosophers and psychologists take a common understanding of minds for granted, without explaining its origins, reasons and development. Perhaps the most insightful story of this from-others-to-self reorientation is that of Wilfrid Sellars, which I will briefly retell and reanalyze in developmental terms in section 6.1.

Like most theorists, Sellars assumes that intuitive psychology is a unified and homogeneous body of ordinary knowledge about minds. I disagree and argue, in section 6.2, that early naive psychology is significantly different in several respects from its successor after 4, which I call commonsense psychology. It is precisely these differentiating aspects that enable the later commonsense psychology of other minds to turn to our own minds. Section 6.3 looks at some new conceptual acquisitions of commonsense psychology that enable—and are symptomatic of—the common understanding of minds emerging after 4. Section 6.4 identifies certain neuropsychological developments after 4 that create the cognitive opportunities and resources for self-understanding and introvert self-consciousness. It will be the job of chapter 7 to explain the new sociocultural reasons for which, and the new cognitive resources (in particular, a new kind of thoughts), thanks to which self-understanding and introvert self-consciousness become mental reality.

A warning before we proceed: this chapter and the next are heavier on the philosophical side than the other chapters. It cannot be helped. For the time being, philosophy remains the main source of insights into and analyses of self-understanding and introvert self-consciousness, as it has been in recent decades in the areas of intuitive psychology and consciousness.

6.1 Philosophical Tales for Children

Despite the major differences surveyed in chapter 3, philosophers and psychologists generally agree that the understanding of minds ends up having a common conceptual framework. Yet, to my knowledge, there is little work on how and why this conceptual commonality comes about. One notable exception is a speculative but insightful account that Wilfrid Sellars proposed in the 1950s. Sellars, it should be added, may have also been the first to propose the theory-theory view of intuitive psychology, which he recruited to vindicate functionalism in philosophy of mind.

This remarkable and influential precedent acknowledged, there are two narrower reasons for discussing Sellars here. The most important is that he proposed a historical transition from understanding other minds to understanding our own, setting a distant and abstract background for the developmental line adopted in this book. A second reason—taken up in section 6.3, below—is that Sellars also identified some key novelties that emerge in this transition, which I associate with commonsense psychology and take to be responsible for the common understanding of minds.

Sellars on the "Evolution" of Self-Ascriptions

In a wide-ranging and influential essay in philosophy of mind and language, Sellars (1956/1963) proposes a thought experiment about how our ancestors might have evolved their understanding of thoughts. He imagines a mythical stage in prehistory when our ancestors spoke a 'behaviorist' language in which they could talk only about the public properties of observable things and events. Language about mental states was unknown. So the question Sellars asks is: What resources must be added to this initial, observational language to allow our ancestors to recognize that others and they themselves think, reason, have sensations and feelings, and so on?

His proposal is that two sorts of resources are needed, and in two stages. The first is a metalanguage, with semantic concepts, in which to describe the intentionality (target-relatedness, in my terminology) of verbal utterances, in the sense that they mean something, are true or false, and the like. Once they develop such a metalanguage, these ancestors can talk *about* thoughts, because "characteristic of thoughts is their intentionality, reference or aboutness, and it is clear that semantic talk about the meaning or reference of verbal expressions has the same structure as mentalistic discourse about what thoughts are about" (Sellars 1956/1963, 180).

Although, in such a metalanguage, one can identify and talk about thoughts in terms of semantic relations, one cannot talk about the mind itself and specifically about thoughts as mental entities. So the next question and stage in Sellars' evolutionary fable: How does one get the idea of thought as a *mental* entity? According to Sellars, this idea of thought as mental is introduced as a *theoretical construct* about internal unobservables that could explain observable behavior, similar to the way in which, in science, the idea of (say) invisible gravitation is introduced to explain observable planetary motions.

Yet the introduction of thoughts as theoretical constructs is not arbitrary. The tribe's resident sage notices that his fellow tribesmen and tribeswomen behave intelligently not only when they think out loud, in language, but also when there is no language output. So, concluding that verbal performances must be preceded by inner episodes of some sort, the sage proposes to model the idea of these inner episodes after the metasemantic construal of verbal expressions, introduced in the first stage. As a result, semantic categories are now applied to those inner episodes as well. The result of this metasemantic exercise is the *public* and *common* notion of thought.

The last episode in Sellars' story concerns applying the notion of thought as public construct to one's *own* mind. He writes that "once our fictitious ancestor . . . has developed the theory that overt behavior is the expression of thoughts, and taught his compatriots to make use of the theory in interpreting each other's behavior, it is but a short step to the use of this language in self-description. . . . Our ancestors begin to speak of the privileged access each has to his own thoughts. What began as a language with a purely theoretical use has gained a reporting role" (Sellars 1956/1963, 188–189). A final and important point: according to Sellars, although thoughts are introduced at the second stage as inner episodes, they are not introduced as immediate inner experiences or linked to such experiences; thoughts are abstract entities, understood semantically and propositionally.

(Disclosure: To the best of my recollection, parts of the preceding summary of Sellars' story may have been influenced by an exegetical account of it that I read, and made notes from, a long time ago. Unfortunately, I have lost the original source and any references to it. So, just in case—my apologies and thanks to the presumed author who, alas, must remain unreferenced.)

To dot an important 'i,' Sellars' main idea is that treating one's own inner episodes as thoughts—that is, as mental states that represent something—originates in so treating the attitudes of others, on the basis of their verbal reports and actions. More specifically, I think, our representations of our own thoughts are actually *modeled* on our representations of the attitudes of others, already understood semantically and propositionally (Bogdan 2000). The implication is that our mental episodes would not look target-related (or intentional) to us and hence would not count as thoughts, any more than hand movements would count as gestures, or inscriptions as symbols, *unless* so interpreted. In the case of thoughts, the interpretation begins with what others say and do, as a basis from which to predict and rationalize their actions. What began as a practically motivated concoction (a "theory" of other minds), intended to make sense of the verbal reports and actions of others, ends up as a way of representing our own thoughts. As a result, we represent our thoughts in the same way, with the same categories, in which we represent the attitudes of others.

Sellars does not talk about attitudes as such, only about thoughts. Yet clearly, to interpret and explain the speech and actions of others, one must ascribe attitudes to them, such as desires, intentions and beliefs. Thoughts alone would not do the job. (This point will be further elaborated below, when discussing Grice's work.) One does not have direct access to the thoughts of others. What their speech and actions normally express or reveal are attitudes. People express or reveal intentions, desires and beliefs in what they say and do. Only rarely are unattitudinized thoughts expressed just for the sake of expressing them, and it is unlikely that intuitive psychology would have evolved just to make sense of such rare and pure thoughts. The older children found by Flavell and collaborators (1995) to be simply aware of their thoughts as mere inner episodes, but not aware of their propositional contents and their affordances (see chapter 2.4), may illustrate the experiencing of thoughts that are not yet structured—or at least not yet recognized as structured—propositionally and functionally by the self-ascription of attitudes.

So, to conclude: I construe Sellars' story as one that purports to explain the transition from a naive-psychological representation of the attitudes of others to a reflexive representation of one's own thoughts and attitudes. Since development is a component as well as a target of evolution, and since self-consciousness emerges during ontogeny, I find a developmental reanalysis of Sellars' account more realistic, without losing its vaguely evolutionary tenor.

A Developmental Reading: Olson

More than twenty years ago, David Olson, a child psychologist with a keen eye for philosophical parallels and the larger picture, proposed such a developmental reading of Sellars' story (Olson 1988). According to Olson, in a first stage, young children are sensorimotor machines whose behavior is not driven by mental states of the propositional sort; in a second stage, the acquisition of language allows them to map sensorimotor schemas onto such states, as inner episodes that cause behavior; and in a third stage, the acquisition of a naive psychology allows them to *think of* the mental episodes of others and their own in semantic terms, as explanatory and predictive of behavior. Notice the implied distinction between having and thinking of one's own mental episodes, in the terms just suggested. It is the thinking-of that matters here.

Olson takes a step further—a bold step, indeed—and suggests that "children actually acquire the cognitive machinery that makes intentional states ascription literally true of them at a certain stage in development . . . A cultural form, a folk psychology, acquired by the child as a theory of mind, may be instrumental in making those mental states [beliefs and desires] subject to awareness and deliberate control" (Olson 1988, 420; my insertion in brackets). Olson further notes that the theory talk of belief and other attitudes (envisaged along functionalist lines by Sellars and other philosophers) acquires through development a mental reality of sorts: "we, in constructing beliefs, make up our minds" (Olson 1989, 620).

I think this is almost right. The qualifier 'almost,' to be further motivated later, points to a distinction I draw between the early and largely innate naive psychology of young children, on the one hand, and the later and culturally assimilated commonsense psychology of older children and adults. According to the next chapter, it is the latter that is responsible for the older children's acquisitions of mental schemas for self-directed thoughts and attitudes, and thus responsible for what will become a reflexive mind. Olson's insight, echoed by a few others (Bogdan 2000, 2001, 2009; Hobson 1993; Tomasello 1999), is that children's intuitive psychology is a crucial mind designer.

Another Developmental Reading: The Model of Others

I turn now to a somewhat different developmental reading of Sellars' claim that our understanding of our own propositional thoughts is built upon the prior understanding of the attitudes of others. I think that this modeling is crucial for the development of self-understanding.

We think reflexively and explicitly, hence metarepresentationally, about our own attitudes not only later than but also on the model of how we first think about the attitudes of others. The temporal argument about *later* has been made in previous chapters; the conceptual and developmental argument about *on-the-model-of* was made in an earlier book (Bogdan 2000). In a nutshell, this modeling can be explained as follows.

Children have been said to enter life with the expectation of coregulation by others through emotional contact, communication, shared attention, word acquisition and other collaborative interactions. The two successive intuitive psychologies—naive and then commonsense—are the main instruments of such mind-to-mind coregulation. Since the earliest years, then, most of the coregulation of children relies on representing the actual or imagined attitudes of others, expressed mostly in communication and behavior, and quite often in a give-and-take exchange with their own thoughts and attitudes.

As Vygotsky (1934/1962) theorized many decades ago, children tend to internalize and mentally reenact adult coregulation, often as dialog with self and even pretend play. Later, as they become capable of deliberate mental rehearsal—particularly after 4, and as the common understanding of minds begins to prevail—children begin to metarepresent their own attitudes as they do those of others. The result is that they understand the target-relatedness and affordances of their own attitudes in terms that are close if not similar to those applied to the attitudes of others. The point here concerns the deliberate reflexive thinking *about* one's own attitudes in a coregulative frame of mind, and *not* spontaneously having or deploying those attitudes. It is the difference between thinking explicitly about my belief that p and simply believing that p.

This modeling strategy can be regarded as a case of *task emulation*, whereby mental schemes handling tasks in one domain are converted and reenacted as schemes that handle different tasks in another domain but in a format similar to the original schemes. One well-known example is the visually friendly Venn diagrams, which are widely used in teaching logic and end up formatting the ways in which many educated people actually think of sets and their properties. Analogies and metaphors also exemplify such task emulation by importing ways of thinking from one domain into another (Bogdan 2000, 99–100). In the case at hand, coregulation is a very potent motive and incentive for children to engage in such modeling by task emulation. Commonsense psychology turns out to be an effective task emulator in the transition from understanding other minds to understanding our own.

6.2 Two Intuitive Psychologies

The distinction between naive and commonsense psychology has been amply anticipated in earlier chapters. The former was said to dominate the first few years of life, while the latter becomes gradually prominent after 4. I will review several features of naive psychology in order to define its successor by way of contrast, and show why the latter alone is capable of making the turn to one's own mind.

Naive psychology is largely (though not exclusively) a sort of procedural *know-how* that young children exercise *spontaneously* in registering and tracking in others first their communicative intents, affects and emotions, then their gaze, bodily posture and attention, and still later simple desires and intents behind others' actions, and beliefs. They do this most often by registering overt expressions, whether facial, behavioral, vocal or contextual. Naive psychology operates *egocentrically* in *situated contexts* and is driven by *current motivation and perception*. This is why naive psychology works *online*. Finally, naive psychology is *metarelational* in the sense that it represents another person's relations to some *concrete, spatiotemporally defined* target. Naive psychology cannot represent how others actually *represent* a target, which is why it is not metarepresentational. This is to say that young naive psychologists cannot represent the propositional attitudes of others, such as intentions or opinions, nor can they represent their own propositional attitudes, past or present, even though (as explained in chapter 2) they register their *experiences* of such attitudes.

For convenience, we can call the attitudes that young children represent object-directed or *objectual attitudes* in order to distinguish them from the attitudes to propositions or *propositional attitudes* whose metarepresentation develops later, after 4, in a new version of intuitive psychology. I call the latter *commonsense psychology* for reasons that will soon become apparent. This distinction, it should be stressed, is about the attitudes and contents that children *represent* (as objects before the mind, in Davidson's (2003) terms) and not about attitudes and contents that children have (as objects in the mind).

Commonsense psychology can be loosely characterized in terms of parameters that contrast with those of naive psychology italicized in the previous paragraphs. This is not a rigorous account, only a working profile for the purposes at hand. In contrasting terms, commonsense psychology is much less a spontaneously exercised know-how, although it can become routinized, and much more an elaborate and inferentially used body of knowledge, a sort of *knowledge-that*, most of it explicit or, if need be, explicitable. Elsewhere, I called its work *reconstruction* because it operates by way of inferences aimed to deliver context-sensitive representations of what other people want, think, intend, do and so on, to be used in interpretation, explanation, prediction or rationalization (Bogdan 1997, chapter 8).

Made possible by new mental capacities (developing after 4) for inference, abstraction, counterfactual imagination and pretense, introspection, reflexive thinking and more, commonsense psychology is bound to be more reflective, in contrast with the reflex spontaneity of early naive psychology and the simplicity of its inferences. It can also be employed offline—and it quite often is. Unlike its predecessor, commonsense psychology can be exercised variably, often with different results, depending on context, motivation, effort, intelligence, experience, insight and other such factors. Casual observation notes that women tend to be better commonsense psychologists than men, older people better than younger, writers and artists better than accountants and football players, and con artists and some politicians are probably the best.

This variability notwithstanding, commonsense psychology is the effective instrument it is—most of the time and in most situations—because most people use it in fairly uniform and shared or common ways, when making sense of other minds and their own. It is a *common* way of making *sense* of minds in general. The main reason it is common resides in the intricate choreography between self-ascriptions and other-ascriptions of attitudes. This choreography, in turn, has a major impact on the development of self-understanding and introvert self-consciousness. Let me unpack this idea.

Commonsense psychology can and most often does operate non-egocentrically, in adopting or reconstructing the stance or perspective of another person. In so doing, it operates metarepresentationally, in the sense that it represents how others represent some event, situation or fact, which is different and more mind-probing than registering metarelationally how others interact (visibly and behaviorally) with some concrete target. Commonsense psychology can also represent offline the unsituated attitudes of others, which are often far removed in space and time from the perceptual and motivational context in which the commonsense psychologist happens to be. Those unsituated attitudes are conceptualized as attitudes to propositions, and not just to spatiotemporally concrete targets, and can be someone else's or one's own. I will say more about propositions and their importance in a little while.

What is important to note now is that the very features that distinguish commonsense psychology from naive psychology are those that make the turn to our own minds possible. Unsituatedness is one of them. When we think of our own attitudes, we just *think* of them and do not need to perceive their visible symptoms, as young children do with their naive psychology. And we can think of our own attitudes independently of the motivational and perceptual context in which we happen to be. Non-egocentricity is essential for the turn to our own minds. Since the current context of perception and action can often be quarantined or inhibited, we can identify and examine our attitudes from various perspectives, including those of other persons, in the same way we do when figuring out the attitudes of others. As noted in the next section, propositions as the publicly distilled and regimented contents of the attitudes offer mighty assistance to the turn to our own minds, as they provide a neutral, abstract and common format in which to represent and talk about the attitudes of others and our own.

So construed, the distinctive features of commonsense psychology suggest the possibility that it evolved procedural and conceptual formats for reasons both external (other minds) and internal (our own minds). Externally, these formats are adapted to the minds of others, whose complexity is more evident to children after 4 and can no longer be managed by their naive psychology. These formats are also adapted to the fact that the attitudes of adults are manifested in ways subtler than overt behavior and most often indirectly, in linguistic communication. From an internal angle, commonsense psychology may have evolved to optimize the goal strategies of selves that operate most of the time in sociocultural contexts, where (as we shall see) they need to implement new forms of self-regulation. Jointly, these two desiderata may go some way toward explaining the turn to our own minds and the common conceptual framework of self- and other-ascriptions.

6.3 A Common Understanding of Minds

Besides its general features that facilitate the turn to our own minds, commonsense psychology uses specific acquisitions as a common format in which other- and self-ascriptions of attitudes can be interactively represented and amalgamated. In different contexts and for different reasons, two of these acquisitions have been anticipated by Wilfrid

Sellars (1956/1963)—the naive-functionalist nature of the concepts of commonsense psychology, and propositions as contents of its attitude ascriptions.

Naive Functionalism

Functionalism in philosophy is a view that construes attitudes solely in terms of interacting conditions, both mental and behavioral, and ignores their hardware substrate. Thus, for example, a 'belief' is functionally understood in terms of inputs, other mental states (desires, intentions), perhaps some dispositions or traits and behavioral or verbal outputs. It is this relational pattern that matters in the functionalist profile of attitudes. A widely held opinion among philosophers of mind is that in a naive and unreflective form functionalism is at the heart of commonsense psychology (Fodor 1987; D. Lewis 1972; Sellars 1956/1963). Many developmental psychologists that espouse the theory-theory view of commonsense psychology agree, and date the emergence of this naive functionalism roughly around the age of 4 (Gopnik and Meltzoff 1997; Perner 1991; Wellman 1990). In this latter posture, naive functionalism enables the commonsense psychologist to take non-egocentrically the perspective of another person's attitudes, to realize that such attitudes can vary from person to person or in the same person across time, and also to distinguish between what another person sees or believes and how things actually are, and so on (Bogdan 2000, 132–137).

There are good reasons for commonsense psychology and (in a rudimentary way) its predecessor, naive psychology, to be functionalist. These intuitive psychologies do not, and cannot access the hardware or inner workings of the attitudes they represent, either in other minds or our own—nor does this limitation concern them. Nor, despite differences in the evidence they use, do the two intuitive psychologies have a distinct or proprietary phenomenal access to the so-called 'cold' attitudes they represent, such as intention, opinion and the like. (I am excluding of course the phenomenally rich and emotion-driven attitudes, such as fear, worry and the like.) The point is obvious for other minds, less obvious for one's own. Yet a case can also be made for the latter. Making this case strengthens the notion that the functionalism of commonsense psychology reflects its genuinely common take on attitudes, whether the self's or someone else's.

To begin with, naive psychology was shown earlier (in chapters 2 and 3) to be extrovert, as is the self-consciousness it sponsors. Young children do not have many, if any, offline attitudes. Their online attitudes are only in extrovert modalities (perceptuomotor, emotional, communicational), and their consciousness extends phenomenally only to the modalities, experiences and contents involved, not to their identity as *target-related* attitudes. A good case can be made—and it has been made—that even though adults are conscious of their target-related attitudes, the consciousness in question need not be phenomenal, even when subjected to phenomenological inspection.

Believing that two plus five equals seven or that 'hat' means 'chapeau' feels like nothing. (Try it!) This is more than saying that our consciousness of our attitudes is transparent, in the sense that it extends only to their contents, not to their mental vehicles. It is to say that the *experience* of believing need not have its *own* proprietary phenomenality. The same is true of other cold attitudes, such as intention, opinion, expectation or often even desire (like the desire for a peaceful and noiseless world). This nonphenomenality claim does not of course extend to the so-called hot attitudes, based on empathy, feeling and emotions. Tellingly, the nonphenomenal cold attitudes are the ones with the widest range of functional links and the least dependence on sensory inputs and sundry perceptual and emotional experiences [more in a note on the nonphenomenality of cold attitudes].

To sum up, the central point so far is that the shared indifference of commonsense psychology to hardware, inner mechanisms and even the phenomenality of functionally rich but cold attitudes is another key piece of evidence about the homogenization and unification of the conceptual framework of other- and self-ascriptions of attitudes after 4. And so, quite significantly, is the format of the contents ascribed to attitudes both in the first and third person.

Propositions

Sellars' "evolutionary" story, we recall, ends with how our ancestors—and older children, on our parallel story—come to think of their own thoughts and report their contents abstractly and semantically in terms of *propositions*. The term 'proposition' means different things to different philosophers, logicians and linguists. A proposition may be what a sentence means or what a that-clause refers to or the content ascribed to an attitude. This multiplicity of roles reflects the commonsense-psychological take on contents. We think of our own thoughts and attitudes *in terms of* what they represent, as their *contents*. And we identify and describe such contents (Sellars' point about reporting thoughts) in the public format of sentences that mean something in propositional terms, usually in the indirect form of that-clauses. This is why the contents of thoughts and attitudes are said to be propositional. All of this is familiar and not much debated. But this is only half of the story, though it is already sufficient to establish the common and public format of content representation.

The other half—which is less familiar and more controversial—is that as contents ascribed to attitudes, propositions are *constructs* of common-sense psychology. In other words, propositions are how the contents of attitudes *look* from the vantage point of commonsense psychology. This does not mean that propositions are *invented* by commonsense psychology. The grammar and semantics of natural languages and its communicational constraints are more basic sources. But it means that commonsense psychology adopts this format for its *own* reasons. To see what is involved in this idea, let us consider the following question: If, from the common-sense-psychological stance, thoughts and attitudes are individuated and ascribed in the semantic terms of what they are about, and if this individuation is made in terms of propositions—does it follow that people actually think propositional thoughts, when their thinking is *not* in a common-sense-psychological mode? A parallel may help guide our way to an answer.

Early in the twentieth century, many philosophers of perception were enamored by the notion of *sense data* as a sort of visual atoms operating as an interface between the mind and the world. Despite what its early advocates thought, the arguments for sense data were about how we *think* reflectively—indeed, commonsense-psychologically—about what we perceive, and not about how perception *actually* works. According to current scientific wisdom, perception does not work in terms of the sense-data model. If it did, it would have had different mechanisms than it actually has—an issue that sense-data theorists never bothered to consider. To borrow a distinction from Donald Davidson (2003), sense data were construed as (sensory) objects *before* but not *in* the mind—indeed, before the *reflective* and commonsense-psychological mind, and not in the perceptual mind.

Another take on the same distinction compares propositions to *numbers* (Churchland 1979; Davidson 2003). The argument is that propositions—and hence the propositional contents of thoughts—are in the eye of the beholder as speaker of a public language reporting on thoughts and attitudes. The fact that we think and talk about attitudes as having propositional contents need not entail that thoughts are *intrinsically* propositional, and that propositions are in the mind and structure its representations, anymore than the fact that numbers are used to quantify physical processes need entail that numbers exist in and structure the physical world. Propositions and numbers are clever devices that enable speakers of a language and scientists to map out and talk publicly about the entities and regularities of mental and physical domains (respectively). But the ontological reification of propositions as actual mental components of thoughts is a mistake, as is the reification of numbers.

There are still other ways to make the point that propositions reflect the stance of commonsense psychology. I will mention two, with little elaboration. One way is to insist that, far from animating actual thought contents, propositions first show up in *reported* speech, in that-clauses following mentalist verbs (e.g., think-that, believe-that, and the like) or in verbs presupposing mentalist ones (e.g., intimate, predict, refuse, and so on). I may actually think something X, where X is more complex than a proposition, as X involves images, memories, anticipations, but I *report* it blandly as 'I think that p'—where p is a proposition (Bogdan 1994, chapter 7; 2009, chapter 5). One can argue that reported speech reflects the stance of commonsense psychology, particularly if one takes a Gricean position on the matter, on which more next.

Another way to relate propositions to commonsense psychology is to note that propositions emerge in public discourse, and then suggest that public discourse, as a form of communication, cannot get off the ground developmentally without the ability to read other minds. Anticipated by George Mead (1934), this is Paul Grice's (1957) famous take on meaningful communication. It is the right take to take, at least developmentally (Bogdan 2000, 2001, 2009; Bruner 1983; Hobson 1993; Tomasello 1999). Reading other minds in order to communicate meaningfully means representing attitudes in naive- and later commonsense-psychological terms. This is to say that the contents of the attitudes are propositional from the stance of intuitive psychology in general and the public communication it underpins.

In sum, as common and public formats for representing the contents of thoughts and attitudes, propositions are constructs of a shared intuitive psychology. So the fact that our ancestors (in Sellars' story) and older children (in mine) end up being aware and thinking of, as well as reporting, the contents of their own thoughts and attitudes as propositions points to commonsense psychology as shaping the representations of thoughts and attitudes.

Davidson on Thoughts and Beliefs

We get still another angle on the common understanding of minds, useful for the argument of this chapter, by reexamining some provocative and apparently implausible ideas of Donald Davidson. Like Wittgenstein and at times Quine, Davidson had the gift of the insightful but cryptic remark—a sure way to get the attention of plenty of decrypting commentators. It surely got mine. But my decrypting here is exclusively developmental.

One of Davidson's most controversial remarks is that "a creature cannot have thoughts unless it is an interpreter of the speech of another" (1984, 157). As if this were not bold enough, Davidson takes one step further and claims that one could not have beliefs without having the concept of belief (1984, 170). According to Davidson, having beliefs requires experiencing surprise when one's own expectations about the world are not met, and also being able to spot one's own mistakes, which presupposes distinguishing between truth and falsity. Making the distinction between truth and falsity in turn is possible only if one has the idea of objective, public truth, and that idea originates in the interpretation of language. A private attitude, Davidson writes, "is not intelligible except as an adjustment to the public norms provided by language. It follows that a creature must be a member of a speech community if it is to have the concept of belief. And given the dependence of other attitudes on belief, we can say more generally that only a creature that can interpret speech can have the concept of a thought" (1984, 170).

A developmental decrypting of these remarks must begin with a clarification. As I read them, Davidson's claims are not—or should not be—about beliefs *minimally* construed as mere information-carrying states or basic expectations materialized in the brain and causing behavior. In this minimal sense, most organisms have beliefs, without having to interpret any speech and without having or indeed needing any *concept* of belief. Davidson's claims must be about beliefs one is *aware* of and *recognizes* as one's own and also recognizes as being target-related and propositionally formatted. One could not spot one's own mistakes or distinguish between the truth and falsity of one's own beliefs, if one was not aware that one's beliefs represent something (the semantic part) *and* that their representing something bears on what one may think and do as a result (the affordance part). Beliefs and other attitudes have both semantic content and affordances, of which the believer must be aware, to fit Davidson's analysis.

To fill in some gaps in Davidson's claims about one's own beliefs, we need explanatory bridges to take us from his premises to his conclusions. I will suggest such bridges in developmental terms. The first bridge combines Sellars and Grice. Sellars' story, as reanalyzed earlier in this chapter, proposed a bridge between interpreting the behavior and speech of others in commonsense-psychological terms, at one end, and becoming aware of and reporting one's own propositional thoughts, at the other end. As Davidson would agree (1984, 150), Grice's analysis supports this Sellarsian bridge with further pillars, by holding that one cannot communicate meaningfully unless one can interpret the speech of others, and one cannot do the latter unless one represents the attitudes of others.

It turns out that Grice's account of meaning can be reanalyzed in plausible developmental terms (Bogdan 2001, 2009; Olson 1988, 1989). Very young children register preverbal meanings by way of detecting the intents and emotions and later attitudes expressed by adult gestures and vocalizations. When normal speech interpretation comes of age, during the second year of life, children are already equipped, with their developing naive psychology, to understand some basic attitudes of others. But it will take several more years and further acquisitions to parlay this understanding into an awareness and understanding of their own attitudes.

Developmentally, a still further bridge is needed to make sense of Davidson's claim that one can distinguish between the truth and falsity only if one has the idea of objective, public truth, which originates only in the interpretation of language. Having this idea requires not only speech interpretation through attitude representation but also, and *antecedently*, shared attention, naive psychology, word acquisition and more (Bogdan 2009). It is precisely these prerequisites that enable children to recognize mistakes, distinguish truth from falsity, and understand surprise as a violation of expectation—first in others and later in themselves—and do so consciously. Many animals and human babies experience surprise or sustained curiosity or confusion when their belief-like expectations are violated, as recent experiments have shown (see Bjorklund 2005, for a recent survey). But that does not mean that they consciously recognize their own beliefs to be false or distinguish between truth and falsity; it only means that they are disposed to react in certain ways when belief-like expectations are violated. Their minimal thoughts and beliefs (if this is what we want to call them) need not be propositional or even conscious for such reactions to occur.

The previous paragraph points to a fundamental fact about mental development, recognized by Davidson in his later work (2003) but known to developmental psychologists for quite some time and anticipated many decades ago by Vygotsky (1934/1962) and Mead (1934). This fundamental fact is that children's conscious ability to detect their own mistakes, distinguish between truth and falsity, and explicitly recognize the violation of their expectations has its roots in the *interpersonal* interactions of early childhood, particularly in the contexts of communication, shared attention and word acquisition (Bogdan 2009; Bruner 1983; Tomasello 1999). These interactions precede language acquisition and the sense of one's own attitudes, and make both possible.

Transition

The turn toward our own minds is made possible by several developments after the age of 4. Three such developments stand out. A first occurs in the children's intuitive psychology. It involves new conceptual resources that animate a novel commonsense psychology and enable young minds to think of their own thoughts and attitudes with the same concepts with which they think of the thoughts and attitudes of others. Self-understanding results from this projection of one's own thoughts and attitudes on a public conceptual map. This map enables the new commonsense psychology to operate non-egocentrically with propositional attitudes—that is, attitudes that are increasingly unsituated, often nonphenomenal and functionally rich, and whose contents are linguistically regimented and formatted as propositions. The resulting common understanding of minds gives older children a firmer grasp and better sense of other minds and their own. These latter developments in turn accelerate the assimilation and mastery of new and more complex sociocultural norms and practices, which pose further challenges and thereby lead to further mental developments.

Second, this arms race is reflected in—and may have contributed to—neuropsychological developments, mostly executive, resulting in a new sort of mind, to be outlined in the next section. It is a versatile and multilateral mind that can operate offline with a vast manifold of mental representations. A third development concerns the ability of this new sort of mind to understand and produce extended and complex sequences of representations of mental states, of others and one's own. Together, these three developments seem to me most instrumental in making the new mind cognizant and conscious of its own thoughts and attitudes.

6.4 A Multiplex Mind

Yielding to the temptation of metaphor, I will use one briefly evoked in chapter 2, to draw a contrast between the child's mind before and after the age of 4. Like most metaphors, this one simplifies and exaggerates in order to highlight the essentials. Metaphorically, the younger mind can be thought of as operating on a single central screen, where various perceptual and memory inputs show up and are constantly updated by new inputs.

Imaginative scenarios, as in pretend play, usually show up in little screens that open in a corner of, and from within, the larger screen dominated by current perception, memory, emotion and motivation. Think of this as a single-screen or uniplex mentation, so to speak, with limited offline capacities that are generally activated, cued and constrained by the deployment of online capacities on the central screen.

Since I am going to milk this 'screens' metaphor some more, as a handy intuition prop, I reassure critics (and worried friends) that it should not be read as suggesting some inner homunculus or unified Cartesian theater, harshly and effectively criticized by Dan Dennett (1991). The screens here just mean transient and widely distributed neurofunctional interactions, whose activation indicates that modalities and mental contents show up and do work. There is no spectator to see the show and no single inner stage on which the show takes place.

Cerebral Opportunities

After 4, the young mind is shaken and transformed by several upheavals that are executive as well as cognitive, and revolutionary in their cumulative impact. Chief among them are the inhibition of current perception and motivation, the linguistic recoding and representational explicitation of earlier procedural competencies, including naive psychology, and a major growth of working memory as the workspace wherein multiple, hierarchically or sequentially organized representations can be maintained, manipulated and flexibly integrated in various formats (Bjorklund 2005; Dennett 1991; Diamond 2001; Donald 2001; Houdé 1995; Karmiloff-Smith 1992). The chief neural platforms of this new mind are the (dorsolateral) prefrontal cortex and the integrative connectivity handled mostly by the right hemisphere and reaching across large regions of the brain. The growth of this platform is most dramatic in the interval between 4 and 6 (Diamond 2001).

Significantly, the self-regulatory range of the prefrontal cortex does not reach the sensory inputs and the online modalities. The prefrontal self-regulation is *intramental*, as are the mental activities it regulates, offline thinking in particular. The independence from input and online transactions, apparently unique in animal mentation, means that the prefrontal executive has the flexibility and even creativity not only to allocate and integrate resources across input-specific domains but also to generate new domains, particularly abstract and fictional. As persuasively argued by Merlin Donald (1998, 2001), against the narrow view that evolution installs only domain-specific modules, the apparently unmodular and certainly domain-nonspecific work of the prefrontal executive is itself likely to be an adaptive specialization responding to new, uniquely human evolution-ary pressures—which I take to be mostly sociocultural. The intramental reach and domain-versatility of the new prefrontal self-regulation generate several cognitive novelties that have a cumulative impact on the develop-ment of self-understanding and introvert self-consciousness.

Explicit Thoughts about Thoughts

One critical novelty is the liberation of the young mind from the captiv-ity of uniplex mentation and its ongoing and situated inputs, and the resulting ability to entertain—often simultaneously, and in different but interconnected perceptual as well as intramental screens—nested sets of alternative and at times conflicting representations of actual and non-actual, current, past and counterfactual states and situations across various domains. A multi-screen or *multiplex* mind thus, quite literally, comes of age.

As far as our story is concerned, the most important novelty brought about by the multiplex mind, after 4, is the ability to form explicit thoughts about other thoughts or attitudes and to embed further thoughts into explicit thoughts and attitudes. For lack of a better term, I will call this ability *explicit thought embedding* or ETE. It is an ability that is crucial to the development of self-understanding and (on my hypothesis) of intro-vert self-consciousness. To understand one's own thoughts and attitudes, one must be able to form thoughts about them, represent them explicitly and, equally explicitly, link them to other thoughts and attitudes, of others and oneself. This is a *reflexive* enterprise, in the sense that one turns one's mind explicitly toward one's own thoughts and attitudes in interaction with those those of others.

An example of the exercise of the ETE ability is to form the following thoughts:

'I think *that* what I wanted to say is *that* very few dogs bark for a good reason'

or

'She thinks *that* Sam realized *that* Maxi would believe *that* p rather than q.'

Both are complex thought contents that I form explicitly. By means of embedding that-clauses, both contents report further propositional thoughts or attitudes or sayings that in turn report still further thoughts or attitudes. According to the next chapter, it is these sorts of reflexive ETE exercises that drive the development of self-understanding, mostly for sociocultural reasons. The question is, what explains the *possibility* of this ETE ability? The multiplex mind is certainly the necessary neuropsychological platform, but is not sufficient to constrain or structure the way the ETE ability works. Other factors must be involved.

Contrary to a widely shared opinion, the grammar of natural language and logical abilities are also necessary but (again) not sufficient for recursive and explicit thought embedding. After all, young children can construct increasingly complex phrases, but not extended sequences of reports of thoughts that include other thoughts and attitudes. The question is not just about recursion or embedding; it is also about the meaningfulness and relevance of the ETE exercise. The development of formal capacities would not explain the latter features. A telling clue to what else is required is that the development of the ETE ability correlates more robustly with the development of narration rather than of the mastery of grammar and logic. This makes sense, as I explain next.

6.5 A Narrative Mind

The ability to narrate is critical in enabling children to assimilate, make sense of, remember and reproduce sociocultural information and practices. In so doing, this ability is equally critical in the children's mental development in general and their self-understanding in particular.

Narration and Recursive Thought Embedding

Young children do not narrate much before the age of 3; they narrate rather poorly for a few years afterward, despite an increasing mastery of grammar; and they limit themselves mostly to descriptions of actions, scenes and events, without particular concern for or sensitivity to the minds of other people or their own. When descriptions of other people do show up, the results tend to be situational, mostly action-oriented and choppily related (of the sort, 'he went there and she did that,' etc.), without a sense of plot or continuous story line and without much reference to attitudes. The minds of other people are not yet narrated about. Indeed, commonsense psychology is barely part of the children's narration—nor is their exercise of commonsense psychology narrative—until about the age of 7 or on some counts even 10 (Bruner and Feldman 1993; Leondar 1977; Nelson 1996; Slobin 1990). This suggests to me that older children's commonsense psychology is still work in progress, as is (on my analysis) the development of their self-understanding and introvert self-consciousness.

Narrations have the vital function of introducing children to sociocultural information and practices, particularly complex and less easily observable ones, most of which become discernible and intelligible in terms of commonsense-psychological narratives (Bogdan 1997, 188–200; Nelson 1996, chapter 7). Narrations also have the vital function of preserving and transmitting the lore of the child's immediate group and larger tribe or nation in various forms (legends, myths, past heroics, and so on). Closer to our present analysis, narrative communication and gossip in particular—narratively reported speech and narrative interpretations and rationalizations of attitudes, all involving commonsense psychology—are vital to social interactions. All these vital uses of narration may have started as powerful selection pressures for a narration capability. In tandem with commonsense psychology, the narration capability is likely to drive the development of the ETE ability.

At least from a Western perspective, it may look to psychologists dealing with (mostly) kindergartened and schooled children, trained in the tasks and obligations of recent culture, that mental development takes place along independent tracks, such as reading and writing, solving problems in physics or logic or simple mechanical engineering. This, I opine (but not argue here), is an evolutionary illusion. Literate culture is a recent historical novelty. Preliterate children were for millennia naturally trained to master language, communication and sociocultural practices, rather than measure volumes in different containers or arrange disks in a Hanoi-tower style or make abstract deductions or, more recently, absorb computer lore. Indeed, if anything, the latter accomplishments and tests actually measure advances in the former and more vital mental endeavors.

It makes sense to think that it was the ancestral and evolutionarily vital pressures of communication, socialization and the assimilation of culture, enabled and reflected by the development of intuitive psychology and narration, that may have stimulated the neuropsychological developments resulting in a multiplex mind after 4. On this reading, progress in problem solving, planning, imagining, reasoning and other such aptitudes may well be *byproducts* of the children's mental abilities that responded to those ancestral and vital pressures.

Why are the *narrative* uses of commonsense psychology in thinking and communication so important to the development of self-understanding and, by implication, introvert self-consciousness? The basic reason, I think, is that it is such uses that *first* pressure and, once mastered, enable young minds to engage in *explicitly and reflexively represented* recursive embeddings of thoughts and attitudes, as applications of the ETE ability. Mere linear deployment of sequences of thoughts about actual or imagined states of affairs, which don't involve attitudes in their contents, are not going to make much of a difference. Chimpanzees are said to be capable of linear and attitude-free deployments, and so are young children (Bjorklund 2005; Tomasello and Call 1997; Whiten 1991). What makes the difference is explicit thinking about thoughts and attitudes. Commonsense psychology is the competence that *first* forces and enables older children to think explicitly about thoughts and attitudes—initially those of others, and later their own. The narrative deployments of attitude concepts push such reflexive thinking about attitudes toward meaningful and topic-relevant (as opposed to merely formal) recursive embedding. This is why, I think, older children's powers of narration can be said to reflect and measure their progress in the development of the latter (ETE) ability.

Review

This has been a sort of bridge chapter aiming to explain the various factors that make possible the turn to one's own mind. The chapter first prepared the ground for the next by recalling, and reanalyzing in developmental terms, earlier accounts of how commonsense psychology, initially oriented toward other minds, turns toward one's own mind. The chapter also distinguished between an early naive and a later commonsense psychology, and argued that only the latter has the stance, the properties and the resources to deliver a common understanding of minds and thus become a bridge for the intense traffic, in older childhood and adulthood, between other- and self-ascriptions of attitudes. The multiplex mind, neurologically in place after 4, provides the platform from which self-understanding and introvert self-consciousness take off, mightily helped by new and powerful narrative abilities. The next chapter tells the story of the actual developmental journey in that direction.

7 Minding Our Own Minds

Around 4 or 5, children undergo a mental revolution that, among other things, has two remarkable and, on my analysis, related outcomes. They become able to construct a new kind of reflexive or self-directed thoughts —*self-thoughts*, as I will call them. These are the kind of thoughts that sequence and coordinate representations of their own attitudes and those of others. Self-thoughts are mental structures that enable self-ascriptions of attitudes, thus providing self-understanding. The initially self-regulatory deployment of self-thoughts in turn activates and assembles the suite of executive abilities, now with intramental reach, that installs introvert self-consciousness. This is the general idea.

Section 7.1 suggests that most of the executive abilities involved in the installation of extrovert self-consciousness also operate in the new mental environment defined by the multiplex mind and commonsense psychology. Section 7.2 samples the new sorts of sociocultural activities that call for self-ascriptions of attitudes, which initially operate in a self-regulatory mode. Section 3 examines several kinds of self-regarding thoughts and distinguishes among them the self-thoughts that sponsor self-ascriptions of attitudes. To conclude, section 4 examines and illustrates how, in regulating older children's sociocultural activities, the means-ends operation of self-ascriptions of attitudes assembles the executive abilities that install introvert self-consciousness.

7.1 Introvert Novelties

Looking at mental developments after 4 from the perspective of the multiplex brain, there are new offline screens to be generated and sequentially and often simultaneously supervised. These offline screens often display contents that project targets out there, except that the targets are not *quite* out there, literally, but are imagined. Even though we often say that the targets and affordances imagined offline are in the mind only, what we actually mean—or should mean—is that they are mentally projected out there, *beyond* the confines of the mind, but that this 'out there' is not the one revealed by sensory or memory inputs. The brain does not 'think'—in the minimal sense of *simulate*—that the targets and affordances are actually *inside* the mind. Except perhaps in deep meditation, the brain is not in the habit or business of locating the targets and affordances it projects *in* the mind. It projects them in a possible world, a possible out-there. It is the out-there of "intentional inexistence," as Brentano phrased the idea inelegantly but aptly.

Older children become (and adults are) conscious of these introvertly generated contents but again transparently—that is, conscious of the targets projected, not of the encodings of the contents or the processes that generate them. Transparency, in this case, ensures that there is nothing we access introvertly that would reveal the underlying mental mechanics, in particular, the executive mechanics that I take to be instrumental in installing introvert self-consciousness.

For current science, the intramental work of the self-regulatory machinery was said earlier (in chapter 4.3) to be mostly shrouded in mystery. Fortunately, what matters to the argument of the present chapter is not knowledge of the details of that work. What matters, rather, is the idea that introvert self-consciousness develops out of the new intramental work of executive abilities that are recruited and assembled in the formative period after 4 by the new commonsense psychology. There are good reasons to take this idea seriously, as argued below.

A first step is to ascertain the intramental range of the executive abilities deemed to contribute to the installation of introvert self-consciousness. Beginning intuitively, it seems obvious that older children and adults deploy and regulate their offline mentation by *intending* some thoughts or train of thoughts to do a specific job, as *means* to some end, *monitoring* and *controlling* the sequencing of these thoughts, paying *top-down attention* to them and, if necessary, activating or including other pertinent representations *from other modalities, searching memory* for relevant items, and *multitasking* by attending to any other pressing offline or online tasks. The italicized words, we recall, refer to executive abilities found in online mentation and responsible for extrovert self-consciousness.

The novelty here—indeed dramatic—resides mostly in the new mental environment in which the executive work is being carried out. This is the environment of the multiplex mentation operating mostly with and on explicit data structures, across various mental screens, according to our earlier metaphor. Also new, of course, is the commonsense psychology that activates and coordinates this executive work. Yet it is likely that for a few years after 4, most of children's offline mentation would still tend to gravitate toward mental imagery, as a sort of displaced perception, and inner speech, as a tangible and public prop for thinking. Both are known to develop significantly after 4, and both appear to exploit earlier resources—perception, in the case of the former (Kosslyn et al. 2001), and imaged linguistic forms in the case of the latter (Carruthers 1996). As a result, it is also likely that the simulative self-regulation of the target-relatedness and affordances of mental images and linguistically expressed thoughts might operate in ways rather close to how it operated in earlier online and extrovert mentation.

There is also the distinct possibility that a good deal of what happens in young minds after 4, at least for a while, is a sort of unpacking and explicitation of what was eminently procedural and implicit in the mostly how-to and motor-bound cognition of earlier years. Largely autarchic or rigidly linked behavioral categories turn into gregarious concepts that link various data structures across several modalities and domains in a flexible and inferential manner. Annette Karmiloff-Smith (1992) has plausibly described and explained this transformative process after 4 in several domains of early activity. There is evolutionary wisdom in this process: evolution most often proceeds by way of change through continuity; and as a stage and locus of evolution, development is likely to meet new challenges by first tinkering with available and well-proven resources.

If this line of thinking is on the right track, we could expect the executive abilities that installed extrovert self-consciousness in the first years of life, under the guidance of the children's intuitive psychology, to continue their work after 4 by adjusting to the new modus operandi of after-4 minds. As acknowledged, the adjustment is largely a matter of scientific speculation. What should not be a matter of speculation, however, is the following objection.

The Circularity Objection

The executive abilities that operate offline after 4 are, on my hypothesis, instrumental in installing introvert self-consciousness. We are now talking about *intendingness* in the form of elaborate planful intentions, introspection as intramental top-down attention, metacognition operating often on explicitly represented thoughts, deliberate means-ends initiative, deliberate memory search, deliberate multitasking, and so on.

A question that comes to mind, as an objection, is how could some of these abilities purposely operate offline without already *presupposing* introvert consciousness? And if they do presuppose introvert consciousness, then surely they could not be its premises, as my analysis proposes.

Here is my answer. First of all, these executive abilities are not conscious as such; they are just dispositions. They are installed as dispositions and so is their interaction. The question is whether we are conscious of their *exercise*. In general, we are not. That was the earlier-noted point about transparency. We are not conscious of how vision or grammar or even thinking works. We usually become conscious of their *outputs* only. I think the same is true of the introvert deployment of the executive abilities considered at this point. We are conscious of what we intend (the output), and not of how we intend (the process as exercise of the ability). Often, as the Libet-type experiments suggest, we are not even conscious of when we intend or start intending certain actions (on which more in chapter 8). The same can be said about the other executive abilities.

Second, it is known intuitively and is becoming experimentally more evident that mental activities once deemed paradigmatic of conscious thinking, not only intending and deliberating but also decision making and problem solving, are actually carried out and often completed *before* we become conscious of their outputs. Third, on my analysis, the executive abilities examined here operate collectively *when* they install introvert self-consciousness as a *competence*, and not necessarily when the competence is already in place and normally exercised. I argued in chapter 4.1 that Cartesian intuitions about the primacy of consciousness are *performance* intuitions that presuppose the competence for consciousness. Once the competence is installed and operative, the contributing executive abilities need not be exercised in any particular configuration and certainly not collectively, in order to be conscious.

There is much more to introvert self-consciousness than this bare-bones picture but it will serve for now. The question to pursue next is what explains its development. Why introvert self-consciousness?

7.2 Dealing with Self

The proximate reasons for introvert self-consciousness, I am about to suggest, originate in commonsense psychology's turn to self in later childhood, and the resulting reorientation of the executive abilities it employs to do its self-regulatory job. But *why* such a turn, and hence *why* self-ascriptions of thoughts and attitudes in the first place? And why only after

4? These questions call for exploring deeper reasons. My answer picks out two interacting challenges that children face after 4. Both challenges emerge out of a new sociocultural climate (an ontogenetic Zeitgeist, so to speak) that children encounter and discern after 4, and in which they must learn to operate.

Reasons for Self-Ascriptions

In order to see what generates these new challenges, I will engage in an intuitive and familiar sort of naive social psychology (sorry: no experiments, no statistics, no referenced data but no need for them, really!). I begin with a brief list of new mental activities that older children often initiate and manage successfully. The more trivial these activities look, the stronger my point: they are the bread and butter of adult mentation engaged in sociocultural practices that call for self-ascriptions of attitudes. Here they are:

- rehearsing what to say and what to do
- thinking how others think of you
- planning how to relate to others and how to react to their reactions
- deliberate and planned lying
- self-involving gossip
- elaborate narratives or communicative exchanges mixing reports of one's attitudes with those of others
- justifying publicly one's motives and actions
- autobiographical memory
- fantasizing about what one could do in the future
- self-criticism
- self-deprecating humor
- talking/writing about oneself
- self-advertising
- defending one's opinions
- choosing one's words carefully
- deliberate and sustained self-control
- interpersonal diplomacy

It does not take much reflection to see that these activities—and many others, along the same lines—occupy older minds most of their waking hours. Both ordinary observation and professional investigations concur that these mental activities enter the repertory of children after 4, and that their exercise matures gradually, some reaching normal competence only in adolescence (Bjorklund 2005; Dunn 1988; Nelson 1996; Rogoff 1990).

These mental activities call for projecting explicitly a distinct self to which one, as a current I, can relate mentally, offline in thinking, remembering, imagining, evaluating and so on, and to which the same current I can ascribe various attitudes. This new gambit requires a new kind of self-directed and self-ascribed thoughts, The handling of this new kind of thoughts is instrumental in calling for executive abilities that generate introvert self-consciousness.

The mental activities on the above list no longer involve just cooperative, dependence or protective relations with others—all of which are fairly typical of early childhood. The new sociocultural games are increasingly competitive, more unpredictable and occasionally confrontational, and often reflect differences or even conflicts of interests, desires, perceptions, values. How the self appears to oneself and is projected to others—the so-called 'self-image'—becomes increasingly important to older children as they negotiate the new sociocultural world in which they enter after 4. To handle optimally the attitudes of others—cooperate with them, influence or manipulate them, render them favorable to oneself or to someone one likes or unfavorable to someone one dislikes, and so on—one must frequently include in one's others-directed goal strategies one's own self with its attitudes, as envisaged by one but also as potentially envisaged by the relevant others. Such inclusion requires self-ascriptions of attitudes.

Just think of (or remember) how an older child prepares for an interview on which depends the admission to a select school or summer camp. It is similar to how an adult prepares for a job interview. Think of the intricate interplay between the self-image one naturally has and the one that will be carefully advertised to the interviewer: 'What would he think if I say that? Would he think that I believe that p rather than q? And would that do me any good?' Or think of the advice a student or adult gets from colleagues or teachers when one prepares for an interview or some important discussion: 'Make sure to say that you like that idea, even if you don't—and don't show your dislike of this other idea, because they like it.' And so on. This is one major reason for the commonsense psychology's turn to self: to optimize one's goal strategies in sociocultural contexts by factoring self-ascriptions of attitudes in one's ascriptions of attitudes to others.

Another major and related reason is coregulation. Interpolating self-ascriptions into other-ascriptions, and vice versa, plays an equally vital role in one's mental and behavioral self-regulation in terms of the attitudes and reactions of others. It is the old gambit of coregulation and interaction with the virtual other (described in chapter 5.1), which is so critical in early childhood. After 4, this gambit requires and uses new mental tools in new conditions. Young children often coregulate their behavior by way of social referencing, checking for the adult's approval (or indifference) before engaging in some action or reacting to a certain state of the environment. Young children often engage in social pretend play in order to coregulate their mastery of some practice by mimicking how others do it. Older children (and adults) coregulate their thinking, their attitudes and behavior by rehearsing what others would think or believe and how they would react.

Gradually, the coregulatory role of others is also played by neutral and publicly shared standards, such as norms, interpersonal obligations, communal perceptions, publicly available information, accepted ways of behaving, handling conflicts, making amends and so on. These public standards often replace an individual coregulator, such as mother or teacher, with an invisibly social coregulator of the sort, 'What would people think if I say this or do that?' or simply 'Is this the right thing to do?'

I trust that, illustrated by this informal foray into an intuitive social psychology, the argument of this section has identified the key reasons for children's turn to their own minds after 4. They are the basic external challenges that lead to the development of self-understanding. The next task is to inquire into the mental resources that respond to these challenges and manage the turn to the children's own minds, help implement self-ascriptions of attitudes and thereby contribute to the development of introvert self-consciousness.

Before proceeding, it is important to repeat that children's turn to their own minds *begins* as a turn to the self of attitudes, to their own attitudinal minds, so to speak. This is a *metarepresentational* turn because one's own attitudes are now explicitly ascribed to a self and represented in terms of their target-relatedness and its affordances.

7.3 Kinds of Thoughts

Except in some pathological cases, thoughts do not float freely and unmoored in one's mind. They are normally anchored at and by one's self—deep down, anchored at and by one's self-mechanisms (in the minimal and basic sense of chapter 4.3). Yet self-anchored thoughts are not of one kind only. For the purposes at hand, I discern three kinds, each with its own developmental schedule and each resulting in a different kind of self-conscious thought. The differences bear both on what the self is conscious of, and on the relations of the self to the thoughts in question. These differences show up in development and help explain what is specific to and unique about the offline, introvertly conscious and self-ascribed thoughts that emerge after 4.

For convenience, I label these three kinds of thoughts *me-thoughts*, *I-thoughts* and *self-thoughts*. They are distinguished and analyzed in terms of the capacities responsible for their mental ownership (me-thoughts), mental agency (I-thoughts) and self-ascriptions (self-thoughts). It is these capacities that explain when, why and how children become conscious of their own offline self-directed thoughts and attitudes. I will suggest that only the self-thoughts are reflexive and self-ascribable. With reference to schizophrenia, I begin my analysis with the first two sorts of self-conscious thoughts, before turning to the third and the most important in our inquiry—namely, self-thoughts.

Me-Thoughts and I-Thoughts: Insights from Schizophrenia

Consider the phenomenon of *thought insertion* that is typical in many cases of schizophrenia. A schizophrenic patient is prone to ascribe a thought of his to someone else, who is suspected of introducing and controlling this thought from outside (Frith 1992). There are disagreements about how to analyze thought insertion, which are well surveyed by Gallagher (2005), Stephens and Graham (2000), Vosgerau and Newen (2007), and, from a developmental angle, Young (2008). I favor the following diagnosis.

The schizophrenic patient who claims thought insertion is aware of the thought being his, in the sense of its occurring in his head and thus being one of his mental states. He does not take this thought to be an extramental entity. The *ownership* of the thought is therefore not in question, if for no other reason than that the thought is privately and introspectively available only to the patient. The thought is necessarily and exclusively a first-person, inside-the-mind sort of thought, which the patient cannot and does not miss. I will say that a thought claimed introspectively to be inserted is a conscious it-belongs-to-me sort of thought or simply a *me-thought*. A me-thought is registered as one's own and distinct from outside physical events and objects. But a me-thought is not yet a thought that one intently and actively initiates and pursues in terms of interactions with other mental states. The latter sort of thought is an I-intently-produced-it sort of thought or simply an *I-thought*. The schizophrenic may think and claim that the inserted thought is not intended, initiated and managed by him. He is not the *author* of the thought, not *in control* of it, and hence is not a mental *agent* with respect to the thought. The inserted thought is his own, a thought in his mind, but is not in his mental power or agency. In other words, the inserted me-thought is not *also* an I-thought. In different terms, this point was convincingly argued by Shaun Gallagher (2005).

A conscious thought is normally authored and controlled by one. It is an I-thought and thereby, necessarily, also a me-thought, occurring in one's head and recognized as one's own. But normal thinkers also get to be conscious of me-thoughts they have not intently and actively produced—for example, in the passive form of flash memories, daydreams or images that come and go as a passing show, or even thoughts they form spontaneously by listening to somebody. In contrast to schizophrenic me-thinkers, however, normal I-thinkers can nevertheless appropriate, re-represent and transform an initially passive and unauthored me-thought *into* an I-thought, if they so decide—thus bringing a me-thought under their mental agency.

What should be added, though, is that one has *conscious* me-thoughts, either normally or schizophrenically, because one is an I-thinker, to begin with, in the sense of having that competence, and because one's self-regulation operates in terms of appropriate executive abilities. One daydreams consciously because one's I-thinking machinery is turned on anyway and ready to become intentful and active at any moment. Likewise, in many if not most occasions, the schizophrenic is a normal I-thinker, given that schizophrenic events tend to be fairly sporadic. A schizophrenic's normal I-thinking machinery is on, even when isolated inserted thoughts are taken to be intruding.

The schizophrenic's allegedly inserted thoughts are usually very specific in content and may not affect the rest of his thinking. This is why the schizophrenic can regard the inserted thoughts as alien, in contrast with the *rest* of his thoughts, which he recognizes as being *his*. Having normal I-thoughts on most occasions, the schizophrenic is aware of this normal profile of self-conscious thoughts, which is the profile of mental agency. As a result, understandably but mistakenly, the violation of mental agency looks like an intrusion from outside and hence a lack of ownership (Gallagher 2005). But it isn't. It is actually a lack of mental agency and its associated conscious experience, whence the inability to treat an inert thought as a purposed I-thought.

A different analysis of thought insertion, by Gottfried Vosgerau and Albert Newen (2007), separates the feeling of agency (or lack thereof) from the misattribution of agency, and suggests that the feeling originates in self-regulation (or its impairment, respectively), whereas the misattribution results from a rationalization in terms and concepts of commonsense psychology. If documented empirically, this suggestion would be more likely to involve self-thoughts rather than me-thoughts or I-thoughts. Self-thoughts are indeed a creation of commonsense psychology, as seen next. It is significant that schizophrenia doesn't afflict children but manifests itself toward adolescence or adulthood, when commonsense psychology, self-understanding and introvert self-consciousness are all firmly in place.

Self-Thoughts

Consider the following self-directed thought:

I used to believe that philosophy departments are places where original thoughts are being produced

It is an offline, introvertly conscious and deliberately produced thought about a past attitude of mine. The thought explicitly represents my past self, as distinct from my current I (the author of the thought), and is related to a past attitude (here, belief) to a particular proposition, described by a that-clause. The thought could have been about my future self and some future attitude or even a different, possible self imagined to hold some attitude to some imagined fact. The mental act involved in all these various self-ascriptions and its output, the thought self-ascribed, can be schematized as follows:

I-thought: [self $\rightarrow$ (thought/attitude $\rightarrow$ proposition)]

$$\frac{}{\underline{\hspace{2cm}}}$$

now $\underline{\hspace{6cm}}$

content of I-thought = thought self-ascribed

____ self-thought as self-ascriptive thought ____

A self-thought is a self-ascriptive thought whose content contains an explicitly self-ascribed thought or attitude, in which both the *self* that is ascribed and the thought or attitude this self *relates to* could be past, future or imagined. A self-thought is recursively amplifiable. It could contain further thoughts and attitudes explicitly related to self or to others. In our example, the thought that is self-ascribed (i.e., what I used to believe) could be expanded to relate to a propositional content that in turn contains some *further* self- or other-related thought or attitude. Thus, I could reformulate my example as:

I used to believe that philosophers always believed that they should produce original ideas

Now my past belief is about still another belief ascribed to others. In the other direction, the self-thought with which I started could become part of still another self-ascriptive thought, as in the following enlarged self-thought:

My earlier thought that [I used to believe that philosophy departments are places where original thoughts are being produced] was too optimistic to begin with

The point of these examples is not simply to illustrate the recursion ability involved or the capacious working memory needed to hold and compute such concatenated thoughts—both of which are part of the multiplex mind that develops after 4. What matters now, and must be shown, is

a. that self-thoughts are a creation of commonsense psychology, which responds to novel sociocultural challenges after 4; and

b. that older children's resulting mastery and deployment of self-thoughts drives the development of introvert self-consciousness.

The first part of claim (a) is obvious from the definition of self-thoughts. The second part, concerning the sociocultural challenges faced by older children, was examined and documented in the previous section. Claim (b) will be discussed in the next section. To prepare the ground for that discussion, I need to add some further elements to the analysis of self-thoughts.

Self-thoughts are a subclass of reflexive thoughts or thoughts about thoughts. Thoughts in the larger reflexive class need not contain in their contents further thoughts or attitudes explicitly related to self; they need not be self-ascriptive, in other words. I can think reflexively about a thought expressed by someone else or read somewhere or merely fancied. That will not be a self-thought. Self-thoughts can operate in a variety of modalities, from autobiographical recall (as in the above example) to planning future projects or actions of one's own, reexamining a discussion one just had, anticipating how to make amends, rehearsing a talk, letting one's visual imagination fly toward a pleasurable future situation in which the self and its attitudes are explicitly projected, and more. Self-thoughts owe the explicit self-to-thought/attitude pattern to commonsense psychology. More generally, enabled by the computational novelties of the multiplex and narrative mind, the development of reflexive thinking is also driven by older children's commonsense psychology and their mastery of self-thoughts in particular. This is an argument developed elsewhere (Bogdan 2000).

It is worth noting that one's offline I-thoughts are distinct from, and lower-level than, one's self-thoughts and reflexive thoughts in general. Offline I-thoughts are thoughts one does 'offline business' with, self-consciously but not reflexively. One is introvertly aware of one's offline I-thoughts as one attempts, for example, to imagine how the room would look if the furniture were rearranged; one does not confuse these actively formed offline thoughts with online perceptions or memories. The offline modality is recognized as self-initiated and as distinct from online modalities. One is also aware of one's offline I-thoughts representing what they do—that is, conscious of their target-relatedness and affordances, hence (on my analysis) introvertly yet nonreflexively self-conscious of these thoughts. In the introvert mode, this is a sort of ongoing peripheral consciousness of one's offline thoughts having some content. It is somewhat similar to the peripheral awareness that a pedestrian, looking ahead and thinking, has of her legs as they advance on the pavement; she is not looking at her legs and explicitly monitoring their balance, pace and so on; she just uses them for walking, being thus (online) self-conscious of their performance in relation to the pavement.

Likewise, in thinking offline about rearranging the furniture in the room, one need not think explicitly *about* the thoughts involved in this imaginative exercise. Unlike self-thoughts, in thinking offline about possible situations (like the arrangement of the furniture in the room), one is not projecting one's self reflexively and offline in relation to thoughts one has. Nor, importantly, is one thereby explicitly representing these thoughts about the arrangement of the furniture *as* one's own attitudes—say, as an explicitly acknowledged belief about a position of the furniture. One may have an ongoing belief about that position but not think explicitly and reflexively about it *as* a self that believes it. Having beliefs and putting them to work, such as thinking *with* them and acting *on* them, is different from thinking *about* them explicitly and reflexively.

The point of the distinctions among offline I-thoughts, reflexive thoughts and self-thoughts is to indicate that only the capacity for producing self-thoughts, grounded in commonsense psychology, can install introvert self-consciousness. Offline I-thoughts and reflexive thoughts are introvertly conscious because (on my analysis) the installation process is over. Even if it turns out that mental reflexivity in particular results from an endogenous computational or metacognitive development (contrary to what I argued elsewhere (Bogdan 2000), where mental reflexivity, too, was grounded in commonsense psychology), this would still not explain the emergence of introvert self-consciousness. On the present analysis, the latter requires more than reflexive computation or introvert metacognition on both; it also requires the metarepresentational management of self-thoughts and hence commonsense psychology. Only the latter can summon enough executive power to light the bulb of introvert consciousness.

Kinds of Selves

Even though the nature of the self (whatever that may be) is not my concern, beyond the biological roots noted in chapter 4, I want to say a few words about the kinds of selves that are associated with the kinds of thoughts discussed so far. It may help to start by recalling a philosophical truism: selves are inextricably packaged with, and indeed expressed by, types of mental activities and in particular thoughts and attitudes, and do not hang around in splendid isolation. Notoriously, Hume could not spot a self as a separate entity or substance when scanning his own mind; what he found were only perceptions, memories, emotions, thoughts and so on. Quite so. Mindful of Hume's point, Kant opined that the 'I think'—referring to the active and intentful thinker of I-thoughts—refers not to an actual and separate empirical self but rather—to twist his terminology a bit—to an *apperceiver* who is at least mindful of, if not actively synthesizing, one's currently conscious I-thoughts. This apperceiver, in my terms, is the I-self—always present and active when the mental machinery is on. At an abstract remove, the positions of Hume and Kant on selfhood reflect the fact (discussed neuropsychologically in chapter 4.3) that a sentient sense of (what we may call now) 'I-selfhood' and 'me-selfhood' emerges out of the regulatory operation of biologically basic self-mechanisms. This sentient sense becomes conscious when the relevant executive abilities animate one's mental agency and ownership.

The self of the self-thoughts, however, is different from the I-self and me-self, and originates in a different capacity. The self of self-thoughts results from an explicit mental projection produced by and embedded in a reflexive *and* metarepresentational I-thought. Autobiographical recall and self-evaluation are vivid illustrations of this mental projection. This new kind of self is therefore a *mental construct* and not the biological output of specialized neuropsychological self-mechanisms, as are, at a higher level of mental complexity, me-thoughts and I-thoughts and the selves associated with them—me-selves and I-selves. The self of self-thoughts—let us call it *the projected self* (instead of, rather redundantly, the self-self)—is the one that gets intellectually but not neuropsychologically revised, embellished or even contested (as in "I don't recognize myself in what I just said"), as we mature or change contexts or change our minds. It is the self with which, in a reflective or projective mode, we manage many of our sociocultural affairs.

The notion that the projected self is a mental construct should not be taken to suggest a variable invention, varying from culture to culture or varying historically or according to ideology. On the contrary: it is the notion that, pressured by universal sociocultural practices, a universal commonsense psychology installs a mental scheme capable of projecting the selves of self-thoughts. The constructivist claim is that this mental scheme is not part of genetically driven neuropsychological mechanisms. Consider, for a useful analogy, the capacity to read or write: they are not natural gifts of the brain. There are no innate neuropsychological mechanisms for reading and writing. These are cultural practices invented rather recently (a few thousand years ago) and their mental schemes are installed pedagogically, explicitly and gradually, with much effort and sweat, in mid-childhood. With time, they become procedural or how-to routines, almost a second nature. Yet they begin as mental constructs. I want to say the same about the capacities responsible for self-thoughts and their projected selves—they are constructed ontogenetically, but not genetically, as robust and potentially universal mental schemes, and become routinized in the same way as many other mental and behavioral acquisitions.

Having charted the notion of self-thoughts as distinct from other kinds of thoughts, as well as the selves they involve, the next task, posited by our leading hypothesis, is to see how self-thoughts contribute to the development of introvert self-consciousness in older children.

7.4   With the Self in Mind

I begin with some reminders that should help frame the argument of this section in terms already explained—and therefore assumed. The analytic schema introduced in chapter 5.3 to explain extrovert self-consciousness was

sociocultural activities → means-ends mentation → representing naive-psychologically the attitudes of others as tools in self-regulation and the pursuit of one's ends → recruiting and assembling online executive abilities → that install extrovert self-consciousness

Chapter 6 noted that, as maturing commonsense psychologists, older children begin to represent the self and its attitudes, and amalgamate their representations with representations of the attitudes of others. Section 3, above, argued that older children factor the result into their means-ends strategies that manage the new sociocultural activities that are discernible after 4. By parity of reasoning, the new analytic schema looks like this:

new sociocultural activities → means-ends mentation → *representing in one's commonsense psychology one's own attitudes, in coordination with those of others, as tools in self-regulation and the pursuit of one's own ends* → *recruiting and assembling offline executive abilities that* → *install introvert self-consciousness*

It is now the italicized propositions and their correlations that must be explained. This brings the notion of self-thoughts into the center of the play. The basic idea is that without employing self-thoughts, one cannot explicitly represent one's own attitudes, coordinate them with those of others, and reason with the results in a means-ends way, in order to regulate one's mental activities in social planning, self-involving gossip, self-evaluation and others listed two sections ago, and use those results in pursuing one's own ends. And one cannot employ self-thoughts in regulating one's goal strategies without activating the offline executive abilities that end up installing introvert self-consciousness.

Before proceeding, let us remember the structure of the argument used to make the case for the presence and exercise of self-consciousness in general. Functionalism, assumed throughout this work, characterizes consciousness in terms of several defining features or parameters. It turns out that most of them—certainly the most important—reflect the executive abilities discussed in this work. Therefore, showing the presence and work of these abilities in typical instances of offline mentation thereby confirms the presence and exercise of introvert self-consciousness. So, given the direction of this chapter, the task ahead is to show that the employment of self-thoughts in a regulatory mode requires the joint deployment of executive abilities associated with self-consciousness in the functionalist equation.

I propose to illustrate this analysis with the example of deliberate, reflective and well-rehearsed lying. I choose this because it becomes available to children's minds soon after 4 and is a paradigmatic example for the wider class of socioculturally driven mental activities involving self-thoughts that older children (and adults) engage in for the rest of their lives.

The ordinary notion of lying covers a variety of cases, ranging from simply telling something untrue, when knowing the truth, to elaborate and carefully rehearsed narratives meant to induce a false belief. For our purposes, I will consider only the latter sort, which (for lack of a better term) I will label *narrative lying*. To identify the key aspects of the illustration that matter to our argument, I will italicize the executive abilities and capitalize the thoughts that are either reflexive and in particular self-directed or directed at the attitudes of others, as the latter figure in one's own self-thoughts. All of these are involved in narrative lying.

Narrative Lying
To tell a narrative lie, resulting in conveying the information that not-p—one must

- know that p is true and not-p false (factual knowledge)
- *intend* to lie, as a trigger to a complex mental activity
- deploy a narrative that reaches into one's past and future as well as those of the people affected by the lie, thus requiring *holding in mind over some period of time a set of related thoughts that are relevant to the intended activity*
- *combine* thoughts and other mental items *from several modalities* (perception, memory, communication routines, planning, etc.)
- *actively search memory* for the right information to be used
- *mentally plan and rehearse* the lie and its implications

The italicized words refer to offline executive abilities jointly required to handle narrative lies. These executive abilities have simpler online precursors. But narrative lying and other post-4 mental activities involve more than that. To tell a narrative lie one must also

- KNOW that one knows that p is true and not-p is false (reflexive knowledge)
- *INTEND* to produce in someone else the BELIEF that not-p (this is an elaborate and specific intention to produce a particular belief in an audience and is different from the initial intention just to lie)
- KNOW that one has this *INTENTION* with this *means-ends* effect on someone else's BELIEF

And more often than not

• also KNOW that by lying one is doing something wrong—a public standard that children initially construe in terms of the inferred ATTITUDES of others (e.g., what others would think about lying)

• but THINK of some justification, self- and/or other-regarding, usually in terms of further self- and other-ATTITUDES

The capitalized words, we recall, refer to reflexive thoughts as well as the attitudes that those reflexive thoughts are explicitly about. Most of the reflexive thoughts are self-thoughts. These self-thoughts could not be produced unless one is *also* able to

• *introspectively access* one's own thoughts and attitudes as being one's own and being self-regarding as well as other-regarding

• monitor *metacognitively* what one is doing mentally with such thoughts

• explicitly *metarepresent* what one's own thoughts and attitudes are about (target-relatedness) and their affordances

• exercise *intentful control* over the thoughts that constitute the lie and over their affordances in others and oneself

• *manage pragmatically* the delivery of the narrative lie and adjust it to the context

Older children (and adults) could not produce narrative lies without being able to form self-thoughts whose deployment requires such abilities.

On this analysis, animals cannot lie at all and young children cannot lie narratively. Thought to be literally minded (Frith, U. 1989; Happé 1994), autistic people are not known to tell narrative lies. Their naive psychology is rudimentary and misses some early stages in psychological coregulation, intersubjective communication and the resulting shared attention. Their later commonsense psychology seems to be even poorer (Baron-Cohen 1995; Hobson 1993; also Bogdan 1997, 165–167). It seems that many autistic people are not mentally reflexive and possibly not able to form and deploy self-thoughts (Bogdan 2000, chapter 8). If plausible, this diagnosis would suggest possible impairments or limitations of introvert self-consciousness in some autistic people.

I have chosen narrative lying as a paradigmatic example of socioculturally driven mental activity, whose execution and regulation call for introvert self-consciousness, because it is a clear and easily recognizable example of means-ends manipulation of someone else's attitudes, in coordination with one's own attitudes, through mental rehearsal. The rehearsed manipulation is executed with the help and in terms of self-thoughts. This means that the narrative liar—and in general, the author of self-thoughts—explicitly represents his self as related to his own relevant attitudes. Some of these self-thoughts, such as the liar's true belief, his justification (in terms of prior attitudes), his knowledge of wrongdoing (in terms of public attitudes), and his justification of lying in general (based on the belief that the person who is lied to doesn't deserve the truth, or that ends justify means, or the like) provide a sort of background.

In the foreground of the narrative liar's mind are several active self-thoughts that are represented in a means-ends format in the explicit terms of how their target-relatedness (their contents and truth and falsity, respectively) and affordances or implications for further attitudes can be caused to cause the desired effects. These foregrounded self-thoughts include the liar's intention to produce a false belief in someone else, his pretend belief to be conveyed by the lie and his rehearsed anticipation of the impact of the lie on further attitudes in himself and the victim. It is this means-ends format of the foregrounded self-thoughts that makes the difference in the development of introvert self-consciousness.

Other mental activities, such as self-evaluation, self-criticism, interpersonal diplomacy and so on (described in section 2, above), can be analyzed in roughly the same terms as narrative lying. They all involve self-thoughts, made possible by mixing and coordinating other- and self-ascriptions of attitudes (the common understanding of minds). As in narrative lying, the foregrounded operation of such thoughts is what brings offline executive abilities to life.

The interaction of other- and self-ascriptions of attitudes that animates self-thoughts reflects their joint means-ends and self-regulatory roles. As for the former role, self-thoughts represent attitudes in ways conducive to a cause-causation strategy of pursuing one's goals in sociocultural contexts by means of one's own attitudes and those of others. As for the latter, self-regulatory role, self-thoughts enable one to represent what others think, what are the publicly shared attitudes about some matter of concern, and—with an eye to adjustment, coordination, amends or change of mind or plans—factor the resulting representations into one's own attitudes and goal strategies. It is this initial and formative interplay between the means-ends and self-regulatory roles of self-thoughts that developmentally call for intending, metacognition, introspective attention and the other offline executive abilities that install introvert self-consciousness as a durable disposition.

To sum up, suppose that, malevolence aside, the narrative lie illustration is fairly typical of the employment of self-thoughts in offline mentation after the age of 4. Suppose also that italicized and capitalized words in the above lists identify the executive abilities and components of reflexive and self-directed thoughts (respectively) that are involved in such forms of mentation. And suppose, finally, that the functionalist equation is plausible in taking the executive abilities involved as key features or parameters of consciousness in general. *Then* the narrative lie illustration has done its assigned job of ascertaining the presence of introvert self-consciousness in offline mentation, thanks to the means-ends and regulatory job of self-thoughts as creatures of commonsense psychology.

We Are Done, Almost

The official argument of this book is over.

Cues from blindsight, absent-mindedness, some clinical cases and a plausible consensus in the functionalist literature all suggest an intimate link between a select spectrum of executive abilities and consciousness. The question has been: what forged this link, and why?

The search for an answer explored the most likely and potent pressures in young children's environments. These were found to be sociocultural. Their handling calls for an intuitive psychology. The development of this psychology shows a consistent pattern in children's understanding of mind, which matches the development of their self-consciousness.

Understanding other minds precedes understanding our own.

Extrovert self-consciousness precedes introvert self-consciousness.

Is there is a *causal* connection between these developments? The argument of this book has aimed to come as close as possible to showing a causal connection by tightening the correlations as narrowly as plausibly possible. There are surely many other factors involved in the birth of self-consciousness. What can be said with sufficient confidence is that, alongside other factors, the intuitive psychology of understanding minds drives the development of self-consciousness by recruiting and assembling a suite of executive abilities that are involved in installing self-consciousness in ontogeny—first in an online and extrovert form, and later in an offline and introvert form.

The next and concluding chapter contains further ruminations triggered by what has been said, and not said, so far. Also included is a comparative look at other analyses that intersect with the present one.

8 Loose Ends

This final chapter explores some implications and tries to tie up several loose ends. It begins by speculating about how and when the human competence for self-consciousness may have been assembled, as a by-product, out of other competencies that evolved as ontogenetic adaptations to the specific challenges of different stages of human ontogeny. The chapter also recognizes some dark—or at least, penumbral—areas in the story of consciousness as told so far. It concludes with a comparative discussion of several views that cover parts of the same territory that has been traveled here. In the process, some of the main themes of this book will be revisited and reviewed.

8.1 Assembled By-product

Assembly

The argument of this book suggests that self-consciousness develops out of and on the top of a "critical mass" of more basic ontogenetic adaptations, most of which have their own distinct functions, but are brought together by children's intuitive psychology to handle their gradual immersion in sociocultural life. Many of these adaptations have nothing to do with self-consciousness, whether extrovert or introvert. Seen in this light, self-consciousness appears to be a *by-product assembled* out of unrelated ontogenetic adaptations with their own histories of selection.

The prime example of assembly is the very driving force behind the development of self-consciousness—children's intuitive psychology. The early naive psychology, involved in installing extrovert self-consciousness, is assembled out of several abilities for bilateral psychological coregulation and intersubjective communication, as well as (possibly) neural mirroring and forms of empathy. The later development of linguistic meaning and propositional thinking, themselves assembled competencies, helps usher in commonsense psychology, which in turn helps to install introvert self-consciousness (Bogdan 2000, 2009). Barely sketched here, the picture that emerges is that of a pyramid of ontogenetic adaptations with some on the top of others and with self-consciousness at its apex.

If assembled in the manner suggested in earlier chapters, self-consciousness is not likely to be imprinted in the genome, not likely to mature according to dedicated genetic instructions, and hence not likely to be localized in a specific brain site. We should not therefore expect a set of genes and hence dedicated mechanisms *for* self-consciousness. Looking at the literature on the evolution of consciousness, this is a conclusion that echoes that of Dan Dennett (1991, chapter 7) and partly of Merlin Donald (2001), both reached by different but congenial sets of arguments. I return to these views in the concluding section of this chapter.

The assembly and operation of self-consciousness is more likely to be widely distributed and intricately interconnected in a network of nodes and relations that are gradually installed by a suite of ontogenetic adaptations, particularly the executive abilities discussed in earlier chapters. Three elements of my analysis—namely, the assemblist and nongenomic angle on the development of consciousness, its essential dependence on intuitive psychology, and the sociocultural activities the latter evolves to manage by recruiting executive abilities—make it likely that self-consciousness is not the result of a gradual natural selection operating across various species through a long phylogenetic history.

Implications

Several implications, admittedly speculative and telegraphically dispatched, follow from this brief and equally telegraphic analysis.

First, given the unique sequence of causes that explain it (sociocultural practices handled in ontogeny by an intuitive psychology that assembles a set of executive abilities), self-consciousness—as defined in this work—may be very rare in evolution and possibly unique to our species. "As defined in this work" means self-consciousness as a stable and durable disposition that is installed ontogenetically by executive abilities. In other words, far from being a natural experience generated by the nervous system in general, self-consciousness signals an evolved readiness to exercise executive abilities which, at least during the installation period, respond to very complex challenges as selection pressures, primarily sociocultural in nature.

Lacking both the installation history and the pressures for it, it is unlikely that most other animal species evolved *this sort* of readiness. What is possible is that intensely sociopolitical and marginally cultural species, such as nonhuman primates and possibly other intensely social mammals, evolved a very rudimentary online and extrovert consciousness, which is probably further enhanced, under increased pressures, in cultural captivity among humans. The open question is whether such a rudimentary extrovert self-consciousness is of the intermittent, on-and-off or pulsative sort or is a more durably exercised disposition. My analysis suggests that an empirical determination would depend on the intensity and complexity of the challenges faced during ontogeny, and also on how much time such challenges as normal tasks occupy an animal mind on a regular basis. All these factors would be reflected in appropriate executive abilities recruited and assembled as adaptive responses.

Second, human self-consciousness may be a fairly recent historical acquisition. Instead of guessing when it may have evolved, my analysis links its onset to the evolution of its key sources—intense sociocultural activities and an intuitive psychology that handles them. As in ontogeny (but without a recapitulationist subtext), it is likely that a simpler naive psychology, geared to overt expressions of mental states, evolved first among early humans, as did its companion, an extrovert self-consciousness, followed (possibly much later) by commonsense psychology and its companion, introvert self-consciousness. In tune with the extant archeological evidence indicating the beginnings of art, religion, burial and technological progress (Boyd and Silk 1997; Donald 2001; Mithen 1996), which in turn suggest not just an intense sociopolitical life (also present in apes and hominids) but also a rapidly escalating culture, it is possible that modern humans may have evolved self-understanding (as defined here) and hence an *introvert* self-consciousness only during the last 100,000 years or so.

Third, the assemblist perspective suggests that self-consciousness may not be "visible" as such to natural or other forms of selection, in the sense of being a direct response to specific pressures, and hence may not have its *own* evolutionary raison d'être. What may be "visible" to selection pressures are the vital abilities involved in the assembly of self-consciousness —primarily the relevant executive abilities and their chief assembler, the intuitive psychology. On this analysis, then, when one asks what is the evolved function of consciousness one actually asks what was the evolved function of an assembly of executive *abilities*, from intending to multitasking.

On a still more speculative note, I think that the proposed reading of the relation between self-consciousness, executive abilities (or, in technical parlance, the supervenience of the former on the latter) and the simulative activity of the brain may begin to explain the Libet-type phenomena, whereby one becomes conscious of (say) one's intention to move one's arm infinitesimally yet measurably later than the firing of the neural structures involved in the relevant motor intentions. Setting aside the controversies surrounding such phenomena (see Dennett 1991, chapter 6; Gallagher 2005, chapter 10), the implication here is that becoming conscious of a motor intention requires the activation of several other executive abilities, and *that* takes time. Contrary to views criticized earlier (particularly in chapter 4), consciousness is not punctate and does not belong to only a single attitude, such as intention, which is itself not a single mental state anyway. Consciousness is manifested synthetically in a manifold of states and processes, even when the focus is on intention, and the completion of this manifold takes time, no matter how minute. As noted in chapter 5.1, in discussing blindsight, the time required for consciousness in turn suggests complex executive processing.

Finally, since the design of self-consciousness was said to be a functional platform for phenomenal consciousness, the possible human uniqueness and recency of self-consciousness may also extend to its phenomenal side, at least in its normally extended and introvert—as opposed to an on-and-off, pulsative and exclusively extrovert—manifestation. And this brings us to the next topic.

8.2   Dark Areas

Any analysis that journeys through the territory covered in this book is bound to cross areas that are partly or even entirely in the dark. Two such areas stand out.

One has already been acknowledged. It is on the road from simulative self-regulation to self-consciousness. This road crosses the areas of thinking and other high-level mental faculties. Little is known about how simulative self-regulation works in these areas. What is better understood about simulative self-regulation is its role in motor cognition, but the latter operates and produces most of its outputs under the radar of consciousness. And the simulative self-regulation of higher-level conscious mentation has been so far beyond the reach of science. The other, even darker area is all too familiar and has been scrupulously avoided so far.

The Conceptual Black Hole of Phenomenality
How the assembly of the executive abilities responsible for self-consciousness conspires with the biochemistry of the brain and other factors to cause

the phenomenal glow of consciousness remains the deepest mystery. I am *not* talking of the physical (i.e., neurochemical) causation involved, looked at scientifically, from the outside—the so-called neural correlates of consciousness. That is not—or will not long remain—a mystery. I am talking of the relation between conscious experience or consciousness experienced *from inside* (i.e., what it is like or feels like) and its suspected executive as well as biochemical bases. How to explain *this* relation is deemed to be the deepest mystery.

Contrary to widespread opinion, I think that *this* mystery is not really scientific. It is not the business of science to explain it. As I said, neuroscience will discover one day what the functional network of self-consciousness is and how it lights up the mind phenomenally. Neuroscience may even find all the many brain sites that respond to that network activation—the phenomenal switch that lights up the bulb. These will be experience-free discoveries, from outside. Yet, as often noted in the philosophical literature, these discoveries will not tell us what it is like to have phenomenal consciousness from inside, nor will they explain this inside experience of phenomenal consciousness reductively, in nonphenomenal terms.

I think (but barely argue here) that the mystery of phenomenal consciousness as experienced from inside has to do with *not* knowing *how to think of* it rather than with how to explain it reductively and hence scientifically. In other words, I see the puzzle of phenomenal consciousness—and its possible solution or dissolution—as *conceptual* rather than scientific. It is a conceptual puzzle invented by philosophers, historically from at least two perspectives—one reductionist and the other phenomenological. Without getting exegetical, I would say this much about these puzzle-generating perspectives.

The *reductionist* perspective is that of dualism. Since Descartes and thanks mostly to him, dualism promotes the metaphysical immateriality of consciousness by using arguments from *conceivability*. Can we conceive of a conscious thought having a left and right side or having an upper part and a lower part or floating on fat-free milk, for that matter? No, we cannot—so thoughts and other conscious mental states cannot be spatial and a fortiori physical. So, it seems, dualism wins. But it "wins" *from inside*, in the experiential terms supposed to underpin the concepts involved in the conceivability exercise. It is an unfair "win." Here is why.

Thoughts are consciously transparent or accessible as contents (what they are about) but not as vehicles (i.e., as underlying functional or brain structures). The Cartesian conceivability exercise asks the thinker to place a representation of the very vehicle of an occurrently experienced thought in its content position and experientially determine its spatial or other physical properties at the same time as the thinker experiences its content. This cannot be done, given how conscious thought operates. The Cartesian challenge rests on a mistake about how the conscious mind works.

Or take zombies, who again conceivably are organisms like us, both materially and functionally. They duplicate our physical states (say, molecule for molecule) and our functional design that maps inputs onto thoughts and then actions, but lack phenomenal consciousness. If zombies are conceivable, then our phenomenal consciousness cannot be explained in physical and functional terms. Dualism "wins" again—and again from the stance of inside experience, since the concepts this experience underpins, as in Descartes, can be isolated from physical matter and causation only from the stance of an inside experience.

In short, dualism challenges us to *conceive*, from felt experiences, of phenomenal consciousness as fully reducible, without residue, to physical matter and its functional arrangements. Since the challenge cannot be met, the conclusion is that phenomenal consciousness cannot be explained in such terms, which are the terms of science. I simplify, of course, but not too much.

A recent version of the *phenomenological* perspective was made particularly famous by Thomas Nagel's what-it-is-like-to-be-a-bat story (Nagel 1974). Nagel's article challenges us to imagine, again in familiar experiential terms, what it is like to perceive or cognize the world in the way a bat (or some other animal or alien mind) does. Can we adopt the subjective (i.e., echolocational) point of view of the bat, which is essential to understand the bat's experience? No, we cannot—so the bat's experience remains unintuitable and unintelligible to us. Moreover, according to Nagel, as an objective fact about the world of minds, phenomenal subjectivity is alien and unintelligible to science, which does not have a subjective point of view and neither understands nor cares to have one. Fair enough. Science, therefore, cannot explain the phenomenal subjectivity of animal and human minds. I simplify, again—but not too much.

Both dualism (against reductive explanation) and the phenomenology of the subjective point of view (against understanding the subjectivity of minds that are not like ours) are *conceptual* inventions of philosophers. These inventions consist in pitting what is conceivable in the inside terms of the experienced phenomenal consciousness against the experience-free, neutral and public understanding of reality, ourselves included. I am not using the word 'invention' in a derogatory sense, nor am I belittling the value of the enterprise. I am just commenting on how the puzzle of phenomenal consciousness came to be, and insisting on its philosophical as opposed to scientific nature.

It may help to see my point, if we recall some well-known historical facts. First, the great and agenda-setting philosophies of Plato and Aristotle did not seem to bother about phenomenal consciousness, nor did they have a name for it. Plato did not dedicate a dialog to consciousness. Aristotle, who wrote about almost everything under the sun and beyond, did not bother, either. Nor, for all I know, did their ancient or medieval successors. This is one very big dog that didn't bark.

Even Descartes, who placed consciousness on the philosophical agenda, did so not as a result of a deliberate and focused inquiry into the structure of the conscious mind as such but rather as an indirect result of his epistemological quest for certainty. Furthermore, the metaphysical consciousness that Descartes opposed to physical matter was mostly the cold consciousness of thoughts and attitudes, rather than the hot phenomenal consciousness of feelings and qualia that is so popular and mysterious these days. Another (smaller) dog that didn't quite bark.

Of course, philosophers since antiquity have known that the human mind is conscious. Who can miss that? And since they slept, and were absent-minded on occasion, they surely knew the difference between consciousness and unconsciousness. This difference was part of the package they called 'nous' or 'soul' or 'intellect,' but it was not the most defining one. And consciousness wasn't decisive for Descartes either, except metaphysically. The point I am making is this: paradoxically, consciousness is immediately present in and to our minds and yet it was ignored for so long, philosophically; and even when, with Descartes, it began to come into focus, the reasons had nothing to do with its phenomenal nature.

The moral I draw from this historical paradox is that only when phenomenal consciousness *had* to play a role in a larger philosophical game—epistemological and metaphysical games for Descartes and later generations, more recently phenomenological games and games linked to scientific reduction and animal ethics—only then did it move into the philosophical foreground. Phenomenal consciousness is a philosophical invention in this sense.

Having said all this, I do not mean to imply that the problems this invention raises are arbitrary or fake. On the contrary: these may be hard conceptual problems for philosophy, and perhaps also for common sense and ethics, but not for science. And since such problems are conceptual, in philosophical or commonsense or ethical terms, their solutions—or perhaps dissolutions or disinventions—should also be conceptual, in those terms and not in scientific terms.

A good number of works on consciousness may benefit from this diagnosis. For example, Dan Dennett's major oeuvre *Consciousness Explained* (1991), on which more anon, was frequently accused of not explaining phenomenal consciousness but rather explaining it away. My reading of Dennett's account is that there is nothing for science or sustained metaempirical reflection to explain about the phenomenality of consciousness, beyond the simple fact that it is manifested when certain conditions and processes, mostly functional, obtain. End of explanatory story. Most scientists of consciousness take the same line. From a different angle, with a different and narrower focus, a similar story has been attempted here.

It may turn out that solutions to the conceptual problems of phenomenality are simply beyond our mental powers, as they would be according to the semi-Kantian line adopted by Nagel (1974) and elaborated by Colin McGinn (1991a, b). But then again, it is our conceptual and not our scientific powers that are thus shown to be limited or impotent. And, lest we forget, the concepts in question are those of inner experience and commonsense, not of science.

Even though the argument of this book was not intended to tackle phenomenal consciousness, I think it has some implications that narrow somewhat the scope of the dualist and phenomenological challenges, even given the more modest philosophical space reassigned to them by the argument of the previous paragraphs. A smaller black hole of phenomenality may be as much conceptual progress we can expect at this time, or perhaps ever.

Narrowing the Black Hole

One assumption (but not the only one) that makes the problem of phenomenality seem intractable is that both common sense and philosophical reflection tend to view consciousness as unitary and autonomous. This assumption must be challenged. Consciousness is neither unitary nor autonomous. Showing this is going to be a piecemeal work, advancing one step at a time, by puncturing the assumption with all the ammunition one can find, including scientific bullets.

One step in this direction, taken in this book, is to show that self-consciousness is the functional platform for the manifestation of phenomenal consciousness. We are phenomenally conscious *through* the work of simulative self-regulation and of the executive abilities that generate self-consciousness. Cancel the operation of some of these abilities—one at a time, or in clusters—and phenomenal consciousness will be increasingly affected, indeed reduced, as clinical cases indicate. Likewise, the development of executive abilities and other executive centers seems to correlate with that of phenomenal consciousness. Thus, for example, introvert self-consciousness and introspection in particular seem to follow the development of the prefrontal cortex and the working memory.

Even though I profiled zombies as a philosophical concoction, it is worth noting that the executive analysis of self-consciousness proposed in this book challenges their conceivability. If self-consciousness emerges out of self-regulation by means of executive abilities, then, as executive duplicates of ours, zombies *must by definition be* self-conscious. But if they are functionally self-conscious and are also *biochemical* duplicates of ours, then zombies ought to be phenomenally conscious as well. If they are biochemical duplicates of ours but not phenomenally conscious, then they are not self-conscious in the first place—and hence, not functional duplicates of ours. In that case, they are not genuine zombies to begin with. You cannot have your zombies and eat them too.

What is conceivable, of course, is that the alleged zombies are only *functional* but not biochemical duplicates of ours—say, in the guise of metallic robots or plasmatic aliens or the much researched but never achieved artificial intelligentsia. Such zombies may have a rich and challenging sociocultural life, or may be designed to simulate such a life, managed by an intuitive psychology that pushes all the right executive buttons. These zombies would then be self-conscious but not phenomenally conscious, because they lacked the biochemical brains that light up the phenomenal glow. But then, again, they are not total zombies (not duplicates molecule for molecule). In almost Aristotelian terms, executively self-conscious zombies have the form or matrix for phenomenal consciousness but not the right matter, if indeed biochemical matter has a monopoly on the phenomenal *expression* of consciousness.

These remarks targeted dualism. Different arguments are needed to limit the impact of the phenomenology of minds that are different from ours. One strategy is to use neuropsychological discoveries. For example, bats and many other animal species are known to be primarily dorsal perceivers, more like blindsighters, with very fast visual processing. (We recall from chapter 5.1 that it is *fast* dorsal processing, and not dorsal processing as such, that seems to be unconscious.) This is why (*pace* Nagel) bats and other fast dorsal processors are most likely lacking a vital route to consciousness. This neuropsychological fact can reframe the phenomenological take on many sorts of animal or generally alien minds. The problem now is not that we cannot imagine their phenomenal subjectivity, which admittedly we cannot: for even if we could, *there would most likely be nothing to imagine.* Like blindsighters in their blind field, fast dorsal and reflex minds, although sentient, lack a consciously subjective point of view. The issue, then, is not that bats echolocate and we don't. The issue is that bats echolocate unconsciously and hence *without* a consciously subjective point of view—unless unconscious sentience is also blessed with a subjective point of view. But then perhaps plants also have a subjective point of view. Bacteria, anyone? The road to a *reductio* is thus open. My analysis predicts (but has not explicitly argued) that it takes a complex executive and intuitive-psychological matrix of self-consciousness to have a subjective point of view, and that occurs only in minds that are shaped socioculturally during ontogeny.

A related strategy is to minimize the scope of phenomenality *within* human consciousness. One step in this direction, taken by Norton Nelkin (1996), is to dissociate phenomenal consciousness from other forms of consciousness, further undermining the unity assumption. Another step, briefly noted in chapter 6, is to ascertain the (apparently) nonphenomenal consciousness of cold attitudes, such as opinions or conjectures. An exclusively intellectual zombie, with our brain biochemistry but operating only with abstract thoughts and a few cold attitudes—hence self-conscious but not phenomenally so—*is* indeed conceivable. There may be some on a few campuses.

Dissociating in the opposite direction, we can think of organisms, including nearly vegetative humans and possibly infants, who may have an intermittently pulsative phenomenality. The pulsations may be phenomenally vivid—experiencing a shape here, a movement there, a color in between, perhaps an object even. Nevertheless, such organisms would fail to ground their phenomenal pulsations in the larger functional matrix of self-consciousness. The question then is whether such isolated phenomenal pulsations can really be experienced as *con*scious. I underscore the *con* here to emphasize the psychological meaning of consciousness, according to the *Oxford English Dictionary*'s definition evoked earlier: "the state or faculty of being conscious, as a condition and concomitant of all thought, feeling and volition." Here 'concomitant' is the key word. Brief, fleeting, intermittent phenomenal pulsations have no such concomitants, which are required for self-consciousness and hence (on my analysis) for the *normal* phenomenal experience of human minds.

It is possible that human infants enter life with such an intermittent and uncoordinated pulsative phenomenality, without normal *con*sciousness; and it is possible that their phenomenal *con*sciousness is gradually assembled, as they progress executively in building up their self-consciousness along the lines explored in this book. If this is a plausible hypothesis, then we can talk of minimal phenomenal awareness that is not yet full-fledged phenomenal *con*sciousness. Some clinical cases, such as akinetic mutism, seem to support this hypothesis [see note on phenomenal pulsations].

With dissociative steps like these, and with arguments that reduce its size, the black hole of phenomenality may get smaller and perhaps even less black. Its unfathomability may even begin to look less formidable. But don't hold your breath. To the extent that it is associated with the mind–body distinction, the phenomenality of consciousness is more than a deep philosophical puzzle. It is also a very potent and resilient cultural meme that has been invading and running human brains for millennia. There is even a scientific suspicion that (alas!) our minds are biased toward dualism from infancy: we may all begin life as Descartes' babies (Bloom 2004). Dualism is no evolutionary joke, which is why reconceptualizing phenomenality and liberating it from the claws of dualism would be a very good thing indeed. But let us now take leave of phenomenality, and move on.

I started this section with the admission that certain areas of the territory covered in this book are partly or completely in the dark. It is only fitting to conclude by acknowledging and comparing some of the seminal works that illuminated some of the same areas covered in this book and provided a helpful and stimulating companionship.

8.3   Fellow Travelers

In philosophy and in science, one is rarely alone in one's journey. One encounters fellow travelers who have been there before, journeying through the same territory, often along the same paths, at least for a while. Even when aiming at or reaching different destinations, these fellow travelers make the road easier to travel, signal dead ends and point in promising directions. In order to acknowledge the fellow travelers who mattered most in my journey and connect their journeys with mine, I propose to parse the shared territory into four major areas covered by my analysis of self-consciousness. These are sociocultural activities, simulative self-regulation, intuitive psychology and human ontogeny itself, as the unique matrix in which self-consciousness emerges.

What one finds in the relevant literature—at least what I found—are two distinct paradigms that are jointly reflected in the approach taken here. On the one hand, an earlier paradigm, originating in the work of Lev Vygotsky and his school, locates the origins and rationale of consciousness in the self-regulation of sociocultural activities but remains vague about the nature of consciousness and of the self-regulatory mechanisms that make it possible. On the other hand, a recent and neuroscientifically minded paradigm is more inquisitive and specific about the relational nature of consciousness and about its executive design, but remains more traditionally centered on the individual mind and locates the origins and rationale of consciousness primarily in its perceptual, affective and motor involvements. Without attempting an exegesis or critical evaluation, I will limit myself to noting some points of convergence as well as divergence between my analysis and theories operating in these two paradigms. (Thanks to most of the fellow travelers for checking the accuracy of my reports.)

Social Life, Culture, Coregulation and Development: Lev Vygotsky

The earliest and most influential fellow traveler, a groundbreaker indeed, was Lev Vygotsky. A founding father of developmental psychology (alongside Jean Piaget) and of one of its most productive paradigms, Vygotsky pressed most of the right buttons in his theory of mental development, including that of consciousness: the primacy of sociocultural activities, the coregulative role of adults and their culture, the outside-in metamorphosis (which he called "internalization") of representations of social relations into self-directed thoughts, often with regulative functions, and the essential link between executive control and consciousness (Vygotsky 1934/1962, 1960/1981). Vygotsky theorized that "all higher mental functions are internalized social relationships" and that the impetus for such internalization, and hence for mental development, is (what may be called) self-coregulation or self-regulation through an internalized or virtual other.

Self-consciousness, as construed here, is not in the center of Vygotsky's attention, yet I think it is broadly compatible with the overall direction of his thinking. Vygotsky's almost exclusive focus on the cultural and linguistic sources of mental development leads me to believe that he took the higher mental abilities, including consciousness, to be uniquely human and specifically the outcome of a unique ontogeny.

Missing from Vygotsky's analyses is intuitive psychology as the competence that relates to other minds and thus enables children to manage and regulate their sociocultural activities. Without this crucial role of intuitive psychology, particularly when exercised in childhood, the (so-called) internalization process remains rather mysterious (Bogdan 2000, 26–35). In all fairness, though, intuitive psychology was not on the radar of developmental psychology during Vygotsky's short life and actually rose to scientific prominence only in the last thirty years. Specific contributions aside, Vygotsky's general conception of mental development in the executive matrix of social interactions and cultural acquisitions has been immensely influential, and rightly so, and has helped create an intellectual climate in which an analysis like the one undertaken in this book could get off the ground.

Society, Culture, and the Executive Mind: Merlin Donald

If I had to guess a plausible direction in which Vygotsky might have elaborated his views on consciousness, one option would be Merlin Donald's analysis in *A Mind So Rare* (2001). It is a direction broadly followed in this book as well. But Vygotsky might have dissented, as I am inclined to, from Donald's view of animal consciousness. So let me begin with this disagreement before turning to the common points.

Donald's take on the animal consciousness tends to be more liberal than mine. He distinguishes three levels of awareness. A first level extends from the "raw feeling" of awareness—what I called 'sentience'—to complex perceptual binding and selective attention that results in the experience of distinguishable objects, actions and events. The latter is a form of awareness available to most mammalian species but not necessarily to those further down the phylogenetic chain. The second level of awareness reflects the ability to control what is represented on a working memory that is more capacious than the one involved in perceptual binding and able to deploy alternative models as well as inhibit and delay behavioral responses. At this second level we find the emerging functional contours of a global workspace. This level of consciousness is attributed to highly social mammals and nonhuman primates. They are admitted in—what Donald calls—"the consciousness club," as may be some lower mammals. More demanding parameters, such as social intelligence and intuitive psychology, are found only in primates. Finally, the third level characterizes exclusively the human form of consciousness, deeply symbolic and cultural.

Tellingly, Donald calls these levels of "awareness," even though he often means phenomenal consciousness. Despite the immense difficulty of separating the two, particularly across species, we do know that there is unconscious awareness in minds that operate according to many of Donald's parameters of consciousness, such as perceptual binding, selective attention, behavioral flexibility, and some capacious working memory. By

tracking such parameters across species, Donald (like many other theorists) is inclined to push consciousness downward in phylogeny. My inclination, in this book, was to take the opposite tack and push consciousness
upward both in phylogeny and ontogeny, by making it dependent on the
self-regulation of genuinely complex and constantly demanding sociocultural activities. Vygotsky might have approved, for reasons discussed
next.

When it comes to human consciousness, however, Donald's line is
entirely Vygotskian. He triangulates both the evolution and development
of human consciousness, functionally understood, in terms of an executive mind that handles social interactions and cultural acquisitions. In an
interesting move, with implications for the present discussion, Donald
reframes in evolutionary terms Vygotsky's celebrated notion of "zone of
proximal development," which contains young skills that can be redesigned or optimized by interactions with adults and their culture. Switch-
ing to the space of evolution, Donald identifies several mental abilities
that are "just on the edge of a species' capacity" in a "zone of proximal
evolution . . . where evolutionary shifts are most likely to occur" (Donald
2001, 138). Whole-body imitation, pedagogy, mindreading or intuitive
psychology, gesturing and symbolic invention are among those abilities,
subject to strong evolutionary pressures and therefore shifts, that made
human consciousness possible. All these abilities are deeply and intricately social and potentially cultural. On Donald's count, only enculturated apes partially share some of these revolutionary abilities with
humans.

Donald's notion of a zone of proximal evolution is an important insight,
which I read as supporting my take on self-consciousness but less support-
ive of pushing consciousness further down phylogenetically. In a nutshell,
my argument is this. Through inherited traits but also through convergent
evolution, many mammalian species and possibly other species evolved
mental abilities that bring them to the first and second level of awareness,
in Donald's analysis. As noted, these levels are likely to display unconscious awareness or sentience. The abilities operative at these levels do not
seem to enter or even come close to a zone of proximal evolution. Adaptive
as they undoubtedly are, these abilities, alongside unconscious sentience,
seem to be a fairly dead end, when it comes to their chances to morph
into—or at least become a platform for—higher mental capacities. The
metamorphosis—or platform—emerges and probably evolves quickly once
mental abilities enter the zone of proximal evolution; and that—according

to my analysis—happens only when they have to face very demanding social and cultural challenges. I see few if any good reasons to locate consciousness outside of that sociocultural zone of proximal evolution, and hence to push it down the phylogenetic chain.

Further support for this idea can be found in the fact that in human ontogeny self-consciousness progresses from extrovert to introvert precisely because it operates *constantly* in a sociocultural zone of proximal development. The same is true of other higher mental capacities, such as counterfactual imagination, abstract reasoning and autobiographical recall. If we do not find these abilities in other species—and we don't—then neither should we expect to find self-consciousness, particularly of the introvert sort.

The idea of a phylogenetic difference and of a possibly unique human self-consciousness gains still further plausibility when we consider the sort of self-regulation that evolved to handle sociocultural activities. It cannot be the *same* as that of other species—not even more or less the same. We are not talking here of morphologically comparable eyes or legs or even hands. We are talking of totally different activities that are bound to give rise to totally different selection pressures, with totally different mental abilities as a result. Self-consciousness, I think, is one of these totally different mental novelties.

I cannot help but be surprised by the widely shared view that, language aside, animal and human minds are fairly continuous or incrementally different in most essential respects, including consciousness, when it's immediately evident that most of the external activities in which animal and human organisms engage are radically different most of the time. It is as if differences in *activities* make little *mental* difference—which is a very unevolutionary and unrealistic view to have.

One last point. It is a fact, noted by many students of primate behavior and also by Donald, that enculturated apes occasionally show novel and superior mental abilities, compared with those of their conspecifics in the wild, particularly in interactions with humans and their sociocultural practices. This fact suggests that apes in cultural captivity may improvise and assemble new responses to new challenges emanating from a new and biologically unusual zone of (only potential) proximal evolution. Of course, these captive apes do not have the ecological and temporal luxury to assimilate genetically or routinize and scaffold pedagogically these new responses as inheritable or culturally transmissible mental abilities. Hominids and later humans *had* that luxury. Self-consciousness is likely to belong to the suite of novel mental capacities that emerged from the zone of proximal evolution defined by sociocultural activities.

Culture, Consciousness, and Memetics: Dan Dennett

In his imaginative, entertaining and groundbreaking work on consciousness, Daniel Dennett introduces the idea of the cultural design of human consciousness by means of memes (Dennett 1991, chapter 7). For our purposes, a meme (a notion invented by Richard Dawkins (1975)) can be roughly characterized as an idea or representation that operates as a memorable unit of cultural replication. Legends are memes and so are prejudices, slogans, proverbs, memorable melodies and good jokes. Memes invade brains and use them as carriers for their replication, much like genes use bodies for their replication. Memes also install a "virtual von Neumann machine"—more or less like a serial mental computer—in the parallel and plastic architecture of the brain. Imposed on the plasticity of the brain, the operation of this virtual machine in turn installs consciousness through a "myriad of microsettings." This is the rough idea.

Dennett extracts several important implications from this idea, which are also in the spirit of the present book. One implication is that the memetic redesign of the human mind is a recent evolutionary novelty, no older than some 100,000 years, which makes human consciousness (as we know it) biologically unique. Another implication is that consciousness is not innate—that is, wired into the initial architecture of the brain—but is rather installed in early childhood. Dennett's story of installation revolves around linguistic and generally symbolic self-stimulation (e.g., talking to oneself) and self-manipulation. The reader will know by now what my story is. As far as I can see, our stories are similar in positing a culturally induced pattern of neural interactions—in Dennett's story, the "virtual machine" as a mental computer, and in mine, the assembly of executive abilities—as being responsible for the installation of consciousness. These installation stories in turn seem to be complementary: Dennett's focuses on the role and use of language in self-stimulation and self-manipulation, whereas mine focuses on sociocultural activities managed by an intuitive psychology that recruits and assembles the right executive abilities.

I turn next to the other (complementary) paradigm that covers areas traversed by the argument of this book. Here sociocultural activities and intuitive psychology drop out of the picture and the focus shifts to self-consciousness, construed relationally and executively. I will consider three such accounts, which are solidly grounded in neuropsychological data and analyses. Though by no means the only ones, these are among the most comprehensive and sophisticated I have found in the literature.

The Ontogeny of Self-Consciousness: José Bermudez

José Bermudez's *Paradox of Self-Consciousness* (1998) is a historically minded account, with respect to phylogeny and particularly ontogeny. It starts with the ontogenetic paradox of the first-person thoughts using the first-person pronoun: it looks as though self-consciousness requires the ability to think and express first-person thoughts, hence presupposing the mastery of the first-person pronoun, yet the latter could not be acquired ontogenetically without some form of self-consciousness. Bermudez's sensible solution is to look for forms of self-consciousness that are ontogenetically earlier and more primitive than the form required by the acquisition of the first-person pronoun.

Before addressing this solution, I think there may be an equivocation in the way Bermudez sets up the paradox, between a *conceptual* decision to construe self-consciousness in terms of the ability to think first-person thoughts, which presupposes the mastery of the first-person pronoun, on the one hand, and an *empirical* dependence of the mastery of the first-person pronoun on self-consciousness, on the other hand.

As far as I can see, the conceptual decision is not fully motivated. Do first-person thoughts necessarily presuppose the mastery of the first-person pronoun? What sort of *self*-regarding thoughts are we talking about—me-thoughts, I-thoughts or self-thoughts, according to the analysis of the last chapter? According to that analysis, young children surely have consciously extrovert me-thoughts and I-thoughts *before* they master language and its pronouns, and consciously introvert self-thoughts several years afterwards. So what exactly is the mastery of the first-person pronoun explaining, insofar as the young children's thoughts are concerned?

It is a further empirical (not analytic) question—and one not fully settled in the developmental literature—what exactly young children *mean* when they start using the first-person pronoun. It is a question similar to that concerning their early use of the mentalist verbs of intuitive psychology, such as 'think,' 'believe,' and the like. There is a tendency among researchers to assume that the first uses of both first-person pronouns and mentalist verbs are somehow very close to adult uses. But this is not clear and is rather unlikely. The semantics of children's language is not easy to decipher, particularly when it comes to words such as first-person pronouns and mentalist verbs, which even seasoned analytic philosophers and linguists have a hard time defining.

And what about the thoughts themselves? Both in his (1998) and the equally insightful (2003), Bermudez credits all sorts of animal species with genuine thoughts, even of a predicative sort. I have criticized this generosity elsewhere (Bogdan 2009). Important here is the fact that Bermudez uses the presence of genuine thoughts as evidence of self-consciousness, with the result that numerous animal species are self-conscious. As earlier chapters and earlier paragraphs in this chapter would indicate, I am skeptical of this as well.

Bermudez's solution to the alleged paradox of self-consciousness is empirically and historically grounded. He discusses primitive forms of self-consciousness, such as exteroceptive perception, somatic proprioception and self-location, which I would rather characterize as self-sentient than self-conscious. An important merit of his analysis is to recuperate and build on J. J. Gibson's (1979) insight that the self is specified in the very content of perception by setting boundaries to, and protruding bodily into, one's visual field as well as by directly registering the affordances of the visual information. This insight makes the content of perception self-related, thus adding further support to the notion of relational consciousness. But again, I am not sure that the self-specifying information in perception, or some other modality, is necessarily conscious. Many animal species are primarily fast dorsal visualizers, and hence likely to be unconscious—yet surely their visual information would be self-specifying.

Ultimately, I think that the differences between Bermudez's approach and mine originate in the kinds of abilities and the domains where we hypothesize the roots of self-consciousness are planted. Bermudez finds the roots essentially (though not exclusively) in how the body and perception engage the physical world. I find these roots essentially in the simulative self-regulation that operates in social and cultural activities. I noted that Bermudez's emphasis on perceptuomotor relations to the physical world is not exclusive, since he does consider in detail (what he calls) young children's psychological self-awareness in contexts of social interaction, particularly joint attention (see 1998, chapter 9). I fully subscribe to his analysis. But whereas I think that sociocultural contexts are precisely the ones—and the only ones—in which extrovert self-consciousness, including psychological self-awareness, originates, Bermudez appears to count them as part of a plurality of perceptuomotor contexts that generate self-consciousness. This difference may also explain why my analysis is more parsimonious and finds self-consciousness only in humans and possibly (and minimally) in other primates, and ontogenetically only in a few socially oriented modalities, at least in the early stages.

Self-Consciousness and Self-Regulation: Antonio Damasio and Thomas Metzinger

The self-regulation perspective is central to the works of Antonio Damasio and Thomas Metzinger. (For a short history of recent neuropsychological thinking in the same direction, see Metzinger 2003, 414–415.) Metzinger's analysis echoes several of Damasio's themes. Unlike Damasio, however, Metzinger is explicit about the role of simulation in the self-regulation that implicates self-consciousness.

Both authors think that self-consciousness makes input information about various targets salient—worthy of attention and processing, and available to various other modalities—thus increasing or even generating its phenomenality, while at the same time masking the underlying operation of the mechanisms involved. Damasio notes specifically that the second-order mappings of (what I call) self-to-target relatedness enhance the image of the target, of what is perceived and mentally represented in general. This seems to me right, but the critical question is what this enhancement amounts to. Does it amount to consciousness of content (of what is experienced), or just an unconscious awareness of what is salient (attention)? Early human infancy may suggest the former, but blindsight and fast dorsal cognition in general may suggest the latter. Is it also possible that, without self-consciousness, consciousness of content may be very minimal and weak, "a passing show," perhaps in the form of phenomenally pulsative sensations without definite representations? Is it possible, in other words, that only a functionally operating self-consciousness transforms the content of what is phenomenally experienced into a specific structure—vivid, coherent, mentally manipulable and memorable? Again, some readings of early infancy and of absent-minded but successful performances may point in this direction.

Damasio and Metzinger draw the contours of self-consciousness more broadly than I do. Damasio distinguishes two basic forms, which he calls "core" and "extended consciousness," respectively. Both forms require a *second-order mapping* by which the organism represents its own changing state as it goes about representing something else. It is in the area of these second-order mappings that I would place the simulative work of self-regulation. According to Damasio, core consciousness occurs when the brain generates an imaged mapping of how the organism is affected by its processing an object and when this processing enhances the image of the causative object. Specifically, he suggests that "we become conscious when the organism's representation devices exhibit a specific kind of wordless knowledge—the knowledge that the organism's own state has been changed by an object—and when such knowledge occurs along with the salient representation of the object" (1999, 25). What I called here a sense of self-to-target-relatedness is roughly this "wordless knowledge," which Damasio also calls "the feeling of knowing—the feeling of what happens when an organism is engaged with the processing of an object" (Damasio 1999, 26).

Damasio's notion of core consciousness seems to me to fall, or perhaps alternate, between (what I called) a sentient sense of sensorimotor self-to-target relatedness and full-fledged perceptuomotor self-consciousness. It is not clear to me whether the "feeling of knowing" is different from my notion of a sense of self-sentience, which need not be conscious. Core consciousness does not seem to meet, at least not always, the extrovert conditions of self-consciousness, such as intent, intermodal integration of information, multitasking or holding several representations in mind for some period of time. Extended consciousness relies on the same second-order mappings as does core consciousness, but also draws on autobiographical memories and other sorts of representations present in working memory. The mention of autobiographical memory suggests, in my terms, the operation of self-thoughts, and the working memory with a manifold of representations suggests the operation of a multiplex mind.

Thomas Metzinger's analysis is concerned mostly with extended consciousness (in Damasio's sense), which he treats as globally as Damasio, but with a novel, rich and systematic angle on its simulative work. A central and very insightful concept in Metzinger's analysis is what he calls the "phenomenal model of the intentionality relation." This model enables one not only to represent continuously one's own representational relations to targets in the world but, as a result, to be phenomenally conscious of the target-relatedness itself.

Self-consciousness, in other words, has its *own* phenomenality. This is an important insight, shared with Damasio. Understandably, it is not very clear what this distinct phenomenality amounts to. Does it take the form of an explicit representation, as Metzinger seems to suggest, or of a "feeling of knowing," as in Damasio? In my analysis I left this phenomenality question open, with a deliberately open-ended notion of a conscious *sense* of self-to-target relatedness. I would only add that such a "phenomenal model" or "feeling" or "sense" is likely to *extend* to the affordances of one's target relatedness. In other words, when one is conscious of a target (object, event, situation), one is thereby conscious not only of being related to the target in some dominant modality but also of what the relation to the target affords for further thinking and/or action.

Both Damasio and Metzinger propose what looks like a *representational* account of self-consciousness: the second-order mappings (Damasio) and the phenomenal model (Metzinger) represent the target-relatedness and as a result generate its phenomenal consciousness as well as the consciousness of the contents experienced. It may be, however, that the notions of mapping and model (respectively) are more neutral and wide than I am assuming here. Neuropsychological analyses of lower-level motor cognition seem to go in the same representational direction.

Yet I have some doubts about the representational format of self-consciousness, partly because of the still poorly understood story of simulative self-regulation at the higher-levels of mentation. But there is another reason for my doubts. As noted in chapter 4.3, in its simplest form, simulative self-regulation seems to work by structural match or mismatch between brain instructions, encoded in a feedforward copy that anticipates a sensory input, and the information provided by the actual input. As I understand this story, there seems to be no overarching representation directed at the match or mismatch between the feedforward simulations and the actual inputs. It's either match or mismatch, or perhaps degrees of either, when appropriate, and nothing else.

Furthermore, for each bodily motion, action toward a target or perception of a target, there may be very many simulations and inputs to be matched. If— a big, but not totally implausible if—the structural match/ mismatch gambit also operates (mutatis mutandis) at higher and perhaps all forms of simulative self-regulation of target-relatedness and its affordances, then a representational account may not be the one to explain self-consciousness.

As a quick aside, I would extend this critique also to theories that posit a higher-order perception or higher-order thought to account for the consciousness of lower-level mental states. I do not think that mental states are conscious in isolation (see chapter 4.1), but even if they were, I do not think (for the reasons just given) that it would be an overarching, higher-level representation—perceptual, introspective or thought-like— that would make them so.

Returning to the comparative review, I will conclude with some more substantive differences. My analysis differs from both Damasio's and Metzinger's—but is closer to Bermudez's—in taking a *developmental* angle on self-consciousness. As noted before, there is much in the design of the human mind that cannot be discerned in the final product, either intuitively, introspectively or even by experiment and theory. Besides its intrinsic interest, mental development was said to provide a useful methodological tool that enables us to understand the less discernible aspects of the human mind in terms of how it developed and why. Self-consciousness is one such aspect. It is only from a developmental angle that we can see that the self-regulatory machinery of early childhood differs importantly from that of later childhood, with equally important differences in the nature and range of self-consciousness. This developmental difference feeds into the next difference with the views under discussion.

The most important difference concerns the *reasons* for self-consciousness and the *sort* of self-regulation that generates self-consciousness. Metzinger pays significant attention to social contexts and some exercises of intuitive psychology. Damasio factors social emotions in his story. But, as I read them, they will probably not agree with the central notion defended here that the external reasons for consciousness are eminently sociocultural and the internal ones essentially executive.

Concluding with Cats

I conclude with another sort of fellow travelers, who cheered me up along the way to this finale by just being who they are. Despite the pessimistic tone of earlier paragraphs, I would love to say that of all the animals, cats are the most likely—and the most pleased—to be self-conscious. But I fear I cannot.

Yet there may be a glimmer of hope in the familiar fact that cats are so incredibly good at exploiting our sociocultural proclivities. Why do they curl up so closely and purr in our laps when we read or watch TV or talk endlessly on the phone? And why do they insist on stepping on a computer or piano keyboard when we happen to play with one or the other? Did cats, by any chance, domesticate *themselves* in an early sociocultural zone of proximal evolution? It is a question whose exploration the Cats Über Alles Foundation ought to fund.

Notes

Chapter 4: Premises

Consciousness of Target-Relatedness and Its Affordances

Let me begin by amplifying the main points in the text. Intuitively, to be conscious seems always to be conscious *of* something or other—in the outside world or inside one's body or mind. One cannot be just conscious, full stop, or conscious of nothing whatsoever. (If one were just conscious, targetlessly, one should rather worry, medically speaking.) Consciousness-of is relational consciousness. But one is not just conscious-of a target; one is always *modally* conscious of a target. One is always conscious through one's proprorioception (regulating one's bodily posture and motions relative to a target or environment), conation (desires, urges), emotions and affects, and of course cognition (perception, memory, thinking). All of these modalities are relational and directed at some target.

That one is necessarily conscious of a target X in some modality is an aspect of our mental life recognized by many students of consciousness, particularly in the phenomenological tradition of Husserl and his followers. Less recognized is the aspect that is central to the present inquiry, namely, that when one is conscious of X, one is not only modally conscious of X but also conscious of being modally *related* to X. For example, my conscious belief that the moon is full can be read relationally in two ways, both of which indicate consciousness of a modal relatedness to targets. Either I am conscious *of* believing that the moon is full, and hence conscious of being in that modal relation (i.e., believing) to that content. (And this could but need not be an explicitly conscious self-ascription of belief.) Or else I am conscious *of* seeing or remembering the moon being full, and hence conscious of the content implicitly believed through seeing or remembering, without attending explicitly to or even noticing my believing that content. In either case, the consciousness involved in my belief is also of my being related to a target in some modality, be it doxastic or visual or memorial.

One's modal consciousness should not be reduced to one's *experience* of the modality involved or of the target as such. (The reader may recall the earlier argument, made in chapter 2.4, against taking the experience of an attitude as revealing the target-relatedness of the attitude. The earlier argument is relevant to the one about to be made now.) Here is what I mean.

When I see a cat, I have a conscious experience of the cat as target. At the same time I am conscious of my *seeing* the cat, that is, not only of my visually experiencing the cat, but also of experiencing my visual relatedness to the cat. My consciousness of my visual relatedness to the cat becomes manifest to me when I change my position toward the cat, and thus alter my visual angle on it and hence my image of it. But I don't even need to change my position toward the cat to experience consciously my visual relatedness to the lovely creature. I can stay put and still have that kind of experience. This is because our visual brain is programmed for experiences of variations of visual relatedness to targets, such as position, perspective, illumination and so on. And, mutatis mutandis, the same is true of other modalities that generate experiences of how they relate to targets.

It may be tempting to think that my conscious experience extends only to the identity of the modality—seeing, in our example—and not to its target-relatedness. I thus recognize and am aware of my experience being visual and not (say) auditory or tactile. And it may also be tempting to think that I am visually conscious of the cat by merely having the visual experience of the cat. So I have at best a conscious visual experience *of* the cat but not of being visually *related* to the cat. Neither temptation delivers the consciousness of my visual target-relatedness as my self-consciousness.

My reply to these tempting but unconvincing analyses is that the reason I am visually conscious not only of the cat and of experiencing it visually, but also of my being visually related to the cat, is not based just on what my conscious visual experience intuitively tells me or fails to tell me. The data and cases surveyed so far, and others to be surveyed later, as well as theory-driven reflection on self-regulation, further suggest—more convincingly than intuition, introspection or ordinary language—that the conditions in which one regulates one's visual perception and the actions it guides make one conscious of being visually related to the targets seen.

The same is true of other modalities that handle content-bearing mental states, from sensorimotor to abstract thinking. Consider the latter. The relational format of the consciousness of our own thoughts does not imply just being conscious of thoughts *as such*, as mental states in one's head—the way in which, say, one is conscious of a headache. And it does not imply just being conscious of *what* the thoughts represent—that is, conscious of their contents. One is conscious of one's own thoughts as, and to the extent that, they *relate to* their targets. One cannot be conscious of a thought-that-p *without* thereby being conscious of the thought being related to p.

The affordances side of the analysis points in the same direction. It is in virtue of my being visually or imaginatively related to a tool—say, a knife or a pair of binoculars—that I can expect certain outcomes if I act on it in some specific way. Merely representing or modally experiencing a tool—or almost anything else— would not have these affordances. But then, I submit, we are rarely conscious of being modally related to objects, events, situations and people without being thereby conscious of the affordances of this relatedness, such as specific implications for thinking or acting. Yes (I hear you), we can and often do make abstraction of affordances, but the point is that dispositionally, if we care or must, we would spontaneously factor in the affordances.

Another point needs some elaboration. Although not central to our story, it is worth bringing phenomenal states, such as pains and feelings, into this discussion. It may seem that such states are nonrelational, since they do not have informational content and are therefore not about anything. So, it seems, if they are conscious, they are conscious full stop—i.e., nonrelationally. Yet normal experience suggests that pains do signal specific bodily events or their localized causes, which one becomes conscious *of* (or at times not conscious of, if for instance, one is intensely attending to other things). Likewise, feelings do signal bodily or mental conditions one is conscious *of* (or at times not conscious of, due to repression, distracted attention or sheer discipline). There are theories of consciousness that plausibly vindicate this intuition about the relational format of the consciousness of pains and feelings (Tye 1995). Furthermore, there are intuitively obvious affordances of this sort of consciousness. Being conscious of a pain also means being conscious of doing (or refraining from doing) something about it. Being conscious of a feeling, such as frustration, also means being conscious of having to do (or not do) something as a result—to relieve it or hide it.

So much, so far, for the expanded intuitive case for the relational and affordances-sensitive design of self-consciousness. The next section in the text adds neuropsychological support to this intuitive argument by showing that the executive originator of self-consciousness, self-regulation, operates along these two dimensions—target-relatedness and affordances: it needs to "know" what an organism is related to and what this relatedness implies for its actions, reactions, behavioral strategies and well-being in general.

There is still further empirical support for the case made here. The idea that self-consciousness is consciousness not only of targets but also of relatedness to targets and its affordances is echoed in another area of neuropsychological research. Twenty years ago, Wolfgang Prinz introduced and explained the notion of a common code of perception and action (Prinz, W. 1990). The basic idea is that perception represents targets in ways that lead to efficient interactions with or actions on targets. To be successful, the perceptions that guide actions must factor into their representational structure the affordances of relating to the targets in question. A quote from Vittorio Gallese captures this idea very well:

Object observation, even within a behavioral context not specifically requiring an active interaction on the side of the observer, determines the activation of the motor program that would be required, were the observer actively interacting with the object. To observe objects is therefore equivalent to automatically evoking the most suitable motor program required to interact with them. Looking at objects means to unconsciously "simulate" a potential action. In other words, the object-representation is transiently integrated with the action-simulation (the ongoing simulation of the potential action).

If this interpretation is correct, objects are not merely identified and recognized by virtue of their physical "appearance," but in relation to the effects of the interaction with an agent. In such a context, the object acquires a meaningful value by means of its dynamic relation with the agent of this relation. This dynamic relation is multiple, as multiple are the ways in which we can interact with the world by acting within it. The object-representation ceases to exist by itself. The object phenomenally exists to the extent it represents the target of an action. (Gallese 2000, 9)

As suggested in the text (chapter 4.3), when the simulations Gallese is talking about operate self-regulatively under the right executive constraints, one becomes self-conscious of the targets one represents, of being related to them and of the affordances involved. It is the main contention of this book that the first significant targets, interactions and affordances encountered by human children, and the ones that first and most forcefully drive the development of their self-consciousness, are not physical but social and cultural.

Chapter 5: Becoming Self-Conscious

Explanations of Absent-Mindedness

One explanation is that the absent-minded (AM) driver is more like a blindsighter in the blind field, unconscious of what he sees and of being perceptually related to the road. His self-regulation passively and automatically responds to visual inputs from the road, helped by driving routines and perhaps memories of the road. The problem with this explanation is that, unlike the blindsighter, the AM driver has an unimpaired ventral perception that is likely to guide his driving. And ventral perception is widely thought to be implicated in conscious perception. (The blindsighter has an impaired ventral system and uses only the dorsal system in the blind side, even though the dorsal can operate consciously as well, as noted in the text.)

Avoiding this objection, another idea is that the AM driver is conscious of the road but his memory does not retain anything from that experience (Dennett 1991, 137; Carruthers 1996, 181). This may be so, but it is not clear why. Is it because the AM driver is only fleetingly and intermittently conscious of the road ahead (phenomenal pulsations), so that no durable perceptual representations are stored in memory? Possibly. But let us note that we often recall *details* of scenes that we were not conscious of when they were first seen. So why would the AM driver's memory fail to do the same?

David Armstrong, who introduced the example in philosophical discussions of consciousness, thinks that the AM driver is conscious of the road but not introspectively conscious of it (Armstrong 1968). This seems right if the former is extrovert consciousness, as in early childhood, and the latter introvert, as in later childhood and adulthood. As with infantile amnesia, extrovert consciousness does not seem to deliver memorable contents. But if introspection is taken to be constitutive of consciousness in general, then I think the position would be less plausible.

As I understand it, the question of AM driving is how to understand the driver's unconscious visuomotor self-to-road relatedness and its causal effects. I hesitate between two reasonable explanations, but incline toward the second. The first explanation is that the visual images of the AM driver are minimal and rather shallow, allowing behavioral guidance but not full perceptual self-consciousness. This explanation appeals to a distinction between *vision*, as the modular computation of raw or shallow visual images, and conscious *perception*, as the interface of such images with information from other modalities, such as memory, expectations, motor intentions and so on. According to this distinction, the AM driver, like the blindsighter, may be guided by vision but not by perception, whence the lack of perceptual consciousness-of—and the lack of the consciousness of being perceptually related to—what is visualized (here, the road).

A problem with this explanation is that intermodal interfaces among vision, long-term memory, some motor intentions, and driving routines may actually take place and be integrated in AM driving, resulting in fleeting and intermittent conscious perceptions. In this case, why not an equally fleeting and intermittent perceptual self-consciousness? The answer, provided by the second explanation, is that this may not be interface *enough* for perceptual self-consciousness of what is perceived.

The second explanation is that the visual images of the AM driver may be rich enough, and intermodally integrated and self-regulated enough, to allow intermittent visuomotor consciousness of the road, and yet fail to meet the stronger interface condition of showing up and remaining long enough in working memory in order to blend durably and coherently with other kinds of perceptions, categorizations, long-term memories, thoughts, intentions and inferences, in patterns that afford behavioral initiative and deliberate control. The working memory of the AM driver is actually occupied by thoughts that have nothing to do with driving. As a result, the driver's self-to-road relatedness is actually regulated unconsciously only at a lower *visuomotor* level and not at the higher and interface-rich perceptual level. This is why there is no *perceptual* self-consciousness and therefore (on my analysis) no conscious perceptions of the road. Not finding enough room in the working memory and therefore not being self-regulated at the rich interface that this memory provides, the visuomotor contents may be explicit and informative enough to enable routine driving, but not enough to generate conscious perceptions and hence later memories, let alone introspection or verbal report. The main reason for this is the failure of the self-regulation of the visuomotor relatedness to the road, to activate the executive abilities involved in extrovert self-consciousness.

In more familiar terms than blindsight, absent-mindedness shows that a mind can be self-conscious in a given modality and not in others. More clearly than blindsight, absent-mindedness shows that the absence of (extrovert) self-consciousness or its diminution is caused not so much by blockage in the input path (ventral and dorsal streams), as by the failure of the executive machinery to do its work.

Chapter 6: Turning to Our Own Minds

The Nonphenomenality of Cold Attitudes

I propose to amplify the argument about the nonphenomenality of functionally rich but cold attitudes in two stages, the first more intuitive but less accurate than the second.

True, with the machinery of introvert self-consciousness turned on (as it is most of the day), there is a felt experiential *background* to whatever we think and attitudinize about, with appropriately felt changes when these thoughts and attitudes change. True also, there is the experience of the mental images or of the imaged language forms (Carruthers 1996) in which we most often express our attitudes, particularly offline ones. But this, again, is the phenomenality of the experience of the *expressions* of attitudes, and not of their identity or format as attitudes—that is, as mental states that are target-related and have affordances. We experience phenomenally words and images, not the attitudes they express. The phenomenality of attitudes is a *borrowed phenomenality*—that is, borrowed from the phenomenality of its imagistic or linguistic expressions. Furthermore, this borrowed phenomenality is necessarily of the *same* kind for all the expressions of the cold attitudes we have, since the expressive means employed—images, words—are of the same kind. This sameness of phenomenality further suggests that the phenomenality of cold attitudes and abstract thoughts, otherwise so diverse, is not intrinsic—only borrowed.

Now for a more rigorous look at the matter. We are (or should be) concerned here with the *commonsense psychological* stance we take toward our own attitudes and *not* just with the experiential stance noted in the previous paragraph, although (as we just saw) not even the latter delivers an intrinsic phenomenality of the attitudes. We should be concerned at this point with how we *interpret* our own attitudes, and not with how we experience their expression. Whether spontaneously or reflectively exercised, this interpretive stance looks at our own attitudes through functionalist lenses that reveal their target-relatedness and affordances. The contents of the attitudes may be known modally and phenomenally. Yet even the contents are reformatted propositionally from the same commonsense-psychological stance. From this stance, cold attitudes do not glow from inside phenomenally and do not reveal any intrinsic phenomenality, precisely because the stance is functionalist. (Functionalism does not like intrinsicness in general.) A functionalist commonsense psychology is solely interested in and tracks the target-relatedness and causal implications of attitudes. This specialized focus has a developmental if not an evolutionary explanation, which I will not go into here (Bogdan 1997; 2000).

Chapter 8: Loose Ends

Phenomenal Pulsations

Several times reference has been made to the notion of phenomenal pulsations. Here is a somewhat more empirical look at this intriguing phenomenon.

Blindsighters and AM drivers, as well as young children operating in certain modalities (but not in others), have been said not to exercise executive abilities such as intention, initiative, control, sustained and intense top-down attention, and intermodal interactions. Damasio notes the same failures in epileptic and akinetic-mute patients (Damasio 1999, 99). Nevertheless, these patients seem to have something in common with young children (and perhaps the absent-minded), but not with blindsighters in their blind field. In epileptic and akinetic-mute patients, the seizure or stroke may sever the links between specific self-regulatory mechanisms and the contents of visual perceptions, thus impairing their perceptuomotor self-consciousness. Unlike blindsighters, however, these patients do not have an impaired visual system. Thus, even if self-regulatory sites such as the cingulate cortex, implicated in attention and control, are damaged, unimpaired modalities, such as object or face perception, may still generate sporadic perceptions that are phenomenally conscious. Yet these perceptions fail to be broadcast to the rest of the brain, and hence are not brought under control and incorporated into purposive mental and behavioral activities. The result could be a sporadic and fragmented consciousness of perceptual contents—phenomenal pulsations—but *without* self-consciousness.

References

Adamson, L. B. 1995. *Communication Development During Infancy*. Boulder, Colo.: Westview Press.

Armstrong, D. 1968. *A Materialist Theory of the Mind*. New York: Humanities Press.

Astington, J. W., and A. Gopnik. 1988. Knowing you've changed your mind: children's understanding of representational change. In *Developing Theories of Mind*, ed. J. W. Astington, P. L. Harris, and D. Olson. Cambridge: Cambridge University Press.

Astington, J. W., P. L. Harris, and D. Olson, eds. 1988. *Developing Theories of Mind*. Cambridge: Cambridge University Press.

Baars, B. J. 1988. *A Cognitive Theory of Consciousness*. Cambridge: Cambridge University Press.

Baron-Cohen, S. 1995. *Mindblindness*. Cambridge, Mass.: MIT Press.

Baron-Cohen, S., and H. Ring. 1994. A model of the mindreading system. In *Children's Early Understanding of Mind*, ed. C. Lewis and P. Mitchell. Hillsdale, N.J.: Erlbaum.

Barresi, J., and C. Moore. 1996. Intentional relations and social understanding. *Behavioral & Brain Sciences* 19:107–122.

Bates, E. 1976. *Language and Context*. New York: Academic Press.

Behrmann, M., M. Moscovich, and G. Winocur. 1994. Intact visual imagery and impaired visual perception. *Journal of Experimental Psychology* 20:1068–1087.

Bermudez, J. 1998. *The Paradox of Self-Consciousness*. Cambridge, Mass.: MIT Press.

Bermudez, J. 2003. *Thoughts Without Words*. Oxford: Oxford University Press.

Berthoz, A., and J.-L. Petit. 2006. *Phénomenologie et Physiologie de l'Action*. Paris: Éditions Odile Jacob.

Bertolo, H., T. Paiva, L. Pessoa, T. Mestre, R. Marques, and R. Santos. 2003. Visual dream content, graphical representation and EEg alpha activity in congenitally blind subjects. *Cognitive Brain Research* 15:277–284.

Bjorklund, D. F. 2005. *Children's Thinking.* Belmont, Calif.: Wadsworth.

Bjorklund, D. F., and A. Pellegrini. 2002. *The Origins of Human Nature.* Washington, D.C.: American Psychological Association.

Block, N. 1995. On a confusion about a function of consciousness. *Behavioral & Brain Sciences* 18:227–247.

Block, N., O. Flanagan, and G. Güzeldere, eds. 1997. *The Nature of Consciousness.* Cambridge, Mass.: MIT Press.

Bloom, P. 2000. *How Children Learn the Meanings of Words.* Cambridge, Mass.: MIT Press.

Bloom, P. 2004. *Descartes' Baby.* New York: Basic Books.

Bogdan, R. J. 1993. The architectural nonchalance of commonsense psychology. *Mind & Language* 8:189–205.

Bogdan, R. J. 1994. *Grounds for Cognition.* Hillsdale, N.J.: Erlbaum.

Bogdan, R. J. 1997. *Interpreting Minds.* Cambridge, Mass.: MIT Press.

Bogdan, R. J. 2000. *Minding Minds.* Cambridge, Mass.: MIT Press.

Bogdan, R. J. 2003. Watch your metastep: the first-order limits of early intentional attributions. In *Persons*, ed. C. Kanzian et al. Vienna: Holder-Pichler-Tempsky.

Bogdan, R. J. 2005a. Pretending as imaginative rehearsal for cultural conformity. *Journal of Cognition and Culture* 5:191–213.

Bogdan, R. J. 2005b. Why self-ascriptions are difficult and develop late. In *Other Minds*, ed. B. Malle and S. Hodges. New York: Guilford Press.

Bogdan, R. J. 2007. Inside loops. *Synthese* 159:235–252.

Bogdan, R. J. 2009. *Predicative Minds.* Cambridge, Mass.: MIT Press.

Boyd, R., and J. Silk. 1997. *How Humans Evolve.* New York: Norton.

Brownell, H., R. Griffin, E. Winner, O. Friedman, and F. Happé. 2000. Cerebral lateralization and theory of mind. In *Understanding Other Minds.* 2nd ed., ed. S. Baron-Cohen, H. Tager-Flusberg, and D. J. Cohen. Oxford: Oxford University Press.

Bruner, J. 1983. *Child's Talk.* New York: Norton.

Bruner, J., and C. Feldman. 1993. Theories of mind and the problem of autism. In *Understanding Other Minds*, ed. S. Baron-Cohen, H. Tager-Flusberg, and D. J. Cohen. Oxford: Oxford University Press.

Butterworth, G. 1991. The ontogeny and phylogeny of joint visual attention. In *Natural Theories of Mind*, ed. A. Whiten. Oxford: Blackwell.

Byrne, R. W., and A. Whiten, eds. 1988. *Machiavellian Intelligence*. Oxford: Oxford University Press.

Carey, S. 1985. *Conceptual Change in Childhood*. Cambridge, Mass.: MIT Press.

Carey, S., and E. Spelke. 1994. Domain-specific knowledge and conceptual change. In *Domain Specificity in Cognition and Culture*, ed. L. A. Hirschfeld and S. A. Gelman. Cambridge: Cambridge University Press.

Carruthers, P. 1996. *Language, Thought and Consciousness*. Cambridge: Cambridge University Press.

Carruthers, P. 2002. Human creativity: its cognitive basis, its evolution, and its connections with childhood pretence. *British Journal for the Philosophy of Science* 53:225–249.

Carruthers, P. 2005. *Consciousness*. Oxford: Oxford University Press.

Chandler, M. J. 1988. Doubt and developing theories of mind. In *Developing Theories of Mind*, ed. J. W. Astington et al. Cambridge: Cambridge University Press.

Chartrand, T. L., and J. A. Bargh. 1999. The chameleon effect: the perception-behavior link and social interaction. *Journal of Personality and Social Psychology* 76:893–910.

Churchland, P. 1979. *Scientiifc Realism and the Plasticityy of Mind*. Cambridge: Cambridge University Press.

Clayton, N., et al. 2002. Elements of episodic-like memory in animals. In *Episodic Memory*, ed. A. Baddeley et al. Oxford: Oxford University Press.

Clements, W., and J. Perner. 1994. Implicit understanding of belief. *Cognitive Development* 9:377–397.

Conway, M. 2002. Sensory-perceptual memory and its context: autobiographical memory. In *Episodic Memory*, ed. A. Baddeley et al. Oxford: Oxford University Press.

Corcoran, R. 2000. Theory of mind in other clinical conditions. In *Understanding Other Minds*. 2nd ed., ed. S. Baron-Cohen et al. Oxford: Oxford University Press.

Cosmides, L., and J. Tooby. 2000. Consider the source: the evolution of adaptations for decoupling and metarepresentations. In *Metarepresentations*, ed. D. Sperber. Oxford: Oxford University Press.

Currie, G., and I. Ravenscroft. 2002. *Recreative Minds*. Oxford: Oxford University Press.

Damasio, A. 1999. *The Feeling of What Happens*. New York: Harcourt.

Davidson, D. 1984. *Inquiries into Truth and Interpretation*. Oxford: Oxford University Press.

Davidson, D. 2003. *Subjective, Intersubjective, Objective*. Oxford: Oxford University Press.

Dawkins, R. 1976. *The Selfish Gene*. Oxford: Oxford University Press.

Decety, J., M. Jeannerod, and C. Prablanc. 1989. The timing of mentally represented actions. *Behavioural Brain Research* 34:35–42.

Dehaene, S., J.-P. Changeux, L. Naccache, J. Sackur, and C. Sergent. 2006. Conscious, subconscious and subliminal processing. *Trends in Cognitive Sciences* 10:204–211.

Dehaene, S., and L. Naccache. 2001. Toward a neuroscience of consciousness. In *The Cognitive Neuroscience of Consciousness*, ed. S. Dehaene. Cambridge, Mass.: MIT Press.

Dempster, F. 1992. The rise and fall of inhibitory mechanisms. *Developmental Review* 12:45–75.

Dennett, D. 1991. *Consciousness Explained*. Boston: Little, Brown.

De Waal, F. 1982. *Chimpanzee Politics*. Baltimore: Johns Hopkins University Press.

Diamond, A. 2001. Normal developments of prefrontal cortex from birth to young adulthood. In *The Frontal Lobes*, ed. D. T. Stuss and R. T. Knight. Oxford: Oxford University Press.

Donald, M. 1991. *Origins of the Modern Mind*. Cambridge, Mass.: Harvard University Press.

Donald, M. 1998. Mimesis and the executive suite. In *The Evolutionary Emergence of Language*, ed. C. Knight, M. Studdert-Kennedy, and J. R. Hurford. Cambridge: Cambridge University Press.

Donald, M. 2001. *A Mind So Rare*. New York: Norton.

Dretske, F. 1995. *Naturalizing the Mind*. Cambridge, Mass.: MIT Press.

Dunn, J. 1988. *The Beginnings of Social Understanding*. Oxford: Blackwell.

Farah, M. J. 1984. The neurological basis of mental imagery. *Cognition* 18:245–272.

Flavell, J. H. 2000. Development of children's knowledge about the mental world. *International Journal of Behavioral Development* 24:15–23.

Flavell, J. H., F. L. Green, and E. R. Flavell. 1995. Young children's knowledge about thinking. *Monographs of the Society for Research in Child Development* 60:1–96.

Flavell, J. H., F. L. Green, and E. R. Flavell. 1998. The mind has a mind of its own. *Cognitive Development* 13:127–138.

Flavell, J. H., F. L. Green, E. R. Flavell, and G. B. Grossman. 1997. The development of children's knowledge about inner speech. *Developmental Psychology* 68:39–47.

Fodor, J. A. 1983. *Modularity of Mind*. Cambridge, Mass.: MIT Press.

Fodor, J. A. 1987. *Psychosemantics*. Cambridge, Mass.: MIT Press.

Fodor, J. A. 1992. A theory of the child's theory of mind. *Cognition* 44:283–296.

Foulkes, D. 1999. *Children's Dreaming and the Development of Consciousness*. Cambridge, Mass.: Harvard University Press.

Frith, C. 1992. *The Neurological Basis of Schizophrenia*. Hillsdale, N.J.: Erlbaum.

Frith, U. 1989. *Autism*. Oxford: Blackwell.

Frith, U., and C. Frith. 2003. Development and neurophysiology of mentalising. *Philosophical Transactions* 358:459–473.

Gallagher, S. 2005. *How the Body Shapes the Mind*. Oxford: Oxford University Press.

Gallese, V. 2000. The inner sense of action. *Journal of Consciousness Studies* 7:23–40.

Gergely, G., H. Bekkering, and I. Kilary. 2002. Rational imitation in preverbal infants. *Nature* 415:755.

Gibson, J. J. 1979. *The Ecological Approach to Visual Perception*. Boston: Houghton-Mifflin.

Goldman, A. 1993. The psychology of folk psychology. *Behavioral & Brain Sciences* 16:15–28.

Goldman, A. 2006. *Simulating Minds*. Oxford: Oxford University Press.

Gomez, J. C. 1991. Visual behavior as a window for reading the mind of others in primates. In *Natural Theories of Mind*, ed. A. Whiten. Oxford: Blackwell.

Gomez, J. C. 2005. Joint attention and the sensorimotor notion of subject. In *Joint Attention: Communication and Other Minds*, ed. N. Eilan, C. Hoerl, T. McCormack, and J. Roessler. Oxford: Oxford University Press.

Gopnik, A. 1993. How we know our minds. *Behavioral & Brain Sciences* 16:1–14.

Gopnik, A., and A. N. Meltzoff. 1997. *Words, Thoughts, and Theories*. Cambridge, Mass.: MIT Press.

Gopnik, A., and H. M. Wellman. 1992. Why the child's theory of mind really is a theory. *Mind & Language* 7:145–171.

Gordon, R. M. 1986. Folk psychology as simulation. *Mind & Language* 1:158–171.

Gordon, R. M. 1993. Self-ascriptions of belief and desire. *Behavioral & Brain Sciences* 16:45–46.

Gordon, R. M. 2007. Ascent routines for propositional attitudes. *Synthese* 159: 151–165.

Graham, G., T. Horgan and J. Tienson. 2007. Consciousness and intentionality. In *The Blackwell Companion to Consciousness*, ed. M. Velman and S. Schneider. Oxford: Blackwell.

Grezes, J., N. Costes and J. Decety. 1998. The top-down effect of the perception of human biological motion. *Cognitive Neuropsychology* 15:553–582.

Grice, P. 1957. Meaning. *Philosophical Review* 66:377–388.

Groopman, J. 2007. Silent minds. *The New Yorker* (15 October): 38–43.

Grush, R. 2004. The emulation theory of representation. *Behavioral & Brain Sciences* 27:377–396.

Happé, F. 1994. Communicative competence and theory of mind in autism. *Cognition* 48:101–119.

Hare, B., J. Call, and M. Tomasello. 2001. Do chimpanzees know what conspecifics know? *Animal Behaviour* 61:139–151.

Harris, P. 1992. From simulation to folk psychology. *Mind & Language* 7:120–144.

Harris, P. 2000. *The Work of Imagination*. Oxford: Blackwell.

Hobson, R. P. 1993. *Autism and the Development of Mind*. Hillsdale, N.J.: Erlbaum.

Houdé, O. 1995. *Rationalité, Développement et Inhibition*. Paris: Presses Universitaires de France.

Humphrey, N. K. [1976] 1988. The Social Function of the Intellect. In *Machiavellian Intelligence*, ed. J. Byrne and A. Whiten. Oxford: Oxford University Press.

Hurley, S. 1999. *Consciousness in Action*. Cambridge, Mass.: Harvard University Press.

Jacob, P., and M. Jeannerod. 2003. *Ways of Seeing*. Oxford: Oxford University Press.

Jeannerod, M. 1997. *The Cognitive Neuroscience of Action*. Oxford: Blackwell.

Jeannerod, M. 2003. Simulation of action: a unifying concept for motor cognition. In *Taking Action*, ed. S. Johnson-Frey. Cambridge, Mass.: MIT Press.

Jeannerod, M. 2006. *Motor Cognition*. Oxford: Oxford University Press.

Karmiloff-Smith, A. 1992. *Beyond Modularity*. Cambridge, Mass.: MIT Press.

Kosslyn, S. 1994. *Image and Brain*. Cambridge, Mass.: MIT Press.

Kosslyn, S. M., et al. 2001. Neural foundations of imagery. *Nature Reviews. Neuroscience* 2:635–642.

Kriegel, U. 2004. Consciousness and self-consciousness. *Monist* 87:185–209.

Le Bihan, D., et al. 1993. Activation of human primary visual cortex during visual recall. *Proceedings of the National Academy of Sciences of the United States of America* 90:11802–11805.

Lehrer, K. 1997. *Self-Trust*. Oxford: Oxford University Press.

Leondar, B. 1977. Hatching plots: genesis of storymaking. In *The Arts and Cognition*, ed. D. Perkins and B. Leondar. Baltimore: Johns Hopkins University Press.

Leslie, A. M. 1988. Some implications of pretense for mechanisms underlying the child's theory of mind. In *Developing Theories of Mind*, ed. J. W. Astington et al. Cambridge: Cambridge University Press.

Leslie, A. M. 1991. The theory of mind impairment in autism. In *Natural Theories of Mind*, ed. A. Whiten. Oxford: Blackwell.

Leslie, A. M. 1994. How to acquire a representational theory of mind. In *Metarepresentations*, ed. D. Sperber. Oxford: Oxford University Press.

Leslie, A. 2000. Theory of mind as a mechanism of selective attention. In *The New Cognitive Neurosciences*, ed. M. Gazzaniga. Cambridge, Mass.: MIT Press.

Lewis, C. 1994. Episodes, events, and narratives in the child's understanding of mind. In *Origins of an Understanding of Mind*, ed. C. Lewis and P. Mitchell. Hillsdale, N.J.: Erlbaum.

Lewis, D. 1972. Psychophysical and theoretical identifications. *Australasian Journal of Philosophy* 50:249–258.

Lillard, A. 1994. Making sense of pretense. In *Children's Early Understanding of Mind*, ed. C. Lewis and P. Mitchell. Hillsdale, N.J.: Erlbaum.

Lopes da Silva, F. H. 2003. Visual dreams in the congenitally blind? *Trends in Cognitive Sciences* 7:328–330.

Lycan, W. 1996. *Consciousness and Experience*. Cambridge, Mass.: MIT Press.

Mandler, J. M., and L. McDonough. 2000. Advancing down to the basic level. *Journal of Cognition and Development* 1:379–403.

Mead, G. H. 1934. *Mind, Self and Society*. Chicago: University of Chicago Press.

McGinn, C. 1991a. Consciousness and content. In *Mind and Common Sense*, ed. R. J. Bogdan. Cambridge: Cambridge University Press.

McGinn, C. 1991b. *The Problem of Consciousness*. Oxford: Blackwell.

Meltzoff, A. 1995. Understanding the intentions of others. *Developmental Psychology* 31:838–850.

Meltzoff, A., and A. Gopnik. 1993. The role of imitation in understanding persons and developing a theory of mind. In *Understanding Other Minds*, ed. S. Baron-Cohen et al. Oxford: Oxford University Press.

Meltzoff, A., and G. Moore. 1977. Imitation of facial and manual gestures by human neonates. *Science* 198:75–78.

Meltzoff, A., and J. Decety. 2003. What imitation tells us about social cognition. *Philosophical Transactions of the Royal Society: Biological Sciences* 358:491–500.

Metzinger, T. 2003. *Being No One*. Cambridge, Mass.: MIT Press.

Milner, D., and M. Goodale. 1995. *The Visual Brain in Action*. Oxford: Oxford University Press.

Mitchell, P., U. Teucher, M. Bennett, F. Ziegler, and R. Wyton. 2009. Do children start out thinking they don't know their own minds? *Mind & Language* 24:328–346.

Mitchell, R. 2002. Imaginative animals, pretending children. In *Pretending and Imagination in Animals and Children*, ed. R. Mitchell. Cambridge: Cambridge University Press.

Mithen, S. 1996. *The Prehistory of the Mind*. London: Thames & Hudson.

Morin, A. 2006. Levels of consciousness and self-awareness. *Consciousness and Cognition* 15:359–371.

Nagel, T. 1974. What it is like to be a bat? *Philosophical Review* 83:435–450.

Nelkin, N. 1996. *Consciousness and the Origins of Thought*. Cambridge: Cambridge University Press.

Nelson, K. 1996. *Language in Cognitive Development*. Cambridge: Cambridge University Press.

Nelson, K. 2007. *Young Minds in Social Worlds*. Cambridge, Mass.: Harvard University Press.

Nichols, S., and S. Stich. 2003. *Mindreading*. Oxford: Oxford University Press.

Ofen, N., et al. 2007. Development of the declarative memory system in the human brain. *Nature Neuroscience* 10:1198–1205.

Olson, D. 1988. On the origins of beliefs and other intentional states in children. In *Developing Theories of Mind*, ed. J. W. Astington et al. Cambridge: Cambridge University Press.

Olson, D. 1989. Making up your mind. *Canadian Psychology* 30:617–627.

Olson, D., and D. Kamawar. 1999. The theory of scriptions. In *Developing Theories of Intention*, ed. P. D. Zelazo, J. W. Astington, and D. R. Olson. Mahwah, N.J.: Erlbaum.

Onishi, K. H., and R. Baillargeon. 2005. Do 15-months-old infants understand false beliefs? *Science* 308:255–258.

Perner, J. 1991. *Understanding the Representational Mind*. Cambridge, Mass.: MIT Press.

Perner, J. 2000. Memory and theory of mind. In *The Oxford Handbook of Memory*, ed. E. Tulving et al. Oxford: Oxford University Press.

Piaget, J. 1964. *Six études de psychologie*. Geneva: Éditions Gonthier.

Piaget, J. 1974. *Understanding Causality*. New York: Norton.

Poulet, J. F. A., and B. Hedwig. 2006. New insights into corollary discharges mediated by identified neural pathways. *Trends in Neurosciences* 30:14–21.

Povinelli, D. 1996. Chimpanzee theory of mind?: the long road to strong inference. In *Theories of Theories of Mind*, ed. P. Carruthers and P. K. Smith. Cambridge: Cambridge University Presss.

Prinz, J. J. 2004. The fractionation of introspection. *Journal of Consciousness Studies* 7–8:40–57.

Prinz, W. 1990. A common coding approach to perception and action. In *Relationships between Perception and Action*, ed. O. Neumann and W. Prinz. Berlin: Springer, 167–201.

Quine, W. V. O. 1960. *Word and Object*. Cambridge, Mass.: MIT Press.

Rogoff, B. 1990. *Apprenticeship in Thinking*. Oxford: Oxford University Press.

Rosenthal, D. 2005. *Consciousness and Mind*. Oxford: Oxford University Press.

Rizzolatti, G., L. Fadiga, V. Gallese, and L. Fogassi. 1996. Premotor cortex and the recognition of motor actions. *Cognitive Brain Research* 3:131–141.

Russell, J. 1996. *Agency*. Hove, U.K.: Erlbaum, Taylor & Francis.

Savage-Rumbaugh, S. 1991. Multi-tasking: the pan-human Rubicon. *Neuroscience* 3:417–422.

Searle, J. 1982. *Intentionality*. Cambridge: Cambridge University Press.

Searle, J. 1992. *The Rediscovery of the Mind*. Cambridge, Mass.: MIT Press.

Sellars, W. 1956/1963. *Science, Perception and Reality*. London: Routledge & Kegan Paul.

Slobin, D. 1990. The development from child speaker to native speaker. In *Cultural Psychology*, ed. J. W. Stigler, R. A. Schwede, and G. Herdt. Cambridge: Cambridge University Press.

Smith, E. E., and S. M. Kosslyn. 2007. *Cognitive Psychology*. Upper Saddle River, N.J.: Pearson/Prentice Hall.

Smith, J. D., W. E. Shields, and D. Washburn. 2003. The comparative psychology of uncertainty monitoring and metacognition. *Behavioral and Brain Sciences* 26:317–339.

Sperry, R. W. 1950. Neural basis of the spontaneous optokinetic response produced by visual inversion. *Journal of Comparative and Physiological Psychology* 43:482–489.

Spivey, M., M. Tyler, D. Richardson and E. Young. 2000. Eye movements during comprehension of spoken scene descriptions. *Proceedings of the 22nd annual conference of the Cognitive Science Society*, 487–492. Mahwah, N.J.: Erlbaum.

Stephens, G. L., and G. Graham. 2000. *When Self-Consciousness Breaks*. Cambridge, Mass.: MIT Press.

Stich, S. 1983. *From Folk Psychology to Cognitive Science*. Cambridge, Mass.: MIT Press.

Stone, V. 2000. The roles of the frontal lobes and amygdala in theory of mind. In *Understanding Other Minds*. 2nd ed., ed. S. Baron-Cohen et al. Oxford: Oxford University Press.

Taylor, M. 1988. The development of children's understanding of the seeing-knowing distinction. In *Developing Theories of Mind*, ed. J. W. Astington et al. Cambridge: Cambridge University Press.

Tomasello, M. 1999. *The Cultural Origins of Human Cognition*. Cambridge, Mass.: Harvard University Press.

Tomasello, M. 2003. *Constructing a Language*. Cambridge, Mass.: Harvard University Press.

Tomasello, M. 2008. *The Origins of Human Communication*. Cambridge, Mass.: MIT Press.

Tomasello, M., and J. Call. 1997. *Primate Cognition*. New York: Oxford University Press.

Tomasello, M., M. Carpenter, J. Call, T. Behne, and H. Moll. 2005. Understanding and sharing intentions. *Behavioral and Brain Sciences* 28:675–735.

Trevarthen, C. 1993. The self born in intersubjectivity. In *The Perceived Self*, ed. U. Neisser. Cambridge: Cambridge University Press.

Tye, M. 1995. *Ten Problems of Consciousness*. Cambridge, Mass.: MIT Press.

van Gulick, R. 1993. Understanding the phenomenal mind. In *Consciousness*, ed. M. Davies and G. Humphreys. Oxford: Blackwell. '

Vogeley, K., and G. R. Fink. 2003. Neural correlates for first-person perspective. *Trends in Cognitive Sciences* 7:38–42.

von Holst, E., and H. Mittelstaedt. 1950. Das reafferenzprinzip: wechselwirkungen zwischen zentralnervensystem und peripherie. *Naturwissenschaften* 37:464–476.

Vosgerau, G., and A. Newen. 2007. Thoughts, motor actions and the self. *Mind & Language* 22:22–43.

Vygotsky, L. S. 1934/1962. *Thought and Language*. Cambridge, Mass.: MIT Press. (Originally published in Russian, in 1934.)

Vygotsky, L. S. 1960/1981. The genesis of higher mental functions. In *The Concept of Activity in Soviet Psychology*, ed. J. V. Wertsch. Armonk, Maine: Sharpe. (Originally but posthumously published in Russian, in 1960).

Wellman, H. 1990. *The Child's Theory of Mind*. Cambridge, Mass.: MIT Press.

Whiten, A., and R. W. Byrne. 1991. The emergence of metarepresentation in human ontogeny and primate phylogeny. In *Natural Theories of Mind*, ed. A. Whiten. Oxford: Blackwell.

Wimmer, H., and J. Perner. 1983. Beliefs about beliefs. *Cognition* 13:103–128.

Wolpert, D., R. Miall, and M. Kawato. 1998. Internal models of the cerebellum. *Trends in Cognitive Sciences* 2:338–347.

Young, G. 2008. On how a child's awareness of thinking informs explanations of thought insertion. *Consciousness and Cognition* 17:848–862.

Index